MINDS ON FIRE

MINDS ON FIRE

HOW ROLE-IMMERSION GAMES TRANSFORM COLLEGE

Mark C. Carnes

Harvard University Press

Cambridge, Massachusetts
London, England
2014

LIBRARY OF CONGRESS CATALOGING-IN-PUBLICATION DATA

Carnes, Mark C. (Mark Christopher), 1950–
Minds on fire : how role-immersion games transform college/
Mark C. Carnes.
pages cm.
Includes bibliographical references and index.
ISBN 978-0-674-73535-4 (alk. paper)
1. Education, Higher—Effect of technological innovations on.
2. Education, Higher—Social aspects.   3. Fantasy games—Social
aspects.   4. Role playing—Social aspects.   I. Title.
LB2395.7.C38 2014
371.33'7—dc23   2014008416

For MEK

CONTENTS

MINDS ON FIRE

Debate at Dawn

"If it's okay with you, Professor, can we begin class thirty minutes early?"

Paul Fessler gaped. As an instructor and department chair, he had fielded plenty of odd questions, but this one floored him. Class normally started at 8:00 A.M.

The strangeness had begun three weeks earlier, when Fessler replaced his usual Western Civ lectures with an elaborate role-playing game, one of dozens created by scholars in the Reacting to the Past consortium of colleges and universities.[1] Fessler had distributed role packets, assigning students to various political factions of the National Assembly of France in 1791. Students spent two weeks slogging through a 200-page game book, consisting of the rules and historical context, as well as Rousseau's *Social Contract* and parts of Edmund Burke's *Reflections on the*

Revolution in France. Fessler lectured on these topics in class. Then the game began, and Fessler retreated to the back of the room. A student took his place at the front, where she presided over the Assembly. Over the next two weeks, students debated and voted on one issue after another. But the debates became heated and lasted longer than Fessler had expected. Many continued after class and spilled into the hallway and dorms. Soon Fessler realized that the semester would end before the game had run its course. He told the class that he had no choice but to cut the game short, omitting the final debates and sessions. The students protested. Some suggested he extend class by an hour, but others had classes immediately after Western Civ. Several days later the students came back with their startling proposal: to begin the class at 7:30 A.M. for the remainder of the semester.

Fessler told this story to professors at a Reacting to the Past training workshop in 2007. When they asked him to explain his students' odd behavior, Fessler said he couldn't. When I pressed him, he suggested I ask them myself. I agreed, and Fessler tracked down several of their names and email addresses. First I interviewed Nate Gibson.[2]

Nate, who had graduated from Dordt College several years earlier, remembered the game well. He even recalled the discussion of the extra sessions. He explained that someone had initially suggested the 7:30 A.M. start time as a joke, but when no other time worked, the idea caught on. "Every student felt a strong personal investment in their roles," he noted, adding that everyone voluntarily came to all four of the early-morning sessions. Perhaps "voluntarily" is not quite right: Nate conceded that he "sort of forced" a sleepy-headed friend to go to class.

"Keep in mind that we'd already lost a lot of sleep in playing the game," Nate explained. "We read more in the weeks of the game than we had at any time before in the class. We plowed through the game manual, our history texts, Rousseau, you name it. We spent hours writing articles. I spent several all-nighters editing my faction's newspapers, and the other editors did too. It had become more than a class to us by that point. The early-morning sessions were the only way to honor the sacrifices that everybody had made."

Nate's story might be filed in the back drawer of the Cabinet of Undergraduate Oddities were it not echoed by the equally bizarre accounts of dozens of other professors who use Reacting games. Many cite classes with perfect attendance—for an entire semester.[3] Pat Coby, a political scientist at Smith College, reported that his most recent Reacting course included three unregistered students. Each attended every session, gave speeches, and submitted twenty pages of written work for the class—even though they received no credit for the course. He also told of a student who had had her lung reinflated in the hospital emergency room but insisted on delivering her speech on Machiavelli a few hours later.[4] Elissa Auerbach, an art historian at Georgia College, mentioned that when she wanted to fill three roles for her game on art in Paris in the 1880s, former Reacting students volunteered to do so, including one who had already graduated and had to drive an hour each way to class; none were enrolled in the course. John Moser, a historian at

Ashland University, observed that his most recent class included six auditors—all of them Reacting veterans who wanted to experience more games. On February 22, 2014, Rebecca Stanton's students at Barnard College held a class dinner at a restaurant in New York. They had taken Stanton's Reacting class seven years earlier; this was their sixth anniversary dinner.

Why do Reacting classes generate, almost spontaneously, such strange levels of engagement? When I first interviewed Nate, the answer seemed obvious. Reacting classes are configured as games. Games are play. People enjoy playing. I decided to write an article developing this simple point. To gain further perspective, I interviewed more Reacting students. I also surveyed the writings of philosophers and psychologists who championed the educational benefits of play. I began with Plato, who endorsed play in the *Republic*—"Let your children's lessons take the form of play"—and went even further in the *Laws:* "Life must be lived as play."[5] Then came Locke and Froebel, followed by a host of educational reformers in the twentieth century. From Rousseau to Dewey, and from Piaget to Erikson, philosophers and psychologists have encouraged teachers to tap the motivational power of play. So I scoured their writings, thinking such works would provide a suitably scholarly gloss on what was otherwise blindingly obvious.

But soon I encountered a problem. Many of the great writers on education insisted that play should push young people along an appropriate developmental path to adulthood. Young children often played in ways that were silly and nonsensical, rooted in make-believe and characterized by competition and aggres-

sion. Though tolerable among the young, such play was fundamentally bad—"foolish and disordered" (Dewey),[6] "infantile"
(Piaget),[7] "destructive and delusional" (Erikson).[8] Bad play
prevented children from making the transition to the real
world of adult work. The educator's task, as Dewey put it, was
to "introduce positive material of value" in order to "lead the
child on," allowing him to "pass naturally, and by continuous
gradations" from play to "more definite study."[9] "The play attitude," he added, "should pass to the work attitude."[10] Piaget similarly proposed to "discipline" play, whereas Erikson sought to
promote "true play." Good play—purged of absurdity, make-
believe, and competition—would prepare young adults for reality, cultivate their reasoning faculties, and encourage them to
embrace the requisite discipline to succeed in college and the
workplace.[11]

   But the students I interviewed delighted in the aspects of
Reacting that the theorists regarded as retrogressive. Students
relished times when Reacting games careened into absurdity,
such as when a young woman, as a Ming scholar, delivered a
persuasive speech on why women should not speak in public,
or when a disciple of Gandhi denounced modernity while re-
ferring to notes on his iPad. And though initially skeptical of
"playing weird roles," Reacting students found the experience
of immersing themselves in the mind-set of someone else to
be peculiarly fascinating. They further insisted that Reacting
became compelling when its competitive elements—a difficult debate, a pivotal vote—culminated in moments of heart-
pounding intensity. These young adults (and plenty of older
ones) were entranced by bad play.

The philosophers and educational theorists warned that if young people failed to acclimate themselves to work, they would never succeed as adults. But students reported that they worked harder while playing Reacting games than while doing course work for other classes. Most Reacting faculty agreed with the students' assessment, and this judgment has repeatedly been confirmed by researchers. In a study of twenty-eight first-year seminars at Washington and Jefferson College, for example, an assessment team found that students in the seven Reacting seminars outperformed students in the twenty-one "Thematic" (traditional) seminars on nearly every measure, including a common essay testing critical thinking skills.[12] But one set of survey responses baffled the researchers: although Reacting students rated their course more highly than did the Thematic students, the Reacting students also indicated that they would be *less likely* to take future Reacting-type courses. The explanation, the researchers learned, was that Reacting students had worked much harder than their peers in regular seminars.[13] A confidential guide to courses at Smith College similarly warned prospective Reacting students:

> Reacting seems like it will be fun and easy. But it tricks you into doing more work than all your other courses combined. Be careful.

"Bad play," in other words, can generate hard work.

Which does not make much sense. Then I realized that many of the students' observations were equally nonsensical, such as claims that they:

- understood themselves better by imagining they were someone else (Chapter 4);
- learned more when teachers said less (Chapter 5);
- found failure to be a pathway to success (Chapter 6);
- experienced strong community bonds through fierce contention (Chapter 7);
- embraced moral thinking when teachers stopped preaching (Chapter 8);
- acquired leadership skills by becoming teammates (Chapter 9); and
- understood the past better by filtering it through their own present (Chapter 10).

Such assertions were counterintuitive if not downright illogical. Moreover, many contravened the basic precepts of higher education.

The experience of playing a Reacting game seemed the antithesis of the pedagogy of higher education. This underscored another point that was becoming increasingly evident. The rationalist foundations of American higher education, though perhaps barely discernible in the modern edifice, had been set down by Plato 2,500 years ago. The critics of bad play, moreover, had borrowed many of their arguments, often explicitly, from the early works of Plato.

Plato's Socrates insisted that a rationalist perspective could prevail only in a state whose citizens had learned, through "chaste and serious play," to work hard at their proper adult roles.[14] In his Athens, however, adults continually surrendered to the natural magic of *mimesis*—the role-playing acumen of playwrights and actors and rhetoricians. Athenians delighted in imagining themselves to be gods and kings, statesmen and jurists; they hooted and howled during raucous competitions in the assembly, law courts, and theaters. Infatuated with bad play, they wallowed in a "morass of ignorance."[15]

That is why Socrates proposed to banish anyone who was adept at transforming himself "into all sorts of characters and representing all sorts of things."[16] Indeed, the suppression of those skilled at role-playing constituted the highest excellence of his utopian scheme. Freed from such seductions, the young could experience, under the guidance of a masterful teacher, the rational play of the mind.

American higher education today may bear little resemblance to Socratic pedagogy—indeed, many insist that therein lies its current deficiencies; but a central Platonic precept—opposition to role-playing—remains deeply embedded in the institutional structures and norms of higher education. Nowadays role-playing is thought to be so obviously wrongheaded that many college educators dismiss it out of hand. When asked to explain why, they usually invoke the arguments of Plato, Dewey, Piaget, or Erikson without citing them by name. Indeed, the subject of role-playing is so far removed from academic discourse that thoughtful arguments on the subject, for or against, are hard to find.

To be sure, some forms of role-playing have sneaked into the ivory tower, usually slipping into its upper chambers. The Harvard Business School's predominant pedagogy—the case method—consists almost entirely of simulations: "You are

CEO of U.S. Steel in 1959 and a strike looms." Many graduate programs in international relations and foreign policy also feature simulations: "It is October 1962 and Soviet missiles have been found in Cuba." But these exercises are simple in structure—Harvard Business School cases average a mere seven to twelve pages of text[17]—and they seldom take up more than a single class. More important, these simulations place students in new situations but not in new "selves." The simulations use what might be called the Connecticut Yankee Mode, in which students are briefly dispatched to the past in order to fix it, carrying a tool kit of contemporary problem-solving skills.

Role-playing simulations have also surfaced in undergraduate education. The most common curricular context is political science, but even then they are rare. A survey of "gateway" political science courses in 238 colleges and universities revealed that fewer than 8 percent of those courses included simulations; and often these occupied a single class.[18] Many undergraduate simulations are little more than exercises. Sociology students "experience" the maldistribution of wealth by playing Monopoly—but with players being allocated unequal assets; and students of science study the problem of building hypotheses by speculating on the contents of a lumpy fabric bag without touching it.[19]

Yet even simple role-playing exercises are often effective, a reason why they are included in the growing buffet of recommended active-learning pedagogies.[20] But these brief simulations lack the motivational and imaginative power of role-immersion games. The students I interviewed explained that Reacting games didn't catch fire until the second or third week, when their new identities and ideas, superheated by competitive pressures, penetrated their minds. That is when they "lost themselves" in the experience. Exactly as Plato had warned: for he had seen how Athenians had succumbed to the "spell" of role-playing—a "childish and vulgar passion."

Plato advanced a reasoned argument in support of a rationalist objective, and it resonated with my own, lifelong immersion in the academic world. He and subsequent theorists pointed in one direction, wholly logical, while the Reacting students seemed to be talking nonsense. But in the end, I followed the students. They were addressing the problem at hand—the strange power of role-immersion games. And the world they described, though alien and somehow forbidden, was also fascinating. Moreover—and I tremble to use the f-word—what the students were doing was fun. Eventually I came to perceive that this seemingly nonsensical realm, when examined from an antirationalist perspective, possessed coherence and power. That's when I decided to write this book, and to base it largely on the opinions of the students. So I threw my net farther, interviewing over the course of four years over ninety students from thirty colleges and universities. This book lists me as author, but the ideas are mostly theirs.

Most treatises on education begin with philosophical first principles, from which are derived the main elements of pedagogical practice. Plato's Socrates, in search of philosophical truth, devised an educational system (and an entire social order) to sustain it. Rousseau, intent on ensuring that Emile remained uncorrupted by society, insisted that the boy be educated in the countryside and denied books.

By contrast, Reacting did not grow out of educational theory; it instead arose almost by accident, when several students transformed a structured debate into an exercise in deep role-playing. Chapter 1 ("All Classes Are Sorta Boring") shows how this innovation paved the way for others. Then the concept spread and evolved rapidly. Faculty from hundreds of colleges and universities proposed further modifications, nearly always based on practice: "This role didn't work very well, so I changed it." The accretion of innumerable improvements and additions transformed Reacting into an ever-evolving system of role-immersion games.

This reliance on innovation-by-practice exacerbated the problem of explanation. In the absence of a theoretical framework to guide and justify decisions, Reacting faculty were continually thrown back on students to determine what worked. Similarly, I have relied on students to explain the appeal of bad play.

Lest academic readers slam this book (or iPad) down in fury, I hasten to acknowledge that the case against bad play is formidably strong. I agree with much of it. In fact, Chapter 2 ("Subversive Play: The Bane of Higher Education") contends that for the past two centuries higher learning has suffered precisely because American students have been fully immersed in bad play—the boozy debates and theatricals of the early literary societies, the hazings and initiations of fraternities, the football craze, beer pong and binge drinking, and a host of competitive, role-playing online worlds, among other obsessions. But this book also contends (Chapter 3: "Creating an Academic Subversive Play World") that the motivational power of bad play—of "subversive play," as I have termed it—can energize students and help them flourish—in college and in life.

Chapter 4 ("Critical Thinking and Our Selves") argues that we experience deep learning by acquiring additional selves; these internal conversations generate deep critical thinking. Chapter 5 ("Overcoming the Silence of the Students") explains that professors talk too much, not because they are fond of speaking but because students often suppress their classmates. Reacting reverses these psychological dynamics. Chapter 6 ("Learning by Failing") proposes that the competitive structure of role-immersion games ensures that students fail, perhaps by stumbling in a speech, by misunderstanding a crucial point, or by losing a game. But these failures, mitigated by being situated within a game, help accommodate students to the risks that help them grow.

Chapter 7 ("Building Community and Global Citizenship") argues that the competitive pressures of role-immersion games generate the strong bonds that build community. Following up on this concept, Chapter 8 ("Inculcating Morality and Empathy [!]") contends that when students immerse themselves in the mind-sets of others, they become more empathetic. Chapter 9 ("Teaching Leadership through Teamwork") maintains that Reacting helps students learn to work within groups—the ideal preparation for leadership. Chapter 10 ("Teaching the Past by Getting it Wrong?") shows how role-playing

games based on historical figures promote imaginative understanding of the past.

The rationalist merits of higher education are well known, intoned by college presidents and commencement speakers, reiterated in institutional mission statements, and endorsed by
most professors—including me. There's no need to restate them
here. This book instead advances what might be called the antirationalist perspective. The central argument is not that
higher education is all wrong, but that it is only half right. Our
predominant pedagogical system—rational, hierarchical, indi-
vidualistic, and well-ordered—often ignores aspects of the self
relating to emotion, mischievous subversion, social engagement, and creative disorder.

Role-immersion games, when configured as an intellectu-
alized pedagogical system, provide access to these often un-
tapped wellsprings of motivation and imagination. This book
can perhaps be regarded as a sort of divination manual, a practical guide to locating those wellsprings and also a primer
on explaining how the magic works.[21] To be sure, a pedagogy
based on role-immersion games has limitations and shortcomings: sometimes the magic fizzles, and class ends with bewildered students staring at the professor–gamemaster in the back
of the room; and sometimes the magic is too potent, and entranced students play too hard, clinging tight to their roles and
bruising the feelings of other students. Longstanding arguments
against role-playing are not without merit. But if the pages
that follow give off a potent whiff of advocacy, it is because the

strong case against role-playing has gone mostly unchallenged for over two millennia.

Many Reacting professors believe that role-immersion games already revitalize our classrooms. They imagine that in the future such games will supplement traditional pedagogies while promoting further experimentation in active learning.

Over the past decade, however, most higher education pundits have envisioned a different future, with online education towering over everything else. The latest rendering is breathtaking in scope, though the blueprint is smudged with erasures. Long gone are the early plans, according to which most colleges would create their own online courses; no longer, too, does it seem inevitable that the University of Phoenix, Coursera, or other for-profit providers will dominate online learning. Increasingly the future is being written by powerful consortia of research universities, headed by Harvard and Stanford, featuring Massive Open Online Courses (MOOCs). Freely available during the years of development, MOOCs are now becoming monetized, the first step in their evolution into McCROCs (Massive Closed Credit-Bearing Online Courses).[22] What will happen next is a source of speculation. Some say that these courses will usher in a new millennium, making the finest teachers available to the entire world at low cost and supported by interactive learning tools beyond our imagining; others predict that when millions of students opt for low-cost online degrees from HarvardX and StanfordX, hundreds of colleges and universities will shut their doors. Higher education may then go the way of Detroit, which clung too long to the past when the future beckoned.[23]

But history unfolds in mysterious ways; the causal arrows are never as unidirectional as pundits think. Already it is becoming clear that many students, subjected to an incessant barrage of Tweets, Facebook summonses, and invitations to fight off aliens or marauding warriors, find it well-nigh impossible to watch a video of even a world-famous professor. (It is also true, of course, that many students, while sitting in a classroom, pay more attention to their electronic devices than the instructor.) But online education is evolving rapidly. José Antonio Bowen rightly notes that its learning products are in their early stages—the equivalent of the Honda circa 1970. "What," he asks, "will its Acura look like?"[24] Many visionaries of online education have already shifted from imitating conventional pedagogies—videos of lecturers—and now plan to embed higher education content within multiplayer games. This will take years and cost billions, but venture capitalists are already moving forthrightly in this direction. (We know, because online education designers have sought access to the Reacting community of scholars.)[25]

Now, as never before, faculty and administrators are determined to make the classroom experience more vital. They know that halfway measures—interactive "clickers" or new versions of PowerPoint—will not make much difference. They're looking to ensure that students *want* to come to their (bricks-and-mortar) institution. Increasingly, these faculty and administrators snap to attention when they hear strange tales of student engagement in Reacting classes.

Reacting will not and cannot supplant the rationalist pedagogy of higher education; but it is already revitalizing the classroom experience at hundreds of colleges and universities. Some Reacting enthusiasts believe that in the future rationalist pedagogies will commonly be supplemented by role-immersion games, a dynamic fusion of Apollonian reason and Dionysian imagination. When this happens, we will become accustomed to weird happenings on our campuses, such as students hurrying off to class, blinking sleep from their eyes, eager to engage in debate at dawn.

CHAPTER 1

"All Classes Are Sorta Boring"

I was late for class, the last of the fall semester, 1995. As I made my way across campus, I leaned into a raw December wind. Leaves skittered along the brick walkway. A few clutched at my shoes and then slipped away. That's how it was with students. They hurtled with manic energy toward uncertain futures while teachers plodded along a set path of professional advancement. Briefly, our lives intersected.

As I entered a stately Georgian building, I looked at the clock above the door. It confirmed my tardiness. But I could do no better than a purposeful trudge up the unevenly worn marble steps. When I reached the classroom, most of the students were clumped at the far end of the table. I took my place at the nearest chair, opposite them. A handful more hustled in a few moments later, obliged to sit near me, as if in penance for their lateness.

I opened my copy of Plato's *Republic,* which bristled with fearsome yellow Post-it notes. I took a deep breath.

"What," I lobbed, "do you think of Plato's attempts to define justice?"

A chill descended. Eyes lowered. Pages fluttered, unencumbered by Post-it notes.

One student hesitantly volunteered a comment; another made a passing observation. A discussion lurched forward. Once or twice a student's perceptive remark gave me hope. But further discussion revealed the patchiness of the students' reading of this masterpiece. They had approached the text as if gathering pebbles at the beach, reaching to grab this or that glittering aperçu to be plonked down during discussion, before it escaped from their minds.

I gazed out the window. The sun had slipped behind the concrete cube of nearby Union Theological Seminary. When I looked back toward the class, I was staring failure in the face, all thirty-two eyes of it. Within a week the semester would be over and they would be gone. Had the class meant anything to them? To me?

I brooded over that class during the winter break. When the students returned in mid-January, I sent an email asking each to stop by my office to chat. Nearly all eventually showed up. I asked what had gone wrong with the class. Most were puzzled by the question and responded warily, buying time to see what I was getting at. But after a third student told me the class had been her favorite, my exasperation boiled over: "You were bored! I was bored! You could *feel* the boredom in the room!" I blurted, voice rising.

She studied the bookshelves above me, as if to make a selection.

"Well, yes," she said. "But all classes are sorta boring. Yours was less boring than most."

Her words struck like lightning, illuminating scenes from my own undergraduate years: the plastic shards and metal bits of an alarm clock, shattered by my fist; the elaborate doodles in my notebooks, followed by all-too-fragmentary notes; the dull murmur of voices, sometimes including my own, discussing the rhythmic structure of Medieval motets; the prospects of the Ibo in the pending Nigerian elections; the failure of state-run workshops in Paris in 1848—or other issues related to an instructor's current research. A collage of fractured images and disjointed sounds—this was what I recalled of my college classes. But it could hardly have been otherwise, since I had skipped so many.

"You're only cheating yourself," an inner voice had chastised, repeating the mantra that parents and teachers have intoned for centuries—and that slackers have resolutely ignored. But when I did show up, most classes were "sorta boring" and more than a few excruciatingly so. I had always chalked this up to my inadequacies as student; but now, hearing the sober assessment of the bright young woman seated opposite me, I wondered: If classes were "sorta boring," was it because of the student or the teacher?

The question goes way back. Henry Adams raised it repeatedly in his account of his own bungled education in *The Education of Henry Adams* (1918). In 1854 he enrolled at Harvard simply because his Boston friends had done so. He paid little attention to the courses. "In truth," he observed, "hardly any

Boston student" took the classes seriously. While conceding his failings as a student, he also pointed a finger at the faculty, who "taught little, and that little ill." By the time he graduated, he had learned nothing. When he received his undergraduate degree, his education "had not yet begun."[1]

For the next decade Adams acquired a practical education as a personal secretary to his father, ambassador to Great Britain, and as a foreign correspondent for the *New York Times*. In 1871, in a mischievous turn of fate, Charles Eliot, Harvard's new president, hired Adams, formerly a bored undergraduate, to teach undergraduates.

Adams's hiring was part of Eliot's master plan to revitalize higher education. Eliot knew that instruction at Harvard was a shambles, so he eliminated most required courses and encouraged faculty to teach smaller classes in advanced subjects. He regarded Adams as the type of fresh-thinking intellectual who could offer provocative new courses and liberate students from the drudgery of lectures.

Adams resolved to inspire students. Over the next six years he "tried a great many experiments" to stimulate their interest. Yet ultimately his curricular innovations proved "clumsy and futile." He "wholly succeeded in none." But again he refused to accept blame. The overwhelming majority of his students "could not be much stimulated by any inducements a teacher could suggest." In 1877 he resigned from Harvard—and swore off teaching. He titled the chapter on his years as Harvard pedagogue, "Failure."[2]

Adams was by no means alone in his disenchantment with undergraduates. In 1888 historian Edward Channing advised

Eliot to move Harvard College "out into the country where it would not interfere with the proper work of the University."[3] Even Eliot eventually abandoned his conceit that brilliant intellectuals could transform undergraduates. Throughout his presidency, students turned up their noses at Eliot's advanced electives and gorged on guts. Of the class of 1898, for example, 55 percent took introductory courses *and no others* during four years at Harvard.[4] Eliot was unfazed: "It really does not make much difference what these unawakened minds dawdle with."[5]

Eliot's nostrums nevertheless spread rapidly among elite colleges and universities. Presidents elsewhere hired top-flight scholars and instituted elective curricula. But their results were little better than Eliot's. In 1889 Ezekiel Robinson, in a speech marking the end of his seventeen-year tenure as president of Brown, recounted his success at establishing graduate programs, recruiting a world-class faculty, and strengthening the undergraduate curriculum. Yet listeners were likely startled when he observed that none of this had stimulated undergraduates. Neither at Brown, nor in "any college in the country, so far as I can learn," had students become more scholarly or studious. It was one thing for students to ignore the rote recitations demanded by the dry pedants of yesteryear and another to doze through classes taught by the finest minds in the world.[6]

The newly hired research scholars made no secret of their contempt for undergraduates. Then as now, professors wangled deals to free themselves of the "burden" of undergraduate instruction. In 1884 John W. Burgess, a political scientist and the most influential member of the Columbia faculty, saw no reason why undergraduate colleges "will have to exist" in the future. The better colleges would elevate themselves into graduate schools and the lesser ones would become mere "gymnasia."[7] When Burgess asked colleague Ogden Rood why he continued to teach undergraduates, Rood reassuringly explained, "I do as little as I can for these dunderheads and save my time for research."[8] Harvard philosopher George Santayana concluded that teachers and students "seemed animals of different species, like a cow and a milkmaid; periodic contributions could pass between them, but not conversation." The four years students spent in college were "trivial and wasted."[9]

The dilemma of the dunderheads persisted into the twentieth century. A. Lawrence Lowell, Eliot's successor, boasted of Harvard's scholars but complained of its students. "Instead of being thrilled by the eager search for truth, our classes too often sit listless on the bench," he noted. "It is not because the lecturer is dull, but because the pupils do not prize the end enough to relish the drudgery required for skill in any great pursuit."[10] Decades later some professors proposed to purge the dunderheads and make the college "the home of an intellectual elite where only Honors students will be welcome."[11] But the tuition of the dunderheads was the lifeblood of the institution, in whose seminar rooms and lecture halls they continued to snooze. In 1951, when political scientist Judith N. Shklar began her stellar Harvard career, she found the culture of the undergraduates to be "one of protected juvenile delinquency." Students "tolerated" no conversation on subjects other than sports and gossip. Occasionally she encountered some "studious youth," but even these "boasted" of their anti-intellectualism. Most faculty had acclimated themselves to students who aspired only to "the Gentlemanly C."[12] Those of us who enrolled at Harvard in the late 1960s and early 1970s were seldom praised for academic diligence.

When Harvard professor and former dean Harry R. Lewis published his thoughtful book on Harvard, *Excellence Without a Soul,* he subtitled it *How a Great University Forgot Education* (2006) without specifying when Harvard classes buzzed with intellectual life.[13] Many faculty today sympathize with the weary professor in Philip Roth's *The Human Stain* (2000). "Our students are abysmally ignorant," he bemoaned, "far and away the dumbest generation in American history." But such words have long echoed through the halls of academia. Many contemporary critics of higher education similarly posit a Golden Age; but no one knows when it was supposed to exist.[14]

The familiar critique of education during the past decade is chiefly noteworthy for how much it resembles the criticisms raised throughout the past two centuries. In 2005 the PBS documentary *Declining by Degrees* showed students dozing in class and bragging about doing no homework. "I take it for granted that most students don't read and don't work," one professor observed. Another said—on camera: "They just sit there."[15]

Surveys have enabled social scientists to calculate with numerical precision the extent of student disengagement. The annual UCLA survey of hundreds of thousands of entering first-year students nationwide has found that in recent years 40 percent are disengaged with or alienated from the academic enterprise. The National Study of Student Engagement (NSSE) concluded that in recent years 20 percent of the students among its more than 500 member institutions were "fully disengaged" with the academic life of their schools. Two sociologists examining the same data concluded that NSSE, which is funded by member colleges, had interpreted the data in an excessively *positive* light: in their view, 45 percent of college students were "fully disengaged." That is, such students seldom came to class or did academic work.[16] Worse, some studies revealed that students' motivation *declined* during their college years.[17]

Other studies uncovered more alarming details: full-time college students *report* that they study on average ten to fifteen hours a week, although one-third say they put in less than half as much time. Another large study found that over one-third of full-time students spent fewer than five hours a week studying.[18] More worrisome, today's students often *believe* they are studying while watching TV, playing video games, or interacting with social media. Their assumption that they learn while multitasking has repeatedly been proven wrong. It also shows they have no idea what real learning entails.[19]

Students who don't work don't learn. In 2011 the authors of *Academically Adrift* found that after three years of college over a third of full-time students demonstrated virtually no improvement in writing and reasoning skills.[20] After surveying hundreds of studies on learning, Derek Bok, one of higher education's staunchest allies, concluded that while it was wrong to say that students learned nothing, they didn't learn very much. He phrased it delicately: the nation's colleges "underachieve."[21]

Social scientists working "in the field" have confirmed the grim conclusions of the statistical studies. In 2001 sociologist Timothy Clydesdale interviewed 125 New Jersey high school seniors the summer before they went to college and then again after their first year. He found that while they had learned to master many basic skills, such as managing checking accounts, schedules, and relationships, they had also proven "largely immune to intellectual curiosity and creative engagement." "I've never had a class where I was really interested and into it," one student at a "public ivy" told Clydesdale. "I mean, it's really boring," another student added. Such responses were typical.[22]

That same year, young anthropology professor Cathy Small went undercover as "Rebekah Nathan, undergraduate student" and lived in a first-year dorm at Northern Arizona University. She was repeating the study of anthropologist Michael Moffatt, who in 1977 had attempted to pass himself off as an undergraduate at Rutgers. Like him, she found virtually *no* evidence that students derived intellectual benefit from classes. They skipped more frequently than she had expected: in the one large course for which she had solid data, barely half came to class on any given day. The students in her dorm, moreover, almost never discussed academic issues—in class or outside of it. Small's "most sobering" insight was "how little intellectual life" mattered to students.[23]

The most obvious proof of student disengagement is how many students fail to graduate. In the fall of 2010, President Obama warned that the United States could not succeed in a global economy as long as it ranked twelfth in the percentage of young adults with college degrees. "We've done okay in terms of college enrollment rates," Obama explained, but more than a third of America's college students fail to earn a degree.[24] (For the past decade, the actual figure is closer to 50 percent.)[25]

Obama proposed "a college access and completion fund" to reduce the financial barriers faced by students who juggle classes
and a full-time job.

But money alone won't solve the problem. In *Crossing the
Finish Line: Completing College at America's Public Universities,*
William G. Bowen, Matthew M. Chingos, and Michael S.
McPherson discovered that one-third of students from even
the *highest* socioeconomic backgrounds failed to graduate. The
authors concluded that these students (and surely plenty of
others) quit because of "weak motivation or interest."[26]

They found classes "sorta boring."

Professors continue to blame students.[27] When the interviewer
for *Declining by Degrees* asked why students slept during class,
the instructor replied, "They know nothing." In February 2011,
after the *Chronicle of Higher Education* reported the unsettling
conclusions of *Academically Adrift,* many professors lashed out
at students in online comments:

- You can't make silk out of a sow's ear.
- We *do* want to blame the students because students,
  no one else, are ultimately responsible for their own
  learning. It is time for us to face the reality that
  nothing really does work when dealing with college
  students who cannot read, write, or solve single-variable
  equations.
- It's not me, it's not the subject matter, it's not the way it's
  taught, it's not the college. It's a failing on the part of the
  students.

- If students spend their time partying, drinking, social-izing, Facebooking, texting, and so on, don't blame the faculty. Blame the students.

Many added that their colleagues agreed but refused to say so publicly. As if to prove the point, all of those posting comments did so anonymously.

But while professors usually blame students, others—especially state legislators, trustees, and the media—blame the faculty. A striking example surfaced after the professor in the PBS documentary declared that her students were ignorant. Director John Merrow retorted that he had found her to be a boring teacher. He then advanced a familiar thesis: professors are hired and promoted because of their scholarship rather than their teaching ability.[28] Senior scholars, insulated by tenure, pawn undergraduate instruction onto overburdened adjuncts and unprepared grad students. Beleaguered instructors ward off student resentment by offering fluff courses, assigning little work, and bestowing As with glad-handed largesse. This "non-aggression" pact enables students to enjoy the social aspects of college without the inconvenience of doing much academic work, and it allows professors to focus on research (or carpentry or yoga) unencumbered by pestering students. Critics, seeking to shatter the pact, call for a crackdown on faculty: an end to tenure, more rigorous assessment of teaching, and fewer leaves and perks.

Both sides eventually haul out their most powerful rhetorical artillery.[29] In response to the charge that they teach poorly, professors cite the fact that some students attend class, work hard, and graduate with honors. The problem with higher education is the dearth of such students. And students, in response to charges of laziness and poor motivation, insist the superstar professors draw them to class and keep them on the edge of their seats. The problem with higher education is the dearth of such teachers.

These claims, too, have been around forever. Henry Adams, student, regarded most of his teachers as hopeless. Henry Adams, professor, maintained that 90 percent of his students were incapable of learning. Like most faculty before and since, he decided to "cultivate" the one student in ten who was eager to learn.[30] ("Ten percent" surfaces repeatedly, at different times and institutions, as the percentage of motivated students. Harvard was a notable exception: in 1934 Alfred Hanford, Dean of the Faculty, claimed that 15 to 20 percent of Harvard students "were capable of achieving something more than a gentleman's grade of C.")[31]

Adams felt awkward about neglecting nine-tenths of his students; after all, the emerging titan of American letters had himself been a sluggard as an undergraduate. Senior faculty nowadays similarly squirm when former "dunderheads" return to campus to lecture on their prizewinning screenplay or to cut the ribbon for a building funded by their entrepreneurial acumen. How did such dullards metamorphose into geniuses?

The answer, of course, is that many students are dull witted only in the classroom. Even Barack Obama, the future head of the Harvard Law Review (among other singular accomplishments), conceded that he "merely went through the motions" as an undergraduate at Occidental College, "as indifferent toward college as toward most everything else."[32] And what of dropouts such as Bill Gates, Steve Jobs, Mark Zuckerberg, and Sean Parker—and lesser celebrities such as William Faulkner and Robert Frost? Were these "dunderheads" incapable of benefiting from college? In 2011 the growing pantheon of illustrious dropouts prompted a *New York Times* columnist to encourage parents to use family savings to help bright kids start a business rather than go to college.[33] Although few agree that college is for losers, no one can dispute that college fails to stimulate many students with academic potential.

But if most students are capable of learning and most faculty are good teachers, why are so many classes "sorta boring"?

In *Our Underachieving Colleges* (2006), Derek Bok proposed an answer. Most classes, he reported, consist of lectures and loosely structured discussions, forms of education that learning research has shown to be ineffective. Colleges underachieve because the predominant modes of instruction are inadequate learning tools.

Bok called on college educators to experiment with active-learning pedagogies—especially those featuring problem-solving and teamwork—and adopt those that prove successful. But he detected little evidence of the pedagogical transformation he advocated. "Teaching methods," he explained, "change very slowly."[34] Administrators lack the resources to reward innovative teaching; faculty cling to professional conventions; and students are wary of active-learning approaches. Colleges would not become "effective learning organizations" anytime soon.[35]

When Bok wrote these words, however, he was unaware of a pedagogical initiative whose roots grew out of one failed class in December 1995.

Innovation by Accident

During the summer of 1996 I scrapped my usual seminar for first-year students and created some structured debates, with winners and losers, set in particular historical moments. I had no special interest in learning theory or the fate of higher education. Like Henry Adams, I sought a more stimulating classroom experience—for myself as much as for my students.

At the first meeting of the class that September, I explained that we wouldn't just discuss important texts. Instead, students would play three "games"—one each month—that were structured as debates.

Diana Paquin Morel, seated across the table, tilted her head and fixed me with cool blue eyes: "If the first game doesn't work, will you stick with the others?"

Her skepticism brought me up short. I assumed students would be eager to try something new. I didn't know what to say to her. "Of course it will work," I babbled, more than a little unsettled by the anxious glances of the other students.

In the next class I lectured on ancient Athens and Plato's *Republic* and distributed the roles for a game to determine whether Socrates was guilty of "corrupting the youth" of Athens. For the next two sessions, the defenders and prosecutors of Socrates met separately, honing their arguments. Then came the trial, which lasted several classes. Each side scrutinized the other side's positions and tried to pick them apart, culling arguments from the *Republic*. Some of the debates were excellent. Nearly everyone was engaged. I was satisfied.

None of it was all that different from the question–response structure of other seminars. This was just a slightly more stylized way of accomplishing the same end. Many teachers had held mock trials of Socrates. Many students had participated in structured debates for Model UN. My class was not in the least bit special.

But several weeks later things careened in an unexpected direction.

It happened during the second game, set in the Forbidden City in Beijing during the Ming Dynasty. After reading *The Analects of Confucius*, each student was assigned a role as one of the Wanli emperor's top Confucian advisers in the Hanlin Academy. The emperor and his supporters would win if they could prevent a majority of the top bureaucrat–scholars from publishing criticisms of their policies. The Confucian purists would win if they could persuade the bureaucracy to oppose the emperor. In history, the struggle between Confucian purists and the Wanli emperor's faction persisted for decades, fatally weakening the dynasty. The game examined only the origins of the dispute.

Purvi Mehta had been randomly chosen as the Emperor Wanli; and Fiza Quraishi, as first minister and chief scholar-bureaucrat. Students tittered at being addressed as "Academician," and Confucian critics accused the Emperor of running amok among the concubines, thereby generating (literally) a succession dispute. The class was lighthearted and fun. The discussion of the *Analects* was mostly on target.

But as I left the classroom Purvi and Fiza pounced on me in the hallway and poured out their frustrations.

"Nobody is taking this seriously," Fiza complained. "It's all just a joke. This isn't how top scholars would have acted." Purvi nodded.

I conceded their point and thought about it. "Confucius believed that ritual could teach behavior," I finally suggested. "He said that if you perform mourning rituals, you're more likely to feel grief; if you bow to a superior, you're more likely to feel deference. Maybe you should try that."

"You mean, make them bow to Purvi?" Fiza asked. "You'd let me do that?"

"Sure," I said without giving it much thought. "Why not? Purvi's the emperor. Just make sure it's based on actual Ming ritual."

I forgot this conversation over the weekend. When the game resumed on Monday, Purvi was missing from the "emperor's" chair at the head of the table. Fiza rose and walked to the podium with a stately gait that was only slightly undone by her unlaced, black high-top sneakers. She read from a note card: "The emperor was displeased with your behavior at the last session."

"She's one to talk, impregnating all those concubines!" someone shouted.

The class erupted in laughter. Fiza smiled for an instant, caught herself, and frowned. "I was displeased, too"—now her tone was serious—"and we're not going to allow it." She looked up and surveyed her classmates: "I mean it, you guys. It's not going to happen again." Glancing down at a fat, hardcover book, she explained that Hanlin scholars were obliged to treat the emperor with respect. When the emperor entered the Academy, everyone must stand. When he sat, they were to sit up straight, without crossing their legs. No one could make jokes or have side conversations. "You can speak only when I say so," Fiza added. "If you fail to do this, I'll have you removed. And remember: your grade depends on class participation and your grade will suffer."

"She can't do that!" Diana snapped. "She can't silence us!" She looked at me.

Fiza's words had astonished me, too. Drawing on that deep reservoir of feigned self-assurance that sustains teachers in moments of perplexity, I replied, "Sure she can. She's the top minister."

A minute later, Purvi entered the room. Fiza stood, as did those of the emperor's faction. The others, still seated, looked at each other and then at Diana.

Slowly, mindful that all eyes were on her, Diana rose. "I don't want my grade to suffer," she muttered. The others stood too. Purvi, smiling nervously, took her seat.

Soon after the debate began, one of the emperor's critics made a joke. Fiza cut her off. "You can't do that. I'm not kidding. Any more of that, you're out of the room."

Her voice was firm. More glances in my direction. I looked at my notebook and scribbled furiously.

Gradually the tone of the class shifted. Students deferred to Fiza and emulated her seriousness. Critics of the emperor lowered their voices and couched their barbs in flowery metaphors: ("Oh, worthy and most esteemed emperor"). Confucian precepts that in other years I had to tweeze out of students now blossomed in profusion. Shy students spoke. The debate, though conducted almost in whispers, acquired a strange, sharp edge.

No class I had seen even vaguely resembled this one. Never had I "taught" a class without saying a word. Never had students been so engaged and in such a weird way.

Someone piped up, "Does anyone realize that class was supposed to end seven minutes ago?"

Heads jerked toward the clock in the back. Then we looked at one another in mute and slightly embarrassed wonderment, as when the lights come on after a good movie.

We had lost track of ourselves.

Each succeeding class was stranger still. If a student advanced a weak argument or made a mistake, the other faction pounced on it. Teammates would leap to defend the first student with supporting arguments. Students grew more comfortable with their assigned roles and philosophical suppositions. They argued with conviction and force. Their papers in support of oral arguments were informed by texts I had not assigned.

Because the transformation occurred after Fiza and Purvi had taken control of the class, I moved my seat farther from the table each week. By the end of the game, I was sitting alone at the back of the room. No one seemed to notice. Students effortlessly filled the space I had dominated. Before and after class and during office hours, clumps of students besieged me; and I was flooded with email queries. But I hardly spoke in a class that had become the students' world, subject to constraints first established in sixteenth-century China.[36]

I invited Judith Shapiro, Barnard's new president, to visit the class. An anthropologist who had done field research among the Yanomami and Tapirapé of central and northwestern Brazil, Shapiro instantly perceived the game's transformative potential. She had long worried that undergraduates were too absorbed in their own selves; this class showed how they could embrace new ideas and perspectives.

We agreed that Purvi and Fiza had stumbled onto something with pedagogical potential. During a single weekend of research on Ming rituals and governance, they had laid the foundations for a new type of student-run learning experience. What, we wondered, could be accomplished by scholar–specialists who committed months or years to designing such a game? Shapiro swiftly endorsed a far broader pedagogical experiment and agreed to take responsibility if it flopped.

Over the next few years, scholarly specialists from other universities helped transform the original set-piece debates into increasingly complex and elaborate games. The concept spread to other colleges and universities, chiefly by word of mouth. During the next few years hundreds of professors joined the initiative, adding complexity and subtlety to existing games and designing scores of new ones.[37] By 2013, faculty at over 350 colleges and universities were teaching with dozens of Reacting games; that same year, forty of these schools formed the Reacting Consortium, a not-for-profit organization that governs the Reacting initiative.[38]

Nearly everywhere, the results have been much the same. Students work harder than anyone can recall. Students rarely miss class and faculty look forward to it. No one calls these classes "sorta boring."

But why don't traditional classes generate this sort of excitement? What's wrong with higher education?

From the perspective of faculty and administrators, not much at all. Higher education is like a majestic clipper ship, a masterpiece of workmanship and design, the triumph of a civilization. Those of us who have booked nearly lifelong passage gaze on it incessantly, sometimes lauding the workmanship, sometimes scrutinizing its every inch for flaws. When it catches a breeze, our hearts leap, for then it is a wonder to behold. Yet often we stare in puzzlement at the towering sails that hang limply from the masts. To determine why it sometimes moves slowly—why it underachieves—we must force ourselves to look away from the ship itself. And when we do, we will likely detect a stiff wind. The problem, as the next chapter shows, is that the wind has been blowing in the wrong direction. For centuries.

CHAPTER 2

Subversive Play: The Bane of Higher Education

Henry Seidel Canby, a young English professor at Yale, had worked hard crafting a lecture on Robert Browning's "Childe Roland to the Dark Tower Came," and now his words swelled to a climax, powered by the meter of the poem. After the final cadence, he abruptly announced, "That's all for today."

Stunned, the students sat in silence. Canby would never forget that moment—a "somnolent afternoon" when orioles flitted through the trees and a grass-cutter clattered on the college lawn. A few students quietly slipped out of the room. For a time Canby basked "in the pleasant glow of successful achievement." Then a handful of students drew closer, unwilling, no doubt, to take leave of Browning so precipitously.

"What is my mark, please?" one asked, and jarred unpleas-
antly on my optimistic mood. "Am I going to be warned
this month?" said another. "Are we going to have this in
the examination?" a third pleaded. Then up stood, then
out stepped, then in struck, amid all these, a fourth with a
cold, hard-souled look to him. "What is there *practical* in
all this literature, Professor?" he queried, obstinately; and
might have added, "Your answer won't interest *me*."

Canby trudged back to his office "and sat down to think it
out." The words of a former teacher echoed—"the astonishing
power of the undergraduate mind to resist the intrusion of
knowledge." He pondered the "multitudinous articles, essays,
letters, reports 'chronicling' the failure of the colleges." He considered the student response to his lecture on Browning and recalled many more such discomfitures. Canby proceeded to write
a book on the "deathly indifference" that "hangs like a fog-
bank" over the American university.[1] It was published in 1915.

He concluded that the disengagement of the students was
not the fault of the colleges, which had been purged of the out-
moded curriculum of the nineteenth century, nor of the professors, most of whom were far better trained and educated than
their predecessors. The real culprits were society, for failing to
enshrine higher learning, and parents, for neglecting to prepare
sons (!) to work hard. Students consequently arrived at college
expecting to have a good time. When professors demanded
work, students paid them little heed.[2]

A few years later Canby left Yale—and undergraduate
teaching. He served in the Great War, edited several literary

journals, and founded the Book-of-the-Month Club. The former English professor now advocated literary excellence— his selections included George Santayana and Erich Maria Remarque—but readers spurned highbrow offerings. The listless students of Canby's English class had become the undiscerning adults who preferred fluff to serious literature. So Canby continued to brood: Why had colleges failed to stimulate the life of the mind? In a 1936 memoir, Canby revisited the fog bank that enshrouded undergraduate education. But this time he surveyed the miasma not from the professor's lectern but from the vantage point of his own undergraduate experience forty years earlier.[3]

The new perspective produced a revelation. Student disengagement had not been caused by society or parents, as he had argued two decades earlier. The culprit was the social world of the students.

Canby explained that when he first arrived in New Haven in September of 1896 he was "dragging a suitcase full of books and carrying as well a set of illusions about the nature of the experience that awaited him." That all changed when he spotted the other students.

> I picked them out in their turtle-neck sweaters under the briefest of top coats, as a dog sees only other dogs on a busy road. There was an arrogant and enchanting irresponsibility in their behavior which was intoxicating. I longed to get rid of my suitcase with its irrelevant books and into a sweater which I saw to be obligatory—to dress like them, to be like them.[4]

Within a few days he was sucked into the social vortex of clubs and fraternities. Soon he realized he had "entered a state within a state, and joined a faction of that state, the student body, aware really only of themselves, their own life." He and his classmates had become beings "from another world." And in that world, they worked incessantly on club projects, parties, hazings, and contests. "If we had no real hardships, we made our lives incredibly hard," he recalled.[5]

Why did Canby and his peers work so frenziedly at such silliness? Obviously they were engaged in play, but Canby regarded it as different from anything he had ever experienced. This form of play consisted of several distinctive elements, all of which were tinged with a delicious illicitness.

A Theory of Subversive Play

Canby and his peers were engaged in social competition. As soon as he arrived at Yale he sized up the other students *("as a dog sees only other dogs")* and perceived that he was competing with them—and for their approval. He worried about how he measured up, mindful that everyone else was making similar judgments. He joined as many clubs and cliques as would have him and submitted to an almost incessant round of pledging, hazings, and initiations. Most other students were doing the same things. "There was no fiercer competition in the business world than the undergraduate competition for social rewards," he wrote.[6]

To succeed in this competition, Canby was obliged to become an altogether different person. In addition to acquiring a turtleneck sweater *("to be like them"),* Canby realized that he must discard "his tie, his hat, his slang, as a manifesto of his escape from rule, but also of his new allegiance." And thus he was "born again, painlessly and without introspection." He became a fraternity brother, a fanatic of the Yale football team, a roistering young blade eager to do mischief, a carousing Yalie who scorned professors and academics. While playing in these ways, Canby became a different person.

Furthermore, Canby's new self was explicitly antirational. When he reflected on his college years forty years later, Canby, an accomplished writer who chose words carefully, repeatedly described the world of students with metaphors of primitivism, savagery, barbarism, enchantment, and fanaticism. He and his classmates had been "intoxicated" by the world they made, which pulsated with unreflective energy and manic flights of fancy. Canby's "rebirth" into the tribe of college students was accomplished, he remembered, "without introspection." He didn't give it a moment's thought. If college existed to promote the life of the rational mind, the play of the students enshrined its antithesis.

The major elements of the students' play world—competition, identity change, and antirationality—imaginatively undermined the social hierarchies, conventional beliefs, and cultural practices of college officials and faculty. Obviously, few of these Yalies were destined to become anarchists or revolutionaries. (When William Jennings Bryan campaigned in New Haven, Canby's classmates laughed at him.) How, then, can the world of such students be regarded as subversive?

Consider, first, its competitive elements—especially the fraternity rushes and hazings. Some scholars contend that such

practices imbued students with a competitive ethos that ultimately prepared them for a capitalist economy.[7] This argument
would be more persuasive if Canby and his classmates had competed for good grades, or perhaps in starting successful businesses or tracking down investment opportunities. But Canby
and his chums competed by seeing who could come up with
the most outrageous pranks and by brawling in the streets of
"respectable" neighborhoods. Perhaps such activities cemented
the social network of future scions of American capitalism; but
it's hard to posit much functionalist benefit in such idiocy.

Two years after publication of Canby's memoir, Johan
Huizinga, the great Dutch historian, argued in *Homo Ludens*
(1938) that human beings have always been drawn to competitive play. Man's earliest cultural artifacts and language itself
contained ubiquitous references to contests and competitions.
Warfare, law, politics, commerce, science—all were "rooted in
the primeval soil" of competitive play.[8] Huizinga understood
that such play was based on some psychological drive—"this
intensity, this absorption, this power of maddening"—but he
struggled to explain its origin."[9]

What Huizinga hinted at, but never stated, is that the irrational compulsion to compete and win is derived from its
promise of overturning familiar statuses and beliefs. The "stu-
dentry," Canby observed, "constantly practised direct warfare
or passive resistance against its superiors."[10] The details of his
rebellion are telling: the free-for-alls were held in "respectable"
neighborhoods, and the evenings of debauchery were more delicious for having been funded by pawning "good suits." Canby
and his friends intentionally "scorned decorum," publicly flout-

ing their break with (adult) social conventions.[11] That's what made it so much fun.

Huizinga did not underscore the subversive character of competitive play because it contradicted his fundamental thesis: If civilizations had been built by competitive play, then its motivational force could hardly have been subversive in character.

Competition thrills, however, because it contains the *possibility* of subverting existing social hierarchies and cultural assumptions. For Canby and his classmates, college was a churning social maelstrom where young men competed for precedence. Rather than accept the usual criteria for distinction, such as family name and wealth or scholarly attainments, they concocted innumerable competitions based on antithetical standards and principles. A son of an old Boston family might be immensely wealthy, but would he crack during the fraternity's initiatory ordeal? A tall and handsome classmate might get all the best dates, but could he keep his wits after quaffing his tenth beer? An assiduous young scholar might achieve the highest rank in the class, but did he have the moxie to smash a lamp post and run like hell on a midnight revel? The students' competitions re-sorted the ascribed social order according to subversive criteria of their own devising.

The very *existence* of such competitions evokes subversion, because it encourages any competitor to imagine herself as a different sort of person—and that is the deepest form of subversion. ("I am not who I thought I was. I can be someone else.")

But this leads back to the conundrum that Huizinga evaded, and that has bedeviled theorists of play ever since Plato. It would seem to be obvious that the play forms of a society must be compatible with the purposes of that society. "If children play on the right lines from the beginning and learn orderly habits from their education," said Plato's Socrates, then they will grow up to become "serious citizens."[12] From Dewey onward, social theorists of a functionalist bent have agreed that play upholds social forms. How could it be otherwise? How can any society survive if its young people internalize behaviors and values *antithetical* to those they will need as adults?

Some clues to answering these questions were provided by anthropologist Victor Turner and others following in his footsteps. Turner, though trained in the British school of structural functionalism, perceived that the public rituals of the Ndembu peoples of Zambia upheld matrilineality, the dominant principle of Ndembu society. Such rituals focused on the milk tree, whose bark emitted a milky substance that resembled breast milk. But the men's secret initiation ceremonies associated whiteness with semen and male generative power. The symbolism of the men's rites thus turned the dominant beliefs of the Ndembu "upside down." This "antistructural" friction, Turner reasoned, generated much of the ritual's emotional power. By expressing (if only symbolically) subversive, antistructural ideas, the ritual enabled men to experience imaginative liberation from the constraints of society.[13] Turner further assumed that such rituals— he called them "liminal"—appeared in all societies. "From time to time," Turner explained, most people seek to discard their customary clothing and status markers and "don the liberating masks of a liminal masquerade."[14]

Turner's reference to masquerade was likely an allusion to Mikhail Bakhtin (1895–1975), the Russian literary theorist who analyzed the deep play of the folk culture of medieval and Renaissance Europe, especially its masquerades, carnivals, games, feasts, and festivals as described by Rabelais. Like Turner, Bakhtin was struck by the pervasive social inversions that surfaced at such times: fools who discoursed in learned Latin; prostitutes who conducted pseudoreligious rites; buffoons who laughed themselves to death. Often, too, such forms of play shifted from inversion to imaginative subversion: during public festivals, chaste rites yielded to salacious dances; and prudent economy, to lavish consumption and grotesque feasts. In the play world of carnival

> all hierarchies are canceled. All castes and ages are equal. During the fire festival a boy blows out his father's candle, crying out . . . "Death to you, sir father!"[15]

In addition to emphasizing the social inversion of carnivalesque play, Bakhtin perceived another central element. Mind was superseded by bodily imperatives: overeating, farting, defecating, screwing.[16] Reason gave way to unreason; and logic, to absurdity. This inversion of normal thought processes was another reason such ceremonies had so much emotional power.

Turner, who never abandoned his functionalist roots, insisted that antistructural rituals promoted social cohesion by venting frustrations.[17] Bakhtin, a Russian theorist who was obliged to navigate the treacherous shoals of Soviet doctrine, never made it clear whether carnivalesque subversions upheld the social order (as Turner maintained) or provided a destabilizing critique of it. Were the Ndembu men, having symbolically challenged matrilineality, more inclined to challenge it in their daily lives? Were the peasants of early modern Europe, having imagined themselves to be lords, tempted to overthrow their masters? And did Canby and his classmates imperil the foundations of the social and political order of early twentieth-century America?

To pose such questions is to suggest their silliness. Almost surely, subversive play did not prefigure social or cultural upheaval. But we cannot be certain—nor could the Ndembu, the peoples of early modern Europe, or college students a century ago. Who can say when subversive play will subvert its own rules? Sometimes a jester's wit might cut too close to the bone and the king would lop off his head. That uncertainty—that straddling of the boundaries of real and unreal—is a source of the peculiar emotional power of subversive play.

This also explains why subversive play usually operates within an explicitly secret or illicit realm. "Explicitly illicit" may seem a contradiction in terms, but it is one of the characteristically nonsensical elements of subversive play. The secrecy of subversive play always conceals poorly. Ndembu women participated in the (secret!) male initiation ceremonies. Lords and ecclesiastical officials in early modern Europe themselves enjoyed carnivalesque subversions: most people recognized the faces behind the masks. Many of the faculty and officers at Yale had gone through the same initiations experienced by Canby and his fraternity brothers. In such instances, the veil of secrecy was so thin as to be transparent. Cornell president Andrew White observed that the secrecy of the fraternities was "nominal." It concealed nothing.[18]

But why go to all of the bother and rigmarole to impose a spurious secrecy?

Because the trappings of secrecy signify that subversive play is not of the *real* world. Ndembu men and carnivalesque revelers were not engaged in subversion but were merely *pretending* to do so. Similarly, Canby and his classmates were not practicing "direct warfare" on college officials and adults; they were only playing at it, concealing their subversion behind masks of metaphor, secrecy, and make-believe.

Finally, subversive play often is restricted to particular times and places. Within the lines of a football field, for example, a blitzing linebacker is allowed to plow into an opponent with intent to harm; but if he were to charge into the stands and knock down the fans, he would be arrested. Similarly, the male initiation rites of the Ndembu and the carnivals of medieval Europe were allowed only at certain times and places. Then, participants were free to imagine a world turned upside down, where men's power trumped matrilineality or peasants ruled over lords; but everyone knew that at the end of the day, things would be set to rights. This allowed people the thrill of subversive imaginings without admitting such thoughts into their *real* selves and everyday lives.[19] Canby recalled that "in a leap of the imagination" he was "naturalized into a new government, more vital than any I had known."[20] He could confess this so easily because it was only for play.

Canby harbored no illusions about the subversive play world the students built and tirelessly sustained. Shallow and unreal, its juvenile verities were mere "shams." Worse, it deprived him of a college education, much as it later produced undergraduates incapable of appreciating "Childe Harold" and college-educated citizens bereft of intellectual curiosity.[21]

Yet Canby could not "think of that life now except with affection."[22] And that was his main insight: the subversive play world of the students was nearly addictive. When arrayed against such formidable potency, his painstakingly crafted lecture on "Childe Harold" did not stand a chance.

The Other History of Higher Education

The familiar history of American higher education is a chronicle of institutional growth and expansion, of improvement in faculty education and training, and of the rationalization of texts and curricula. But this comprises only half the story. Much as medieval people "built a second world and a second life" distinct from the "serious official, ecclesiastical, feudal, and political cult forms and ceremonies" (in Bakhtin's words), generations of college students have built and inhabited subversive play worlds that are distinct from the official institutions of higher education.[23] Two centuries of improvement in higher education have largely been undone by the parallel strengthening of the students' subversive play. Faculty teach better; but students play harder. Students have made their social competitions more intense, their identity transformations more exotic, their subversions more delicious, and their absurdities more mind-blowing.

The story can be sketched here only in broad strokes, but a likely beginning in the United States is with the rise of debating and literary societies in the early nineteenth century. Each week members competed as debaters, orators, singers, joke-tellers, and drinkers. Within a year or two of the establishment of a debating society at a college, a rival society emerged on campus to challenge it.[24] Now members not only competed with each other, but also against the rival society. To improve their chances of prevailing in the increasingly prolific debates, orations, and theatricals, members paid special dues to establish society libraries. By the 1830s, the libraries of these societies usually held more volumes than the libraries run by the colleges themselves.[25]

It might seem that the debating societies were compatible with the educational purposes of the colleges, but nearly everywhere presidents and faculty fought to suppress them. Officials carped that society members nearly always met off campus, often in taverns, and shrouded their activities in oaths of secrecy. The officials assumed—rightly—that students drank (a violation of college rules) and spent much of their time lampooning faculty and criticizing their institution's religious regimen. Administrators complained, too, that the intense rivalry between societies led to campus-wide melees. And because students put so much time and effort into society activities, they neglected their classes. Despite persistent opposition from college authorities, the societies flourished.[26]

After the Civil War, however, a far more powerful subversive play world elbowed out the debating societies.[27] Fraternities borrowed some of the elements of the debating societies—such as the oaths of secrecy—but intensified the competitive elements by instituting pledging and hazing.[28] Failure to be admitted to a fraternity became a badge of social ostracism, what one observer in 1882 called "a silent exclusion, stern and cold as death and about as hopeless."[29]

Pledging and hazing were merely the competitive prelimi-
naries for a new element, an elaborate ritual that transformed
initiates into brothers. Often fraternity initiates were blindfolded and stripped; sometimes they were branded, dumped
into tubs of cold water, administered electrical shocks, forced
to ingest disgusting substances, or otherwise obliged to undergo
painful, embarrassing, and even dangerous ordeals. Humiliation, initiates were told, was necessary to persuade them to repudiate their former, defective self. The ceremony climaxed in
a setting associated with death: often initiates found themselves lying in coffins or blindfolded in cemeteries, surrounded
by skulls and skeletons.[30] Their former selves were now dead
and buried. Then came a flash of light, an explosion of sound,
cheers and laughter, and a boozy celebration. The initiate was
reborn into a new family as a brother. A final element in the
appeal of the initiations was their craziness. In 1863 Edward
Hitchcock, president of Amherst, described fraternity members
as "deranged": they acted as if "under strong hallucination, if
not partial insanity."[31]

Alarmed by the mysterious power of the fraternities, college presidents and faculty vowed to stamp them out. As early
as 1849, professors at the University of Michigan denounced
fraternities as "a monster power" that threatened "debauchery,
drunkenness, pugilism, and disorder and ravagism." The university expelled the fraternities and their organizers; but when
students threatened a mass exodus, college officials relented.[32]
President James McCosh of Princeton similarly acknowledged
the threat of fraternities—their secrecy, interference in the
"plans of the college authorities," and tempting "young men to

drink and dissipation." "Nearly every professor acknowledges them to be an evil," he added, "but is afraid of them."[33]

The subversive character of the fraternities intensified their appeal. Andrew D. White, president of Cornell, concluded that the fight against fraternities could not be won. Indeed, the more that faculty and administrators attempted to ban fraternities or denounced them as a "monster power"—the phrase recurs—the greater their popularity.[34] A banned super-secret fraternity, White concluded, became "a wretched, occult, demoralizing power."

By the 1880s, the triumph of the fraternities was nearly complete. College officials now sought to resuscitate the debating societies as a lesser evil, but it was too late. In 1880 a Yale student recalled that after the arrival of the fraternities nothing could make students "take an interest" in the debating societies.[35]

By then, too, students were adding another room to the funhouse of their new subversive play world: intercollegiate football. Students themselves established athletic associations to build facilities and rent equipment, schedule games, and arrange travel. Like fraternities, football neatly subverted the academic enterprise. While colleges and universities were hiring faculty with advanced degrees and enshrining the life of the mind, football celebrated brute strength. In 1892 Harvard president Charles Eliot denounced football as an "evil" that sapped students' energy and diverted them from study.[36] "Worse preparation for the real struggles and contests of life can hardly be imagined," he added.[37] Yet the more that college officials inveighed against the sport, the more popular it became. College officials bemoaned their "powerlessness" to regulate a sport run by the "crude and boyish devices" of the students themselves.[38] As historian John Thelin observed, attempts by faculty and administrators to take control of intercollegiate athletics were "usually derailed by determined undergraduates."[39]

Early in the twentieth century, the appalling toll of football injuries and fatalities emboldened some college administrators to demand its eradication. Criticism peaked in 1904, when twenty students were killed in collegiate football games. After more deaths the following year, Columbia president Nicholas Murray Butler cancelled the sport and called on other college presidents to do likewise. But students, supported by alumni, rose in defense of football; and no other Ivy president joined Butler's crusade. Ten years later, Columbia restored the sport.[40] By then, fraternities and intercollegiate football stood as the twin pillars of student life, the crowning achievements of the world the students made. In 1907 Woodrow Wilson, president of Princeton, resolved to dismantle the "sideshows" of student life—fraternities, eating clubs, and athletic associations—because they were

> so numerous, so diverting—so important, if you will— that they have swallowed up the circus, and those who perform in the main tent must often whistle for their audiences, discouraged and humiliated.[41]

But Wilson was stymied by the combined opposition of students and influential alumni such as Joseph Pyne, Princeton's richest benefactor (and member of dozens of Princeton clubs and sporting groups). To Pyne and countless others, the student-built world mattered more than professors and academics. Discouraged and humiliated, Wilson fled Princeton and set his course for the less obdurate realm of politics.[42]

After World War I, most college officials abandoned efforts to eliminate the "side shows" and instead brought them into the main tent. They wrested control of football from the students by promising to build football stadiums and recruit better athletes and coaches. In the intensely competitive world of the students, the appeal of a winning team clinched the matter. College administrators negotiated similar deals with fraternities: in return for some modest degree of college oversight, the fraternities could stay. Administrators gained a cheap and easy way to recruit, house, and feed students, while fraternities were free to concentrate on subversive play, nearly always to the detriment of academic performance.[43] Fraternities became "entrenched" in college life, historian Helen Horowitz observed, with a "strength and intensity" that has "baffled observers for over a century."[44]

Nowadays, fraternities and sororities remain a major factor in college life.[45] But in recent decades their predominance has been challenged by new forms of subversive play. *Animal House* (1978), starring John Belushi as "Bluto Blutarsky," showed how students could create a subversive play world with little more than a few kegs of beer. But while Bluto and his fellow frat-house rejects tried to outdo each other as gross-outs, they lacked a clear framework for competition. Big Alcohol fixed this by promoting beer pong, a drinking game in which students bounce ping-pong balls into plastic cups, triggering a round of obligatory drinking. In the 1980s Anheuser-Busch mounted a forty-seven city advertising blitz in which it distributed beer pong kits to fraternities and college bars.[46] Other drinking games proliferated; in the 1990s, *The Complete Book of Beer-Drinking Games* sold half a million copies.[47]

Through such ploys, Big Alcohol changed the subversive play of students. The most obvious result was a marked increase in competitive drinking. In 1999 John Eskovitz, the editor of the *Indiana Daily Student,* explained that students on his campus "try to outdo each other in drinking games." Students constantly boast about "how much they drank and how fast, and how many crazy things they did while drunk, even how they passed out."[48] Students at Dartmouth told researchers that the appeal of drinking was largely derived from its competitiveness. "I don't like just sitting down and drinking," one student explained. "I love competition, so for me pong is perfect."[49]

In 2005 Barrett Seaman, a reporter on assignment for *Time,* spent months living with students at several different colleges. He was astonished by the frequency and intensity of beer-drinking games. And Seaman was no ingenue, having been president of a fraternity as an undergraduate at Hamilton College two decades earlier. But the drinking of his day was "nothing like the array of games now deeply embedded in campus culture."[50]

A senior anthropologist at Dartmouth similarly explained that binge drinking on campus had become a cultural rite. He described how, during regular Wednesday fraternity "meetings," the chapter president initiated the rite by guzzling beer until he vomited, to the thunderous cheers of its brothers. Then they joined in, and soon lost all inhibitions, urinating or vomiting in cans "throughout the meeting." Binge drinking was "a kind of carnival" in which students competed as gross-outs, inverted social norms, and surrendered to animal impulses.[51] Recent studies show that nearly half of college students are binge drinkers or, as one researcher put it, "situational alcoholics."[52] Nearly one in four students acknowledges having gone on a drinking binge *three* times or more within the previous two weeks.[53] Alcohol poisoning is so common that major universities keep multiple ambulances on alert on most weekends. Over a three-year period at Penn State, for example, 585 students were hospitalized for alcohol poisoning.[54] Nationwide, alcohol is cited as the main cause of 70,000 sexual assaults and the deaths of nearly 1,700 college students each year.[55]

In recent years, undergraduate videographers have released "I'm Shmacked" videos ranking the distinctive party scene—drugs, drinking, and sex—of different colleges. But unlike the *U.S. News and World Report* rankings, these videos assess colleges according to what matters most to many students: the craziness of their subversive play.[56] Hard-drinking students have subverted nearly every social convention save one: they buy plenty of booze, exactly as the corporate marketers planned.

For decades, a nationwide annual survey of tens of thousands of entering college freshmen reported that the "coolest" thing on campus was drinking. But in 1999, executives of Big Alcohol recoiled in shock: the new crop of first-year students enjoyed logging on more than getting wasted.[57] And what they logged onto, chiefly, were video games. In the past few years, studies have shown that between two-thirds and three-fourths of college students play video and online games every day.[58]

All games featured explicit competitions—"leveling up," in the argot of the genre—as players gain experience points and ascend to higher status levels. Many students, in pursuit of some higher game level, describe themselves going "snowblind" in the final hours of marathon sessions. "It's the grind sometimes but then you get there," one reported.[59] The rise of massively multiplayer online role-playing games such as *World of Warcraft* has socialized the competitive elements. While playing online, moreover, college students are engaged in activities that often repudiate the professed values of the institutions they attend. The most popular games contain strong misogynistic elements, continuous violence, coarse language, and sexual and racial stereotypes.

This was not true in the early years of video games, which featured hand–eye coordination and strategy (*Pac Man* and *Donkey Kong*). But games evolved in progressively more subversive ways. *Grand Theft Auto,* first released in 1997, illustrated this development. Virtual car racing had been popular in video arcades since the 1980s, but *Grand Theft Auto* transformed the driver into a car thief, pursued by police in wild chases through city streets and highways. Players now rack up points by evading the police or running them over, leaving behind a carnage of shattered cars and mangled cops and pedestrians. Some nations have banned the game as "depraved." But the antisocial elements have contributed to its popularity.[60] Chock-full of the basic ingredients of any subversive play world, the game has become a favorite among college students.

The Internet has provided students an opportunity to compete anytime and anywhere, instantly and anonymously. Several studies have found that college students who regularly play video games do worse than their peers in academics. Strong correlations have been found between students who play video games and high-risk behaviors, such as binge drinking.[61] In 2009, after faculty and administrators at the University of Minnesota, Duluth, attributed online gaming to be a "hidden cause" for academic failure, FCC Commissioner Deborah Taylor Tate identified *World of Warcraft* (11 million users) and other games as one of the "top reasons" for high college dropout rates.[62]

Facebook is so much a part of everyday life that it's easy to forget that it originated as a form of subversive play when undergraduate Mark Zuckerberg hacked into Harvard's information system, uploaded thousands of pictures of female students, and invited viewers to judge which were hottest.[63] Facemash, as Zuckerberg called it, was a sensation—a ruthless social–sexual competition, outrageous *and* illicit. From that concept Zuckerberg created a subversive play world in which competitors choose an avatar based on their own self.

Many students compete on Facebook by accumulating "friends" and by creating dauntingly cool virtual selves.[64] "The social pressures within Facebook are immense," a student at Columbia explained.

> You can tell almost immediately if a friend hosted a party without you. The pictures are posted online, people chat

about the evening on each other's walls. All of a sudden, you wonder why you were left out or how you could make yourself "cooler." Much of what I'm describing is incredibly superficial, but it seems to be a part of life to care about how many friends you have. The site becomes a breeding ground for human competition.[65]

Students massage their Facebook self-image by manipulating *everything*. They search for photos of themselves that others have posted; if these are unflattering or show embarrassing behavior, students "untag" or delete them. By pumping up their accomplishments and smoothing over deficiencies, students construct idealized versions of themselves. "You create your own identity in a cyber world," the student continued, "so that you can be more 'successful' in the real world."[66]

The subversive elements of Facebook, especially lurking and stalking, are subtle but profound. And the entire premise is gloriously absurd. One student noted that it made no sense to spend many hours a day "mindlessly" stalking people with whom she had little personal contact. "Above all," she added, "the idea that you are 'learning' about someone—their likes and dislikes, family life, social life—through a mechanism in which you have no contact with that person is bizarre." For millions of college students, however, Facebook has become the ultimate subversive play world—an unbounded arena for competition, identity manipulation, subversion, and absurdity. It has become the fastest growing addiction on campus. At least until 2013, when two viral apps—Lulu and Tinder—ratcheted up the social competition by encouraging students to rate (and comment on) the attractiveness and sexual prowess of classmates.[67]

Some students grew bored with online lurking and stalking and decided to undertake such activities in the flesh. In the late 1990s, a strange form of tag known as "Assassins" or "Mafia Assassins" spread through many campuses. Rival teams would attempt to assassinate their opponents, "shooting" them with Nerf balls or balled-up sweat socks or stabbing them with spoons. "Assassins" spent countless hours strategizing, plotting, hiding, and searching for enemies. Because their "weapons" consisted of spoons or socks (rather than large Nerf blasters), players found it easier to fly under the radar of campus security. The concept spread and now "assassins" games are played at hundreds of colleges and universities. At Columbia the "Assassins" website shows photos of student players who were killed the previous week. The concept is so wrong-minded, so antithetical to the university's professed commitment to civil discourse and collegiality, that students find it irresistible.[68]

In 2005 students at Goucher College invented a wacky variant of "Assassins" called "Humans vs. Zombies (HvZ)." Players representing either group, identified by different swatches of cloth, eliminated the other by "shooting" them with Nerf balls or sweat socks. To avoid being "killed," players remained in their rooms for days, sneaking out at odd hours for food. Sometimes scores of combatants fought pitched battles on the college green.

The game caught on and spread. Nearly everywhere, campus security officers were outraged at the spectacle of students hiding in bushes or stairwells and prowling the campus with scary Nerf blasters. After the shooting at Virginia Tech in 2007, many colleges banned the game. Driving it underground, of course, only enhanced its appeal. Nowadays hundreds of campuses have regular (and mostly unauthorized) "Humans v. Zombies" competitions.[69]

In a video released by the designers of "Humans v. Zombies," Sandy Ungar, then-president of Goucher College, defended the game as "harmless if somewhat mischievous." He added, with a slight shrug, "We need to find new things to do on campus—to make this a lively, vibrant place." Doubtless his faculty winced at these words: Wasn't the classroom supposed to be that sort of place?

But the awkward truth is that over the past two hundred years many students have been so immersed in subversive play they haven't chanced upon the deeper fascination of the life of the mind. In 2004 sociologists Elizabeth Armstrong and Laura Hamilton began their multi-year study of fifty-three first-year students who lived on the same floor of a dorm at one of the "top one hundred" public universities. The scholars found that the overwhelming majority of these students got caught in the powerful undertow of the campus party culture. Five years later only seven had managed to leave the university "with the kind of credentials or human capital that many expect all college graduates to acquire."[70] A century earlier, Henry Seidel Canby summed it up best: "We resisted the intrusion of abstract ideas because our skin was full to bursting of our own affairs and our minds hot with our own enthusiasm."[71] After their minds have been set on fire by subversive play, many students take little notice of the professor at the front of the classroom furiously striking stone against flint, trying without much success to ignite a few sparks.[72]

Students have changed considerably since Canby's day. Many do not live in dormitories, belong to fraternities or sororities, or have the time or inclination to participate in "college life." Nor do they all indulge in binge drinking, play video games, or spend entire weekends hunting down "Zombies" or skulking about as "assassins." Many earn college credits while working full-time and raising a family. Some "attend" college by logging on. Many are fully committed to academic study.

Yet many excellent students from the "most selective" colleges and universities complain of being stressed from juggling courses *and* competitive social play—maintaining a high GPA and putting in their work-study hours while regilding their Facebook wall and holding their own at the bimonthly drinking binge. Adult learners, too, often concede that the lure of subversive play complicates their impossibly harried lives.

Subversive play has long functioned like a black hole, pulling hard at the minds of students, sapping their intellectual and physical energies and sometimes drawing them wholly within its orbit. Faculty and administrators have attempted to obliterate these play worlds, to drive them from campus, or to warn students of the danger they pose. In 2013 sociologists Armstrong and Hamilton, having witnessed the harm caused by the pervasive party culture, called for the elimination of the Greek system and a "scaling back" of college athletics; but they knew of no schools that were moving in this direction.[73]

If teachers and administrators refuse to fight the battles their predecessors lost over a century ago, can anyone blame them? But if students' minds remain trapped in the labyrinthine worlds of subversive play, does higher education have much purpose?

CHAPTER 3

Creating an Academic Subversive Play World

The issue raised at the outset of this book—why Nate and his classmates volunteered to attend a class before sunrise—now has an obvious answer. As the French Revolution game approached the final weeks, Nate explained, everyone had gotten caught up in the drama. Imagine, he said, a heated debate with friends over stem cell research or abortion; then superimpose on that debate the final minutes of a close basketball game. That was how Reacting felt. "It was a story that required closure, a game that needed completion," he added. To end it early would be like walking out of a good movie before the last scene, or kicking basketball players off the court before the final buzzer. Much as fraternity pledges endure unimaginable humiliations to become "brothers" and video game players sacrifice sleep to climb to the next level of *World of Warcraft,* Nate and his classmates crawled out of bed and went to a voluntary class in order to enter a subversive play world.

This one differed from most others in that it occurred in a college classroom.

But how does a classroom become a subversive play world?

By definition, subversive play worlds exist outside the boundaries of everyday life. The early nineteenth-century debating societies met in taverns; fraternities built their own "houses"— and committed most of their resources to maintaining them; "Humans v. Zombies" defines precisely which parts of campus are off-limits for "kills." College classrooms, however, are controlled by college authorities. How can such a space belong to students? How can a play world be subversive if faculty design, regulate, and supervise it?

The explanation is that subversive play worlds do not destroy hierarchy, authority, and order; they depend on it. Without clearly identifiable authority—dominant elites, social conventions and systems of belief—there would be nothing to subvert. College football, for example, is a big business, largely funded by corporate advertisers and media companies. Strong-willed coaches call the plays and subject players to brutal training regimens. Referees initiate the action and enforce the rules. Players are seemingly mere pawns of powerful adults. Yet when a ballplayer puts on a uniform and steps onto the playing field, he becomes a different person. As he surveys the other team during warm-ups, he can feel the adrenaline pumping. When the ball is hiked, he exults as the ordered formations dissolve into mayhem, and he delights in the antisocial thrill of knocking an opponent "on his ass." In postgame interviews, he may tell a reporter of his commitment to work—of giving 110 percent—or he my cite his loyalty to the school and coach; but the truth is that once the subversive play begins, he's having fun.

Most people are eager to seize every opportunity to engage in subversive play—even when it happens in a seemingly unlikely place such as a college classroom. Students realize that Reacting games have been designed by scholars, that their instructor functions as coach, referee, and grader, and that many of the activities are academic in character (researching and writing); yet students usually transform the class into their own subversive play world, and when they do, the walls of authority seem to dissolve.

But creating a subversive play world in a college classroom can be tricky. In Nate's class, it began with a change in the instructor's attitude. For his first eight years as a college teacher, Paul Fessler had worked to perfect his lectures. "I rarely, if ever, had students falling asleep," he noted, "yet at times it all felt a bit ephemeral." When former students came back to reminisce about college, they never mentioned his lectures. Fessler himself recalled only vaguely the lectures he sat through as an undergraduate. But he never forgot a simple Civil War simulation one of his instructors had done. So as a professor, Fessler searched the Internet for historical simulations, but most of these involved re-enactments, during which students wound up "parroting historical figures and ideas—not debating them." Eventually he happened upon the Reacting website. When he saw that Reacting games included primary sources, major texts, and debates on big ideas, he decided to give it a try. The next semester—the fall of 2002—he committed a month of his Western Civilization class to the French Revolution game.

"But I was still skeptical," he admitted. As a new professor at Dordt College, Fessler knew he was taking a gamble. For one, he harbored doubts about group projects. It was not just that slackers coasted while others did the work. He also worried that a student-run class would turn into "a cringe-worthy nightmare" where "students who knew nothing instructed students who didn't know the difference." He found it impossible to trust the game manual's advice to allow students to take charge. He envisioned an epic failure that might torpedo his career. He therefore resolved to do everything possible to make the game work. During the three setup classes, he lectured feverishly, outlining the history of the *ancien regime,* discussing the first two years of the French Revolution, and describing the central concepts of Rousseau's *Social Contract.* During the fourth class, when students received their roles and were assigned to factions (Feuillants, Jacobins, "Friends of the King," and others), Fessler raced from group to group, trying to ensure that the students in the groups understood "their" positions. But he knew they didn't. The next class included a quiz, and the student performance was no worse than with other classes, but it was also no better. And in normal classes, students weren't expected to take charge and articulate the main ideas. Fessler's concerns mounted.

With the next class, the game began. Fessler reluctantly yielded the podium to the student who had been randomly assigned the role of the president of the National Assembly in

France in July 1791. After taking a seat in the back of the room, Fessler furiously wrote notes to prod students to speak and act as their roles prescribed. But it didn't work. "No matter how hard I tried," he recalled, "the game had too many pieces and too many roles for me to control." Realizing he could not dictate all of the ideas and possible actions, he sat back and watched. And "the quieter I got," the better the game went. Students ceased looking to him for the right answers and guidance. "They had to find it themselves—or they would fail," he observed. From that first game, Fessler learned that in Reacting he needed to be a "drill sergeant" while setting up the game, but during the six game sessions, he had to sit back and let students take control. After the final game session, Fessler led a postmortem class in which he explained what happened in history and guided students in a discussion of how and why their game differed from the historical reality.

After teaching with Reacting games in 2003 and 2004, Fessler had become comfortable with the approach, although he was still nervous at the start of each game and anxious somewhere in the middle: Would students figure it all out and drive the game to a conclusion? They always did, and he continued to be astonished by what they accomplished. So in the spring of 2005 he was confident that Nate's class would be equally successful.

Nate, on the other hand, wasn't so sure.[1] To his dismay, the game book was several hundred pages long. "I basically skimmed it," he recalled. During the first two weeks, too, he skimmed Rousseau's *Social Contract* and Burke's *Reflections on the Revolution in France*, also required for the game. On the day of the quiz, Nate barely scraped by. But once Nate received his twenty-page role packet, his interest perked up. He was to lead one of the sections of Paris, charged with mobilizing the urban poor to action. His role packet also revealed that as a section leader, he had a bizarre special power. On a few occasions, he could rouse the poor of his section of Paris to concerted mass action; if his speech were powerful and inspiring (and the subsequent die roll favorable), his section would riot, sending that district into chaos and prompting conservative members of the National Assembly to flee Paris—and even France. When other section leaders joined in, the rising of the *sans culottes* could be momentous (as happened in August 1792).

As leader of all the sections, moreover, Nate was editor of the faction's newspaper. Among his tasks was to produce, each week of the game, a newspaper that would be distributed to the entire class; as editor, Nate assigned essay topics and prodded team members to submit their essays in time for him to produce and photocopy the newspaper.

For the first game session, the agenda was the Civil Constitution of the Clergy, a cluster of provisional laws that nationalized the Catholic Church: priests were to be paid by the national government, and church officials would take orders from the National Assembly rather than the pope. Nate and the section leaders were supposed to pressure the National Assembly to pass the Civil Constitution.

Before the first game session, Nate and the other editors distributed their factions' newspapers to the class. Then Nate and the other section leaders, who did not belong to the National

Assembly, moved to the "balcony"—the back of the classroom. The "president" of the National Assembly opened the session by inviting members to speak on the Civil Constitution.

Nate watched as the debate unfolded among the delegates. Some read speeches almost directly from their newspaper. Other students, more confident, spoke freely or glanced at notes. "King Louis XVI" insisted that the National Assembly return lands it had seized from the Catholic Church. Otherwise, deprived of its chief means of sustenance, the Catholic Church would collapse. "King Louis" cited Edmund Burke's assertion that Christianity provided a "deep and firm foundation of virtue" without which France would fail. "Father Francis," another conservative delegate, agreed and enlisted Rousseau to attack the Civil Constitution: religious and political authority could not be combined. "Lafayette" (Linda Schroedermeier) disagreed. "He" pointed out that the Civil Constitution had legalized seizure and sale of church property; without that revenue, the new government would be bankrupt. Leaders in the Jacobin faction challenged the conservatives. Rousseau, they said, had insisted that the general will was incompatible with sectional associations. Catholic priests who retained their allegiance to the pope constituted a "particular" interest that subverted the "social contract." The conservatives, citing Burke, insisted that utopian social schemes were folly. To extirpate a religious faith rooted in centuries of belief and custom and replace it with a state-run religion was madness.

Nate and the other section leaders nodded or shook their heads in response to the speakers, but mostly they sat quietly "on the edge of the classroom," as Nate recollected. Then Fessler, seated nearby, passed Nate a note: "Don't be afraid to be obnoxious." Nate pushed it to the two other students in his faction; they exchanged glances. "Now," Nate observed, "the game really started for us." When a conservative spoke against the Civil Constitution, Nate and his teammates booed. Then they drew crude cartoons on the blackboard at the back of the room. Sometimes, unbidden by the Assembly president, they delivered impromptu speeches. Nate took it upon himself to stir things up by shouting, chanting, singing—"whatever I could do." This class, Nate realized, was unlike any other. "That realization," he said, "was the start of the adrenaline rush."

Nate's raucous behavior infuriated the conservative delegates. Insults flew back and forth. In response to Citizen Nate's reference to "a travesty of justice," another delegate commented that the unlettered Citizen Nate knew "neither the definition of travesty nor the definition of justice." The Assembly president was hard-pressed to keep order. The first class ended without a vote on the Civil Constitution.

At the outset of the next class, the conservatives mounted a counterattack: the "irresponsible" behavior of the section leaders proved Edmund Burke's point—the illiterate poor of Paris, having been incited to break free of the customary ties that bind society, had become an unthinking and bloodthirsty mob. The conservatives then turned Rousseau's words against Nate, who could think of no reply. The conservatives had come up with solid arguments, backed by Rousseau, that hadn't occurred to Nate or his team.

Instantly Nate realized that he couldn't prepare for class as in the past,

> where I could tune in for a minute, say something smart, earn my credit for the day and tune out. I realized that for every class I would need to pay attention, work hard, and contribute. It really was sink or swim.

Toward the end of that session, Lafayette threw his support to the Jacobins, and several indeterminate delegates also endorsed the Civil Constitution. When the votes were tallied, the Civil Constitution was approved. The Catholic Church had been crushed. The conservatives groaned. The Jacobins and section leaders cheered. Nate, a track runner, recalled that that moment was

> similar to passing a rival in the last hundred meters of a long distance race—you've been neck and neck, it could go either way, and it went your way. I probably pumped my arm, cheered, and started a chant mocking the conservative faction.

Nate and his allies now planned to destroy the monarchy and complete the revolution.

But over the final two weeks—the early morning sessions, in fact—things did not go as Nate had hoped. As in history, Lafayette changed sides, using his power as commander of the National Guard to move against the Paris sections. Meanwhile,

the alliance between the Jacobins and section leaders unrav-
eled: rumors circulated that a Jacobin planned to arrest Nate
and the other section leaders. Nate, who had become immersed
in the history of the revolution, perceived that Robespierre had
eventually turned on Danton in exactly this way. What was the
best strategy—in history—and in the game? Nate wasn't sure.
It was all a complex and rapidly changing puzzle. "That was
part of the fun," Nate explained.

Through it all, Fessler functioned as cheerleader, guide, and
gamemaster. During class, he passed notes encouraging shy
students to speak and others to consider a particular text or historical perspective. After class, he met with the factions to provide encouragement and guidance. The conservatives, crest-
fallen after losing the vote on the Civil Constitution, doubted
whether they could devise persuasive arguments in defense of
monarchy. Fessler encouraged them to study Burke and restate
his arguments in their own words. Fessler also graded everyone's written work—their newspaper essays—swiftly, prodding
writers to cite specific texts and bolster arguments with more
facts. (Two-thirds of their grade was based on their written
work, and one-third on class participation. Fessler said that the
winning team would receive a half-grade bonus in their class
participation grade, a mathematically negligible element of their
grade for the course.) As gamemaster, guided by the instructor's
manual, Fessler issued weekly "Gamemaster News Bulletins,"
which introduced new complications (the slave rebellion in
Saint-Domingue, the debate over ratification of the Constitution of the United States, rumors of European monarchs plotting to crush the French revolutionaries).

Each week's newspapers were better than those that came before. The essays showed deeper understanding of Rousseau and Burke, and the articles were informed by more historical details and facts. The newspapers were also wittier. The constitutional monarchists included an advertisement for a "lifelike Jacobin doll" that talked "meaninglessly and incessantly." The ad was paid for by MADD (Moderates Against Dumb Discourse). Another newspaper included a notice in the personals: "Wanted: Pen Pal, 'Lonely King Louis.'" The return address was crossed out and replaced with, "Location Undisclosed." When Austro-Prussian armies, intent on crushing the revolutionaries, approached the borders of France, the conservative newspaper, in a sly endorsement of the invaders, ran the headline "Troops on the Move" accompanied by a photograph of U.S. troops liberating a village in Normandy in 1944.

Nate and Linda recalled that they became so immersed in the game they cared little about their grade for the course. They wanted to make strong speeches and write effective papers chiefly to impress their peers. Everyone knew when a speaker was unprepared or an essay was lame. Conversely, the entire class buzzed when someone made an irrefutable argument or wrote an arrestingly powerful article. Fessler enjoyed guiding students who were eager to do well rather than focused on getting a good grade. Each game session, too, was filled with drama: Would the shy student find his voice? Would the constitutional monarchists come up with a good rebuttal to Rousseau's point about divided sovereignty? Would the defenders of slavery in Saint-Domingue find the economic statistics to make a strong argument? Fessler looked forward to each class, curious to see what would happen and eager to find ways to prod students to do even more.

Nate worked harder than ever before, researching, writing, strategizing, editing, and plotting. He acquired a deeper understanding of the ideas of Rousseau. The plight of the urban poor became "accessible and familiar." "It was like putting on a good pair of glasses, or turning a light on," he explained. "I could see *why* people who lived through the revolution did what they did." No longer was the game just about defeating his hardworking classmates in the conservative faction or outsmarting the wannabe Robespierre in the Jacobin faction. Nate's sense of self had been enlarged: he identified with the poor of Paris. His victory would be theirs; should he fail, they would suffer the consequences.

Even before Nate's classmates had decided on the 7:30 A.M. sessions, their behavior had attracted the attention of other students. One Friday night, when some visiting friends suggested they go to a party, Nate declined. "We've got to have the best newspaper," he told them. "I gotta make the other factions' newspapers look bad." The visitor just stared at him. Nate's campus friends were equally mystified. Usually Nate watched TV or played video games until 2:00 in the morning, procrastinating on schoolwork until the last minute. But now he spent his free time pouring over philosophical tracts and history books.

Nate enjoyed their perplexity. "There's an unwritten rule that you're not supposed to like learning," he explained. "You're supposed to consider skipping and sleeping through."

> While my friends trudged off to their engineering, theology, philosophy, or business classes with this sense of apa-

thy and frustration, I was rushing off to Western Civ, eager to see how that day's session would unfold.

Other students challenged his enthusiasm: "What are you doing in Western Civ that is so important?"

"I need to rally the people of France to overthrow the King!" Nate replied.

"Well, good luck with that," they'd say, exchanging looks.

"I felt sorry for them," Nate added. "They didn't understand because they hadn't done anything in class that had really lit a fire under them."

Much about Nate's class was strange. The intense competition among students; the loss of self-consciousness that prompted him to clamber upon chairs and belt out revolutionary songs; his identification with people who had been dead for over two centuries; and the crazy subversion of student norms and behaviors. Each element, extracted from the context of a normal classroom, seemed bizarre. Looking back on the events that had occurred nine years earlier, Nate acknowledged that it all seemed "very strange." But at the time, and from their vantage point within a subversive play world, his classmates' decision to come to class at 7:30 made perfect sense.

Elements of a Reacting Subversive Play World

Everyone responds to a role-immersion game in a different way. Some are stimulated by the competition, others by the imaginative reach, and others by the absurdity of it all. Gilberto G. Jimenez is among those who mostly enjoy its competitiveness. Gilberto was born in Monterrey, Mexico. After graduating from the local high school, he spent a few years racing a Formula 3 car. Then he went to the University of Hartford, where he took a Reacting seminar in 2007. In the first game, set in Athens in 403 B.C.E., he was assigned a role as a radical democrat. It instantly engaged his competitive instincts.

From the start he sought an edge over the other students. "I knew my peers were doing the same thing, looking for an edge over me," he revealed, "so I had to research topics I knew *they* would bring up so that I could defend my stance." His chances of winning improved if he could persuade the Athenian assembly to rebuild its navy. But Sparta had just crushed Athens and Athenian remilitarization might provoke Spartan intervention. Gilberto went to the library to research the subject. He discovered that while the Spartans committed themselves wholly to war, they also indulged in a long period of recuperation afterwards. Athens could "sneak up" and rebuild its navy and defensive walls while the Spartans were still recovering, or so he argued.

As he delivered his speech, Gilberto noticed that his heart was pounding. "It was silly," he observed. He had raced cars at speeds in excess of 150 miles an hour; he was not in the least intimidated by public speaking. His excitement was "something more": he wanted to win, just "for the sake of it—to be number 1." Perhaps, he suggested, the compulsion to win was rooted in biology—part of our programming as a species to survive in a competitive world. A lust for competition was part of his own makeup: of that he was certain.

Other Reacting students care less about competition and instead enjoy imagining what it's like to be someone else. Eric Welkos, a senior majoring in Asian art history at McDaniel

College (Maryland), is an example. When he enrolled in an art course that included a Reacting game set in Paris in 1888, he considered himself a devotee of the avant-garde. Assigned the role of William Bouguereau, a staunch traditionalist and avowed foe of Gauguin and Van Gogh, Eric considered playing the part ironically: perhaps as a stuffy pedant whose retrograde views would send classmates into hysterics. But once immersed in Bouguereau's writings and paintings, he uncovered more merit than he had thought. Traditional academic painting revealed a disciplined beauty and aesthetic power. Soon he found it easy to denounce Van Gogh and Gauguin "for slopping some paint on a canvas and calling it art." For their part, the students playing Van Gogh and Gauguin tweaked Eric over Bouguereau's rotund cherubs and bare-breasted angels.

Eric enjoyed the competitive banter and the debates. But what appealed to him most was becoming Bouguereau. "I really absorbed him," Eric admitted. "To play Bouguereau, you have to *be* Bouguereau inside and out." Eric eschewed his customary bohemian garb and came to class in a black pinstripe suit, bow tie, and pink shirt. The other students in the class embraced their roles, too. When Eric met them outside of class, immediately they assumed their game identities: Bougeureau chatted with Monet and Meissonier. The student playing Van Gogh took to wearing a Band-Aid on her ear. Becoming other people was *fun*—researching their lives, writing papers from their perspective, voicing their ideas in class.

Often students find this surprising. Accustomed to hiding behind the glittering facade of their Facebook wall, many are initially unnerved by the idea of becoming someone else. For example, when Ashleigh Schap, a sophomore at the University of Texas at Austin, first heard about Reacting she was appalled by the prospect of "weird role-playing games." An upper-class student further warned that the workload in Reacting was "brutal," so Ashleigh resolved to take nearly any other course. But scheduling problems intervened and she had no choice but to enroll in a Reacting class: "I thought it was going to be a pain in the butt."

In the first game, she was assigned the role of Thrasybulus, the general who led the radical democrats in Athens in 403 B.C.E. Her initial task was to persuade the Athenian assembly to punish those who had collaborated with the Spartan army of occupation. Lest she make a fool of herself, Ashleigh worked hard on her speech. At the beginning of the first game session, as she walked to the podium, stomach churning, she worried that the speech would bomb—and that the class would be a dud. But as she spoke, something clicked: her words made sense and she saw several other students—all of them strangers—nodding in agreement. Then, while looking at the impassive faces of the other students, she wanted them to nod, too. She poured emotion into her words, and soon she was hooked. When she returned to her dorm, she started her next paper. She had become Thrasybulus.

> I really bought into it. I genuinely adopted a set of beliefs, and I very genuinely sought to defend them. The game was fake; we all knew that. But the goal—influencing your peers, making your voice heard, saying something worth hearing—that was very real. We weren't actually

in Athens, but we were actively trying to change each other's minds.

Perhaps the oddest aspect of Reacting is how readily students surrender their skepticism and, like Ashleigh, "buy into" Reacting. Partly this is because they take possession of the class. To be sure, students recognize that their sovereignty is illusory. Their thoughts and actions are constrained by the rules of the game, by the requirements of their particular roles, and by the ultimate authority of the instructor-as-gamemaster. Students perceive that the professor who has given them suggestions on how to win or write a persuasive paper has just walked over to their opponents and done the same with them. Students who are on the verge of winning chafe when the gamemaster folds in complications that make their task harder. A major element of all Reacting games is the tension between the students who run the class and the gamemaster who enforces the structure of the game. This dynamic invites students to subvert it and often they do: sometimes they undertake additional research to challenge gamemaster rulings and to propose rule modifications.

Sometimes, however, the subversions are more explicit.

A vivid illustration occurred in Larry Carver's Reacting class at the honors college at the University of Texas at Austin in March 2009. His students had finished *Henry VIII and the Reformation Parliament* and the class was midway through the set-up phase of *Defining a Nation: The Indian Subcontinent on the Eve of Independence, 1945.* The setup included a 100-question quiz on nearly 700 pages of readings: the 200-page game book, large sections of the *Bhagavad Gita* and the *Qur'an,* and a history of colonial India.

On the day of the quiz, Ingrid Norton, a graduating senior, arrived early. Her reading of the materials had been perfunctory. The threat of a quiz had been insufficient to make her study hard, and now it loomed. She grumbled about the quiz with her peers. "Reacting absorbs students into ideas, gives them motivations for reading that are more organic (and internal) than quizzes," she mentioned afterwards. "We all knew we would eventually do the reading." But she was convinced that the forced quiz went against the spirit of Reacting.

Then an idea popped into her head. "What if we hold a nonviolent protest against the quiz today? Like Gandhi?" she asked her classmates. The idea caught fire, Ingrid recalled, because it "tapped into the anarchic inclination" of students.

A few minutes later Carver entered the room, joking about the heat in India. The students stared at him with poker faces. "OK, OK," Carver said. "Must have been something I said, so let's try this again." He walked out and closed the door. The students looked at each other. Then Ingrid hurried to the center of the room and sat down, cross-legged. Everyone joined her, some giggling, others nervous and uncomfortable. When Carver re-entered, the protesters said nothing.

"Ingrid," he asked, "are you behind this?" She smiled innocently. Then he walked out.

"The emotional tenor changed instantly," Ingrid recalled. "He had pulled out the rug from us."

"Go after him!" several students pleaded.

Ingrid and some others leaped up, ran out the door, and caught up with him down the hall. "No," he replied. "I'm not coming back. The offices in India close early. Sorry."

Ingrid saw the glint in his eyes: "I felt frozen out, but I knew he was messing with us." The delegation returned to the classroom and the students spent the next hour in agitated debate. Had they erred in challenging authority? Carver was not just their instructor; he was also head of the honors college. Would he really punish them?

Ingrid, however, put things together. The British, she argued, would have stormed off, too, or thrown the protesters in jail. Gandhi himself had said that those who engaged in civil disobedience should expect to suffer the consequences. The path to justice was never easy. Soon the students were lost in a debate over the tactics and philosophy of civil disobedience.

Carver's ingenious response to the students' make-believe civil disobedience—to pretend that it was *real*—transformed the class into a subversive play world within a subversive play world. Carver was both taking the protesters seriously—and playing with them. "It had us a bit on edge," Ingrid recalled, "but it energized us," eliciting

that lovely feeling of challenging authority, of being encouraged to be anarchic in an educational setting, of taking a class in your reins, and just that cool thing where you're admitted into a realm possessed by authority figures. . . . This was what I felt about the best of my college classes, that I could go out and take on the world.

Most subversive play—because it contravenes normal social structures or beliefs—edges toward man-bites-dog absurdity. And the first thing that strikes observers about a Reacting class is its weirdness: callow young men and women acting as if they were Ming emperors, or eminent scientists in the Royal Society, or Founding Fathers of the American nation. Whenever a Reacting course is first offered at a college, word spreads that something "strange" is going on. Soon a reporter shows up. What draws attention and generates headlines are the unusual happenings, such as Nate's standing on a chair to incite the mob or Ingrid's impromptu sit-down strike. Usually, toward the end of the article, the reporter quotes students on how hard they have worked, but the main point of the story is that Reacting classes are absurd.

As indeed they are. Yet the strangeness of Reacting is not limited to the occasional over-the-top actions of some students. Everything about the experience is weird: coming to class before sunrise; working all night to gain an advantage to win an academic game; identifying with historical figures with unusual beliefs; parading an eager-beaver enthusiasm in a student culture predicated on sophisticated disinterest. The permeating strangeness of Reacting is another reason it's fun.

"An Interesting Place to Spend the Rest of Your Life"

But if we (intermittently) transform the college classroom into a subversive play world, will students ever learn to take their education seriously? Will they acquire the requisite work ethic to succeed as adults?

Sadly, most students in "normal" classes don't work very hard, as was noted in the "Debate at Dawn" section of this book. Even the students cited in this chapter insisted that, before Reacting, they had never done much work in school. "I put precisely as much effort into schoolwork as it would take to get an A, which wasn't much," Nate confided. "I could write convincingly even if I had no idea what I was talking about, or deliver an eloquent presentation about nothing."[2] Gilberto, the former NASCAR driver, said that he had never done more than was required for his college courses, and yet he, too, was consistently at the top of his class. Ashleigh reported that she had been a straight A student in high school, received perfect scores on her AP exams, and was accepted into the intensely competitive honors college at the University of Texas at Austin.

"I'm a great test taker," she explained.

I'm great at guessing what teachers are going to ask, and I can store dates and names like it's nobody's business. It was never a question of how much I knew, but how many correct answers I got. If I had thought about it, I would have realized that I had forgotten most of what I had "learned" three months or a semester later. But I never thought about my education. Why would I? I wasn't going to be a tested on it.

After Reacting, these students perceived that they had been missing something. The French Revolution game was the first time Nate had ever been forced to take his education seriously.

Gilberto explained that in Reacting he was impelled to work far harder than his teachers had required. "And that has *never* happened to me in any other class," he wrote (emphasis in the original). I scoffed at these words. "Never," he insisted, "not even now, and I'm a graduate student in chemistry." Similarly, Ashleigh had always liked school, but after Reacting she realized that "there was so much more to learning that I wasn't getting."

During our Gmail chat, Ashleigh worried that I was missing the point—that I assumed that Reacting had taught her to work harder. She *did* work harder than before—"I was reading hundreds of pages a night and writing thousands of words a week for Reacting," she noted, "but it never felt like work." And *that* was her point. To her, researching and writing for Reacting was like trying to solve a puzzle—"but on steroids!" She did it for fun: "It's not fun in the way that roller coasters or playing with dogs is fun. It's a more satisfying, self-fulfilling fun."

For these students, Reacting was even more fun than their usual subversive play worlds. During the final weeks of the French Revolution game, Nate didn't have time for video games, much to the consternation of his friends. Ashleigh, who belonged to a sorority, skipped mixers to do research. (When I suggested that missing a fraternity mixer was probably no great loss, she set me straight: "Have you ever been to a mixer? They're very fun!") Her sorority sisters thought it strange that she preferred research to partying, and Ashleigh conceded that staying behind "kind of sucks." But she insisted that it wasn't that big of a deal. Not only did she enjoy the work, she also dreaded coming to a Reacting class unprepared: "Now *that* sucks," she noted, "way more than missing a mixer. There's no way to avoid making a mistake."

People can be fully immersed in subversive play worlds without doing things that are obviously pleasurable. Basketball players practice foul shots, hours on end, utterly absorbed in the tedium. Video game players, struggling to break a record or advance a level, skip meals, sleep, and everything else. No one observing them would say that they were having fun. Subversive play worlds commonly oblige players to work harder than ever before. This also explains why the activities that students customarily dread (and often evade)—going to class, reading, researching, writing papers—become "fun" in the context of a role-immersion game.

The students in this chapter insist that Reacting did not maroon them on Pleasure Island, but instead served as a land bridge to the life of the mind. After taking Reacting, for example, Nate changed his major to history and decided to become a teacher. He now teaches history in Japan, incorporating role-immersion game pedagogical principles. I first heard of Gilberto—the former NASCAR driver—when he contacted me via email. He had been elected president of the science graduate student organization at Purdue. Rather than socialize over beer and pizza, he had persuaded the society to host Reacting science games; he wanted my advice on how to pull it off. Ashleigh explained that Reacting had given her "a sense of purpose, a hunger" for knowledge. Ingrid, after graduating from the University of Texas, became a freelance writer; as I type these words, one of her book reviews is appearing in the *Los Angeles Review of Books*.

When Judith Shapiro, president emerita of Barnard College and an apostle (and teacher) of Reacting, was asked by students what they should get from college, she responded: "You want the inside of your head to be an interesting place to spend the rest of your life."[3] Reacting students have absorbed the truth of this maxim, because they have admitted to their minds a host of fascinating characters. This experience is interesting and fun; more important, it enlarges their sense of self—the subject of the following chapter.

CHAPTER 4

Critical Thinking and Our Selves

.

Selves in Conflict

"Shalom," "Fareeda" (a pseudonym) said with a broad smile, her face framed by a polka-dotted black hijab. "I apologize for my lateness. Some of my chickens and lambs ran astray and I was trying to bring them back home."[1]

Some giggles, a few guffaws.

"But that is the issue I want to talk about today. Bringing the Jews back to their ancestral homeland."

Fareeda was playing David Ben-Gurion in a Reacting game set in Palestine in 1936, when British commissioners had been sent to end the escalating violence between Jewish settlers and Arab Palestinians. A bright student with sparkling eyes and an infectious smile, Fareeda told the "commissioners" that Jewish immigration to Palestine accorded with international law; that Jews had purchased the land they occupied; and that the eviction of Arab laborers was justified to provide jobs for Jews fleeing Hitler's Germany. Fareeda effortlessly adopted the first-person voice of Ben-Gurion, often citing his exact words and incorporating details of his life into her articles and speeches ("When I emigrated to Palestine . . .").

In real life, Fareeda was born in Bangladesh to a conservative Muslim family. Her father emigrated to the Lower East Side of New York. When she was young, Fareeda's family joined him; later they moved to Queens. She finished reading the *Qur'an* in Arabic in the third grade and spent much of every weekend at the mosque. She enrolled in the local public high school in September 2001, a month that changed her life. After 9/11, dismayed by the widespread ignorance of her faith, she gave speeches on Islam, founded the Islamic Social Club at her school, and wore a hijab at all times. In college, she became active in the Astoria Youth Group, a subchapter of the Muslim Ummah of North America.

Now, a veteran of many Reacting games, she was playing the Zionist leader many Muslims blame for the current plight of Palestinians. At first she had doubts about the role, but by the time she had finished reading the packet outlining Ben-Gurion's life, they had evaporated: "Oh my goodness," she thought, "this is me!" During the next few weeks her identification with Ben-Gurion intensified. She came to admire his audacity and leadership.

As the game began, other students gravitated to her strong personality and, like the real Ben-Gurion, she became leader of the Zionist faction.

There were moments when I wasn't sure if I was leading my faction as Ben-Gurion the character or as Fareeda-Ben-Gurion. This confusion was partly because the class didn't end at 3:55 P.M. The Zionist faction was spending incredible amounts of time in my suite; I was constantly on the phone or emailing others in the class. There were no boundaries between class and outside of class and night and day to define when Fareeda would be Ben-Gurion and when Fareeda would just be Fareeda. Instead, I was Fareeda-Ben-Gurion all the time.

This complicated her personal life. When she told her Muslim suitemates of her admiration for Ben-Gurion, they gaped at her. "That's when I shut up about Ben-Gurion," she recalled.

Yet she could not deny her feelings: she had unconsciously become a soul mate of the archenemy of Palestinian Muslims. "For me, it was a little bit scary," she said. She decided not to tell her parents about the role.

Fareeda's chief antagonist in the game was "Joshua" (a pseudonym), assigned the role of Awni Abd al-Hadi, head of the radical Arab Independence Party. Intellectually gifted and articulate, Joshua dove into the role wholeheartedly and emerged as leader of the Arab Higher Committee. He denounced Ben-Gurion and Zionism; criticized the Balfour Declaration for giving Jewish settlers, then a small minority, preferred status; and appealed to the British commissioners to halt the illegal Jewish immigration. Alluding to the peril Jews faced in Hitler's Germany, he acknowledged the moral case for allowing their immigration to Palestine. "I can accept them as Jews," Joshua-Awni conceded, "but never as Zionists."

In real life, however, Joshua was a committed Zionist. In high school he had headed a program that raised over $160,000 for Israeli victims of Palestinian terrorism. As an undergraduate at Columbia, he served as an officer of a pro-Israel group and as editor of the *Current,* an undergraduate magazine devoted to Jewish affairs. In 2007 he coauthored an essay, republished by the *National Review Online*, criticizing Columbia president Lee Bollinger for inviting Iranian leader Mahmoud Ahmadinejad to speak.

Yet under Joshua-Awni's leadership, the Arab Higher Committee built a strong case against the Zionists. Nevertheless, the British commissioners in the game proposed to partition Palestine into separate Jewish and Arab states. This was the pivotal moment—in history and in the game. Mindful of the calamity that ensued when Palestinians refused to accept partition in 1937, Joshua-Awni desperately worked for a compromise alternative. But negotiations with the Zionists broke down and Joshua-Awni rejected partition. "I could not betray Awni's life and legacy," he explained.

In the game, violence escalated, forcing a British crackdown and the arrest of key Arab Nationalists. The chances of the Arabs gaining Palestine by force plummeted. A series of die rolls yielded the worst possible outcome. The Palestinian Arabs lost power—and their state. The game, which lasted over a month, had unfolded much like history.

Joshua insisted that he had been able to divorce his pro-Zionist identity from the game itself. "I think I was able to compartmentalize my identities—to separate the fact that I am a Jew from the fact that I was Awni Abd al-Hadi in the game."

But the sudden collapse of the Arab position took him by surprise.

> When everything fell apart, I was crushed. I was feeling the same sort of dumbfounded bafflement the Palestinians felt when they lost their homeland. At that moment I had an inkling of *their* feelings: "I just had my whole world turned upside down." I actually felt like I wanted to take to the streets. I wanted the figurative gun, so to speak. I wanted the power to act. Being at the mercy of the British, and of chance, made me want to throw out the results of the game. I think I felt, on some small level, the devastation that Palestinians must have felt.

"Did you identify with Awni?" I asked.

"Absolutely," he replied without hesitation. "If I had been a Palestinian at that time I most certainly would have been Awni. Awni stood by his principles in a moment of crisis, not really knowing what was going to happen next. I admire that. I think I would like to see myself someday emulate that kind of attitude."

Joshua had identified with an historical figure whose legacy had harmed the cause to which he had devoted his life. Fareeda had come to a similar realization: "I can't explain how eerily I feel a connection to the political personality of BG [Ben-Gurion]," she told me.

"Do you think you were brainwashed?" I asked.

"In some ways I think so," she replied. "What does this say?"

This conversation brought to mind another several years earlier. "Angela" (a pseudonym), an African-American student in my Reacting class for first-year students, had come to my office and announced, "I cannot take this role." She handed me a sheaf of papers.

I looked at the cover: First Pastor of the Boston Church in *The Trial of Anne Hutchinson.*

"This says I'm supposed to give a sermon outlining the orthodox ministers' position, but on page fourteen it says that they believed in the Trinity. I don't. I belong to Jehovah's Witnesses."

"But you're just playing a role," I said. "'Angela' won't be giving the sermon. 'The First Pastor' will be doing so."

"But I would be saying things about the Bible that aren't true."

I considered this.

"If you were in the drama club and you were assigned the part of the First Pastor in a play, would you read your lines in the script?" I asked.

"Not if they went against the word of God."

"But in college you're supposed to try out new ideas, to challenge everything. That's how you grow intellectually," I replied.

"I've discussed this with my father. I won't speak falsehoods about the Lord."[2]

I wanted to ask how she could be so certain. The Puritans, reading the same Bible, arrived at a different conclusion. But I hesitated. Angela's voice was steady; she spoke with quiet confidence. As much as any student I can recall, she possessed "the courage of her convictions." "To thine own self" she had remained implacably true.

Do instructors have a right to thrust students into situations that challenge "their inside beliefs and understandings"? To assign them roles that potentially undermine their self? Does the fact that Fareeda and Joshua came to "believe" their roles prove that they had been brainwashed? Was Plato's Socrates right that those who indulge in *mimesis*—who assimilate themselves into the mindset of others—are being false to their own self?

Why Brainwashing Doesn't Work: The Stability of the Self

Those who study the psychology of brainwashing generally agree that, in the absence of torture or death threats, it usually doesn't work. Among those few whose self is changed by torture, their normal self usually resurfaces after their release from captivity. The explanation is that the self is remarkably stable and persistent; the associations and ideas we acquire early in life tend to endure. We assume that the personality and core identity of friends will remain mostly unchanged even when we haven't seen them in decades, and usually we're right.[3]

But why? Scientists speculate that the early humans with a fixed sense of self were more likely to form the stable relationships and cooperative groups that promoted survival and procreation. Those who lacked a stable self did not last long: How could you trust someone who keeps changing?[4] Over time the brain evolved to give primacy to an "ensemble" of self-referential neural webs.[5] Neuroscientist Antonio Damasio has proposed that the "neural basis for the self" is complicated by linkage of the high-order cognitive webs to our more fundamental in-stinctual and emotional neural networks. A "third set of neural structures"—a "metaself"—adjudicates among the entire cluster of self-referential neural webs.[6]

But if the self arises through the linkage of billions of cog-nitive webs, including those connected to biological and emo-tional networks, who is engineering these linkages? Damasio compares the process to an orchestra whose members begin playing "in the conspicuous absence of a conductor." The perfor-mance *creates* the conductor—the self.[7] This discussion, like most such speculations, soon resembles medieval debates on the nature of the soul.

But scientists have gleaned some tantalizing clues about the neurological components of the self. When test subjects are asked to think about themselves while undergoing neural im-aging, no single part of the brain lights up with neural activity. But when subjects are shown pictures of their own house, clus-ters of neural webs are activated within the cortical midline structure, a part of the brain formed early in man's evolution; but when shown pictures of houses other than their own, neural webs in evolutionarily "newer" sections of the brain are activated. The same is true when subjects listen to recordings of voices. We place information about our self in a more readily accessible storage box than information about others.[8] The likely explana-tion is that from infancy onward, as more and more information is routed along our self-related neural paths, the neurons are primed to make instantaneous connections. We've known this truth instinctively: it's really all about "me" after all.[9]

In 1890 psychologist William James perceived that because our "self" likely grew out of our contact with many different people, it likely had multiple constituent elements: "A man has as many social selves as there are individuals who recognize him and carry an image of him in their head," James wrote in 1890."[10] In 1934 George Herbert Mead elaborated on James's insight. Many selves inhabit our minds, Mead explained, because we have internalized them from countless social situations. "The self is not something that exists first and then enters into relationship with others; but it is, so to speak, an eddy in the social current," Mead wrote. He insisted that the self was

> a process in which the individual is continually adjusting himself in advance to the situation to which he belongs, and reacting back on it. So that the "I and "me," this thinking, this conscious adjustment, becomes then a part of the whole social process and makes a much more highly organized society possible.[11]

Our "self" emerges from our interactions with others.

But then, how does it maintain its solidity? James maintained that most people "carefully" review their list of selves and "pick out the one on which to stake [their] salvation."[12] When push comes to shove—do we go to work or tend to a sick child?— we *decide*, through an act of will, which of our selves is paramount. Our metaself, in Damasio's terminology, mediates among our many selves.

Our metaself protects us from brainwashing. But the solidity of the self poses a problem. How can we ever think in fundamentally different ways? Our neural networks cannot readily unlearn their well-worn associative pathways. When our "inside understandings" are built into our self, how do we get them out? When truths are self-evident, how can we scrutinize them?[13]

Critical Thinking: "Getting the Inside Beliefs Out"

Many believe that the fundamental purpose of college is to encourage students to examine their beliefs critically. Indeed, most colleges and universities claim that "critical thinking" is the main objective of undergraduate education. A survey of faculty at four-year colleges and universities found that 99.5 percent regarded the "ability to think clearly" as "essential" or "very important."[14] The American Association of University Professors proclaimed critical thinking to be the "the hallmark of American education."[15]

Yet mounting evidence indicates that college does little to improve critical thinking skills. A major study in 2004 found that only 6 percent of college seniors were "proficient" in critical thinking and 77 percent were "not proficient."[16] Two years later Derek Bok, former president of Harvard, surveyed scores of studies and concluded that although seniors did better on critical reasoning tests than entering freshmen, they didn't do much better, and two-thirds of college seniors failed to report substantial achievement.[17] Subsequent studies have confirmed these conclusions. In 2011, for example, Richard Arum and Josipa Roksa found that 45 percent of their sample of 2,300 students made *no* gains in critical thinking after three semesters of college—a major reason why the authors concluded that many college students are "academically adrift."[18]

Learning researchers complicated matters by insisting that critical thinking is not a skill to be mastered, like French or trigonometry, but a psychological problem to be solved. From an early age, we are plagued with "illusory understandings"—explicit errors that prevent us from accepting truths—and also with "inert ideas"—equally erroneous beliefs that lurk unnoticed, making them all the more pernicious. "Education," former Carnegie Foundation President Lee S. Shulman observed, "is a *dual* process in which, initially, the inside beliefs and understandings must come out, and only then can something outside get in."[19]

In his first *Meditations* (1641), French philosopher Rene Descartes acknowledged that the "whole edifice" of his thinking had, since childhood, rested upon a large number of falsehoods that he had accepted as true: "I realized that it was necessary . . . to demolish everything completely, and start again right from the foundations." He contrived to obliterate these foundations by hypothesizing that a "malicious demon of the utmost power and cunning" had tricked him into believing what he thought; he had no choice but to scrutinize all of his inside beliefs and understandings, relentlessly rooting out error.[20] But if a demon has sneaked into your thinking, how can you think it out?

Decades later John Locke arrived at a different solution. The mind at birth was a blank slate. If it were inscribed only with truths, the mind would remain error-free. He therefore

advised parents and educators to teach as many truths to infants and children as possible, leaving little room for erroneous
beliefs. Erasmus had used a different metaphor—the mind as
virgin field, ready for cultivation—but the concept was similar:
the teacher's task was to fling great handfuls of seeds onto the
field and nurture them; the more healthy plants, the fewer
weeds.

This agglomerative approach makes intuitive sense, which is
why teachers scrawl masses of words onto blackboards (or upload
them into PowerPoint), spew them out in fast-paced lectures,
and give frequent quizzes to ensure that students are learning
the material. If we fill the empty vessel of the brain with truths,
malicious demons can't find space in which to take up lodging.
But as Harvard's Charles Eliot observed, the mind is more
sieve than empty vessel. Any parent who has offered advice to
a child, or teacher who has graded a test, knows this to be true.
When we can find no immediate use for information, we consign it to remote storage centers. Soon it is "out of mind," subject to the vagaries of our off-site retrieval systems.

And what if the chief sources of error are our parents and
teachers themselves? What if we have been socialized to believe myths and falsehoods? Rousseau, rethinking Locke's
metaphor of mind as empty slate, proposed that infants were
pure and good; they became corrupted through socialization.
In *Emile* (1762), Rousseau proposed to insulate the young mind
of his putative student—Emile—from *all* socializing influences.
Under his tutor's prophylactic guidance, Emile would learn vo-
cational skills, scoutcraft, and little else: certainly not "how to
generalize ideas" or "make abstractions." As he approached

adulthood, Emile, though simple-minded, would be ahead of everyone else in that he would possess his own reason "and not another's."[21]

The implausibility of Rousseau's scheme—how can children be shielded from socialization?—underscores the dimensions of the problem: If selves are shaped through socialization—parents, teachers, religious leaders—and if role models espouse error, how can anyone learn anything important? One solution to this conundrum is probably the oldest and perhaps the most influential pedagogical system ever devised: the Socratic method.

The Socratic Solution: Expunging the Self

Many of those seeking to reinvigorate undergraduate education regard the Socratic method as the gold standard. Bok, in a chapter of *Our Underachieving Colleges* entitled "Learning to Think," proposed the Socratic method as the most powerful of the active learning pedagogies.[22] Calls for wider adoption of the Socratic method have resounded in all quarters, ranging from the conservative Allan Bloom, who insisted that the university existed "to preserve and further" that which Socrates represented, to the liberal Martha Nussbaum, who noted that "liberal education in our colleges is, and should be, Socratic."[23] Columbia English professor Andrew Delbanco insists that the value of "teaching by questioning" was a "pedagogical truth that has never been better demonstrated than in the Platonic dialogues composed some twenty-five hundred years ago."[24] The convergence of Socratic method and higher education makes perfect sense: Plato's Socrates proposed to use reason to uproot error and promote truth, which could stand as an elegant compression of the mission statements of most colleges and universities.

But the Socratic method has withered partly because it never worked particularly well, even when used by the master himself. Nietzsche observed that the Socratic dialectic wasn't persuasive. "Nothing is easier to erase than a dialectical effect," he noted."[25] In 1971 Princeton classicist Gregory Vlastos observed that Socrates was "not persuasive at all": he "never" managed to win over an opponent.[26] Within a few decades this judgment had become the new orthodoxy among classicists. "On the whole," Gary Alan Scott concluded in 2000, "one is bound to come away from [Plato's] dialogues with the impression that his Socrates is not very effective as a teacher."[27] That same year, John Beverslius, in *Cross-Examining Socrates,* put it even more sharply:

> If the early dialogues show anything, they show Socrates' monumental failure. The recalcitrant and unpersuaded interlocutor is not a phenomenon peculiar to some of the dialogues, but a phenomenon common to most of them."[28]

Some scholars, while conceding the point, blamed Socrates's interlocutors for being too dim-witted to perceive their teacher's wisdom. (This argument, of course, resonates with the modern critique of the "dunderheads" in college classrooms; see Chapter 1.) But if Socrates's pedagogical deficiencies arise from the incapacity of his students, how can the Socratic method address the problem of disengaged students?[29]

Others maintain that Plato's Socrates was less interested in persuading his interlocutors than in exhibiting his playful wit and penchant for irony. That's why he sometimes put forth unsound or specious arguments. But this raises even more difficult questions: Why would a teacher toy with students but fail to let them in on the joke? And how can falsehoods advance the truth?

A more plausible explanation is that Socrates failed to persuade because that was never his goal. The apostle of reason understood the limitations of reason as a pedagogical tool. He did not *seek* to lead his interlocutors to truth—at least not directly; instead, he wanted them to declare that they knew something—anything—and then prove them wrong. The resulting *emotional* upheaval would shake the foundations of their self. That's one reason Socrates refused to debate hypothetical propositions and insisted that interlocutors state positions they genuinely believed in: "It's you and me I want to put on the line, and I think the argument will be tested best if we take the 'if' out."[30] By changing the ostensible search for truth into a personal challenge, Socrates could prove that his interlocutor's self was defective.[31]

A Socratic interrogation followed a predictable arc that culminated in the interlocutor's admission that he didn't know what he was talking about. In the *Republic,* for example, after Socrates asked Polemarchus to define justice, Polemarchus confidently supplied a definition. Socrates posed one clarifying question after another. Forty questions later, Polemarchus was reeling. "I don't really know what I did mean," he conceded. But this did not satisfy Socrates, who peppered Polemarchus with two dozen more questions. Polemarchus threw in the towel: "What you say seems perfectly true," he admitted. He wasn't confused; he had been dead wrong. He knew nothing about justice. Worse, he had been ignorant of his ignorance. What other unseen errors lurked among his cherished beliefs? And if his thinking were so shoddy, perhaps his very self was "a morass of ignorance."

Socrates ensured that his students would fail by obliging them to make positive statements on matters they didn't understand. "In what way can you search for something when you are altogether ignorant of what it is?" Meno implored after fumbling through a Socratic interrogation.[32] The resulting admission of cognitive incapacity, of the failure of one's own self, was the most important step toward fashioning a new one.

But to indict one's self so damningly is not easy. Meno, for example, told Socrates that

> you are bewitching and drugging and completely spell-binding me, so that I have become saturated with puzzlement . . . for really I am numb in mind and mouth, and I do not know how to answer you.[33]

The term Plato's Socrates usually used to describe this interrogation was *elenchus,* a word that at the time included strong connotations of shaming and humiliation.[34] The Socratic dialogue culminated in a "public hazing" or a "humbling moment," a shattering of the underpinnings of the self.[35] After having repudiated his former self, an interlocutor would become, under

Socrates's midwifery, a "soul that is in travail of birth *(Theaetetus)*."[36] He would be reborn as a new person.

Sometimes, however, the transformation went awry. Alcibiades and Critias, Socrates's students, were the prime historical examples. Alcibiades, a handsome athlete, compelling orator, and commanding leader, crumbled beneath an interrogation by Socrates. Never before had such a thing happened to him, Alcibiades declared. He had come to see himself as no better than a degraded slave. Critias, another young man of substantial gifts, became so upset during a Socratic interrogation that he could not continue. Socrates, taking over for his "benumbed" student, explained that Critias was ashamed of his ignorance. Alcibiades and Critias had been humiliated, their sense of self demolished.

Rather than adopt a new identity as seekers of truth, however, Alcibiades became a scoundrel who betrayed Athens and Critias sent death squads to round up democrats. According to some scholars, Socrates generally exerted a harmful influence on his students.[37] Anger, one scholar observed, was the most common response to a Socratic interrogation. And if a student ended up hating the teacher, "surely it is bad teaching and a bad form of intercourse in general."[38]

Such sentiments echoed the judgment of the 500 Athenian jurors who, mindful of the depredations of Alcibiades and Critias, convicted Socrates of corrupting the youth. Even Plato conceded that the Socratic assault on the self was fraught with danger. Dialogic argumentation, Plato's Socrates warned in the *Republic,* should not be taught to very young men, for they might repudiate their former beliefs and become subject to "corruption." Socratic instruction should be restricted to those who were orderly and steady in their intellectual habits; others were unfit for it.

Why the Socratic Method Generates Resistance

In the modern world, the Socratic method has had its most visible success in American law schools, where it has served as the predominant pedagogical mode ever since Christopher Columbus Langdell introduced it at Harvard in 1870. Langdell, like Henry Adams, had been hired by Charles Eliot, who disapproved of lectures and endorsed Langdell's plan to institute an "intensely active" pedagogical system. Langdell eschewed lectures and instead "grilled" students by posing a succession of questions relating to legal reasoning. Langdell's version of the Socratic method swiftly spread to other law schools. By 1930 it had become "almost universal" in American law schools.[39] It remains the dominant mode of education for first-year students at American law schools. Many lawyers regard their own interrogation as the transformative moment when they surrendered to the intellectual demands of the profession. They began to think like lawyers.[40]

But even in American law schools, the Socratic method has long had detractors. Langdell's first Socratic class infuriated his students. Many took part in "impromptu indignation meetings." Most stopped coming to class.[41] Student resistance, however, contributed to the method's appeal: law deans intent on proving the supremacy of a law degree over apprenticeship with a local lawyer or judge emphasized the intimidating rigor of the Socratic method.

Student opposition sometimes caused the Socratic method to flop. When singled out before a large audience of their peers, students often cloaked their confusion by spewing convoluted sentences and legal jargon. Classmates, relieved to have been temporarily spared, tuned out as the professorial inquisitor struggled to find enough substance to continue the questioning. Often, frustrated professors resorted to lecturing. In 2008, on the occasion of receiving a teaching award, UCLA law professor Stephen Bainbridge recalled that when he had been a law student the "great Socratic teachers" had abandoned the interrogatory process: "Socrates did almost all of the talking."[42] Similarly, Brian Leiter, a professor at the University of Chicago Law School, gave up on the Socratic method because he found it didn't work. "There is no evidence—as in 'none'—that the Socratic method is an effective teaching tool," he concluded.[43]

The critique of the Socratic method in law school includes a darker narrative. In a blistering memoir of his first year at Harvard Law, Scott Turow, the future novelist, described how his classmates had had "their valued beliefs ridiculed, and in general felt their sense of self-worth thoroughly demeaned." "If you get knocked down often enough," he added, "you learn not to stand up." Eventually his law school friends became "a sad, bitter, defeated lot." Lani Guinier, the first black woman to be tenured at Harvard Law, claimed that the Socratic method was particularly harmful to women. She reported on a study that found that many women were "alienated" and "delegitimated" by it. One female law student told Guinier bluntly, "For me the damage is done; *it's in me*. I will never be the same. I feel so defeated." One of Turow's female classmates equated the Socratic interrogation with rape.[44]

Some law schools have given up on the Socratic method or softened it beyond recognition. "It is clear to me that the Socratic method is dying," declared University of North Carolina law professor Martin B. Louis in 1994. "I think it is dying because an increasing number of young law professors are playing it safe and because we've given much more power to the students to express their unhappiness with the Socratic method."[45]

The retreat of the law schools from the Socratic method suggests its unsuitability for undergraduate education. Of course, most of those advocating the "Socratic method" in college do not propose to grill students in the manner of the law professors; they simply mean to teach by posing questions and stimulating discussion. The interactive advantages of this approach are obvious; but this interrogatory mode has its drawbacks. Teachers, seeking to engage students, naturally ask questions of a personal nature. But many people regard such questions as a potential threat to their self and they immediately withdraw from the questioning.[46]

Plato's Socrates understood this danger, and he adjusted his interrogation to fit the psychological profile of his interlocutors. He toyed with his less able discussants, nudging them along gently, but he took an arch and even sarcastic tone with opinionated speakers. But always he showed his interrogator to be wrong. He did not employ reason to chop away thickets of error so that his interlocutors could find their way to Truth.

Instead, he used reason—along with specious arguments, sarcasm, humor, and a whole panoply of rhetorical tools—to bring about an emotional upheaval that would culminate in a "destruction of assumptions to the very first principle." Once their former self had collapsed, a new one could be erected on firmer foundations.[47] Socrates understood that deep learning begins when the "inside understandings" come out.

But there's the rub: our inside understandings do not readily "come out." Our self-related thoughts are ingrained in us, imprinted upon the neural superhighways of our brain. Our self usually withstands most assaults, including the Socratic interrogation.[48] As Nietzsche and modern scholars have perceived, the Socratic method fails because it arouses mistrust among interlocutors who retreat, turtle-like, within the hard protective shell of their self.[49]

And if the self does not collapse—if the "inside understandings" don't come out—how can anyone engage in transformative learning?

Adding New Selves through Role-Immersion

Pauline Brown, a first-year student at Barnard, enjoyed being the Wanli emperor for the role-immersion game set in Ming China. Most students enjoy the role and for good reason. She was absolute ruler: "her" word on all matters was law. But during the first few game sessions, a group of exceedingly polite but annoyingly persistent Confucian critics in the Hanlin Academy had undermined her power. Just when she began to think that she might lose, spring break intruded and she headed home. On the flight to California she didn't feel quite right. By the time the plane touched down in San Francisco, she had a bad case of the flu and spent much of the next week in bed. One night her temperature spiked. By morning, despite her mother's steady supply of fluids, Pauline had become delirious. She had not fallen asleep, so she recalled "with perfect clarity" what happened next, which she recounted to me:

PAULINE: I saw myself from someone else's perspective, just my upper body, as if I were blankly staring out of a picture frame. I was the Emperor [Wanli]. I was wearing a red gown with bits of gold. It was really beautiful. And this big rectangular hat with gold tassels.

MC: The emperor's hat? Like a shoebox, with the short sides front and back?" [There was a picture of such a hat in Ray Huang's *1587: A Year of No Significance,* a book assigned for the game.]

PAULINE: Maybe that's what it was.

MC: Did you have a beard?

PAULINE: No beard. That's the weird part. It was *me.* I knew I was a *male* emperor yet I was still Pauline the girl. I knew I was supposed to be a man, but it was *my* face. It was very strange.

MC: How did you feel as you looked at yourself in the picture?

PAULINE: I was totally and utterly stressed out! I knew that I was sick—I knew I had the flu—but as emperor I was *sooo* worried that I wouldn't be able to help my people. I thought, "Oh no! I have to prevent the [Yellow] River from flooding and stop the pirates and the poverty, but I can't because I'm sick, throwing up, and just not well." My thoughts were racing the whole time: worry worry worry. Mainly about not being an adequate emperor.

By morning, she added, she was moaning aloud, "My people, my people. What will become of my people?"

"What people?" her mother asked.

"The people of China," Pauline replied. Her mother called a doctor.

Emperor Pauline had hijacked Pauline's physical attributes as well as her emotional and cognitive machinery. But even in her feverish state, MetaPauline was functioning: it regarded Emperor Pauline critically and perceived that much was wrong. Emperor Pauline was staring "blankly" from the picture, imprisoned within a frame, upper torso only and thus incapable of motion, though the real Pauline was vigorous and lively. MetaPauline spotted another major mistake: Emperor Pauline, though wearing the costume of a Ming emperor, lacked a beard and had the face of a girl. Emperor Pauline was a fraud.

Though an obvious imposter, Emperor Pauline had become part of Pauline's self-system. Her selves engaged in a complex and multitiered conversation. When she interrogated her selves, MetaPauline re-examined who she was and what she believed. Emperor Pauline had not dethroned MetaPauline. It just made her work harder.

By the fourth or fifth session of a Reacting game, students commonly report that they are beginning to believe their roles, although they usually qualify such statements with immediate disclaimers: "Well, not *really,* of course, but . . ." This ambivalence suggests that the students' core self has admitted the newcomers to their self system, but only provisionally: it has flagged the interlopers as "unreal." Reacting selves, like all subversive play selves, come adorned with explicit markers—cognitive asterisks, as it were—signifying their unreality: "We're just for play!"

I happened on another illustration of this phenomenon in 2010. I was cleaning out my office and found a VHS tape of a Reacting class from 2000. When I replayed it, one scene stood out. "Citizen Victoria," leader of a Paris section during the French Revolution, called on the poor of Paris to rise up against the king's troops. "Let us bleed and gag, kill and destroy," she declared, her long black hair swaying as she chopped the air with her hands. "Tyranny must die. For without the death of tyrants, we cannot live!" Her voice rose to fever pitch and her body quivered. "We are dead right now!" she shouted, "and if I must die in order to live, in order for France to live, I shall die!"

The class sat in stunned silence. Even as I watched a decade later, a shiver pricked my spine. I recalled Kenneth Branagh's dictum that the "under-the-skin kind of tingle that the audience can feel" does not come about through special technique; it occurs when an actor achieves "an absolute, laser-beam radio-signal connection with the truth." The secret, he said, is to be "as real and as natural and as truthful as possible in the moment."[50] Citizen Victoria elicited the tingle not through her mastery of the theatrical arts. She believed what she was saying.

I wondered what had happened to Citizen Victoria in the ensuing decade. So I tracked her down and interviewed her online. Now she was a lawyer in Paris, having recently been transferred from her firm's New York offices. We joked about her working in Paris two hundred years after she had been a leader of the city's rabble. I then asked whether she remembered the speech in which she roused the sections to fight.

"Certainly," she typed immediately. "Die! Die! Die!"

I was surprised that she recalled it instantly and said so.

"I completely owned the role," she replied. "I didn't feel like I was in a classroom. I didn't feel like a young woman in college. I was in Paris. I felt like I truly was a French revolutionary. I had so completely studied the ideology and the character, I didn't need to think and formulate my answers or find the right words. They just came."

"Had you been brainwashed?"

"Hardly," she replied. "I believed in nonviolence then. I still do."

For a time we discussed other subjects. Then I had an idea: "If it were Paris in 1791 and the King's henchmen arrived on the scene, would you call on the crowd to attack them?"

Long pause.

"Perhaps."

During that pause, I suspect that Citizen Victoria and the real Victoria debated the issue, with Citizen Victoria scoring some points. Victoria had to rethink her pacifism. Her "inside understandings" had not been expunged; they had just been subjected to an internal grilling. She had engaged in critical thinking of the deepest kind.

But if our self is fundamentally stable, deeply rooted in neural networks that ensure its stability, why would it let down its guard and admit outrageous, self-critical interlopers? Perhaps the answer is that we sometimes grow bored with our self. We complain of being "stuck in a rut," a neat metaphor for the well-trodden pathways of our self-focused neural webs. We crave something different. That's when we're drawn to subversive play worlds, which we know will conjure all sorts of mischievous alternative selves. These characters appeal precisely because they are so different. They taunt our metaself for being predictable, for adhering to social hierarchies and conventions. They evoke absurd and outrageous alternatives. They spice up our lives and make us laugh. In a word, they will be fun.

But the neural capacity of the brain is a terrible thing to waste. Our species has advanced partly by adding more neurological processing power to the brain. Why would our brains allocate precious neurons to the invention and maintenance of such silly creatures?[51]

Perhaps the answer is that sometimes our familiar associations and beliefs fall short of our needs. When confronted with unfamiliar problems, our usual self may fail us. And insofar as our self is a product of social and cultural interactions, those around us may think much as we do. How, then, can society respond to unfamiliar challenges and change direction? To return to the idea at the outset of this chapter: When inside beliefs and understandings are linked to the self (literally, through neural webs), how can anyone think differently?

Subversive play selves provide an answer. By definition, they generate ideas that challenge our self and contravene reality. When our self (or society) is trapped in a logjam, we must look for some new means to break it up. We frantically revisit those subversive selves, and ransack the peculiar treasure trove of information and ideas that are part of their baggage. Often enough, we have a eureka moment that causes us to wonder, "Where did that come from?"

Nowadays, however, most of our subversive play selves are conjured by corporate conglomerates: a new video game invites us to acquire the powers of superheroes, and a beer commercial shows how we can become "the most interesting man in the world." Having internalized these subversive play selves, we are unconsciously attuned to information about them. Corporate behemoths obligingly inundate us with pertinent updates: the latest movie provides cool new references that must be added to our Facebook Wall; we Tweet about Snookie's latest exploits; we buy fine clothing for our *Second Life* avatar. If so many of us are distracted these days, it's largely because our subversive play selves continuously lap from these profit-generating information streams.[52]

Reacting subversive play selves demand information, too, but much of it is found in books and libraries. Emperor Pauline was busy searching for information on Chinese history—the flooding of the Yellow River and piracy—and for Confucian *Analects* that supported her position. Emperor Pauline was even soaking up information of which the real Pauline was unaware: the real Pauline had not realized that Emperor Pauline was wearing the proper Ming emperor's hat. *("Maybe that's what it was.")*

Emperor Pauline further suggested that Pauline could become a male emperor, just as Citizen Victoria forced Victoria to rethink her pacifism. In this way, Reacting subversive play selves enlarge students' mental universes by introducing them to new peoples, texts, and worlds.

Dangerous Interlopers

Nearly always subversive play selves amuse us; sometimes they challenge us to think harder; but sometimes, while sparring with us, they land a blow that knocks our metaself out cold. The story of "Isabella" (a pseudonym) is one such example.

Isabella told me that she became a Christian at an early age. She didn't know why, and this mystery has shaped her life. Her parents were not religious, but she was drawn to a neighborhood church and began attending it on her own. Three years later she arranged for her own baptism. "When I was fourteen, fifteen, I tried not to believe in God," she said, "but it didn't last." At sixteen she "got serious" about her faith and studied theology and apologetics. After high school, she attended a community college, studied fashion, and married a devout Christian. At twenty-seven, she enrolled at California State University at Long Beach in preparation for the seminary. By then, Isabella was immersed in a Christian subculture. "All of my friends were Christians," she explained.

> Bible study was our central social activity. I only socialized with Christians (Christian art critiques, Christian rock concerts, Christian game nights). It is quite possible for a young Christian to be completely isolated from opposing world views and belief systems, to live in a stable, reliable world structured by consensus and doctrine. It was a self-preserving way to live.

Then she signed up for David Stewart's course on the Old Testament, a requirement for her major. Stewart's class, following the conventions of academic biblical scholarship, examined the complexities, contradictions, and ambiguities of the text. Isabella carefully noted the "troubling questions" raised by Stewart's lectures, but she "just put them away." Perhaps she would address them in seminary.

Midway through the course, Stewart announced that the lectures were over and the class would play *The Josianic Reform: Deuteronomy, Prophecy, and Israelite Religion*. The game is set in Jerusalem in 622 B.C.E., when workers who had been repairing the temple purportedly discovered ancient religious scrolls—the Book of Deuteronomy. The game recreates the debate among religious leaders and Josiah's court over whether the scrolls contained the true word of God. Isabella was assigned the role of Huldah, a prophetess whose victory objective was to affirm the authenticity of the text.

As Huldah, Isabella was forced to confront a host of textual problems. Why, she wondered, did Josiah solicit the views of Huldah, a minor prophet and a woman, instead of Jeremiah, a male prophet of great repute? Josiah's decision was all the more suspect because Huldah's husband worked as a top administrator for Josiah. "I had to engage these issues, confront them, and truthfully acknowledge the textual problems," Isabella explained, "because others in the class would be attacking my character over precisely these points." She had no choice but to scrutinize the text from multiple perspectives. "To do that, I had to put my own perspective and expectations on the shelf," she noted.

But as so often happens in role-immersion games, Isabella found it impossible to disengage her real self from her role. She sent pointed emails to Stewart: "I honestly have no idea where to start, because I keep coming up against a total lack of evidence in support of Huldah's claims," she wrote. "What is driving me mad," she added on another occasion, "is that I am afraid I have to write a paper that assumes speculation as fact." Her doubts about the Bible mounted. She cried. When her husband offered reassurance, she became irritated. Once, while they were waiting for a campus bus, she poured out an agony of doubt. When he reminded her that she was merely playing a game, she lost control.[53] What happened next she related in a Gmail chat:

ISABELLA: By that point, it had ceased being just an assignment. Huldah's prophecy begins the process of canonization on which the texts that I put my faith into as scripture began to take their shapes. If she was a false prophet, if the whole "Scroll of the Teaching" was nothing more than a political move by Josiah, then what of the rest of the Bible? Suddenly I felt like I couldn't trust anything, and all the little inconsistencies and ambiguities that we believers like to skip over or ignore seemed to be glaring at me. I started yelling at my husband. We were making a scene for sure!

MC: You? So soft-spoken? I cannot imagine you yelling.

ISABELLA: It was a sort of high, nonstop hollering.

MC: Because you were wracked with doubts?

ISABELLA: Yes, in the text. I realized two things. I thought I knew the Bible, but I only knew it as I could fit it into my world view, my belief system. I was on a path to seminary, to biblical studies. After [playing] Huldah, I realized that I needed to look at the text with my own eyes, not just be taught. Is this clear? I had never allowed myself to admit that I had unanswered questions. Second, I stopped trying to justify my belief in God through validation of the text. I allowed faith to play a larger role in my life. I gave up a little bit of that need to have all of the answers, but not the task of looking for answers.

MC: Your certainty in your beliefs was eroded?

ISABELLA: Yes.

MC: You ceased to be who you thought you were?

ISABELLA: My identity is tangled up with my faith, and my faith was shaken up and restructured. So, yes.

MC: Did this hurt?

ISABELLA: Yes.

MC: Because?

ISABELLA: Because my former self, my earlier faith, was really sure of itself! I had all the answers I needed to maintain my beliefs.

MC: You experienced an identity crisis?

ISABELLA: Oh, yes. Absolutely.

MC: So Reacting made you cry, yell at your husband, and plunged you into an identity crisis? Great experience, huh?

ISABELLA: All true. But I like my faith better now. Is that weird? I never even knew I could *like* my faith! Because it is real! It is messy and full of questions and focused on God. Just like the Bible.

Before the Josiah game, Stewart had lectured on the "troubling problems" unearthed by biblical scholars; Isabella, an outstanding student, had "learned" of these problems. But she had not admitted them within her self. She had just "put them away"—"out of mind," as it were. But after Huldah had taken lodging within Isabella's self system, the ensuing identity conflict caused her to rethink the text that served as the bedrock of her identity. The experience had not simply enlarged Isabella's self; it had changed it fundamentally.

Perhaps Isabella's story illustrates why Plato's Socrates denounced actors and poets. When you take on someone else's identity, you are false to your own self, and that which rests upon falsehood cannot lead to truth. A person who assumes alternative identities cannot remain at unity.

Plato's notion of a unitary self has had a long shelf life. Philosopher Charles Taylor has argued that Plato's goal of attaining "unity with oneself" constituted the "dominant family of moral theories in our civilization."[54] Rousseau agreed with Plato: "He who begins to become alien to himself does not take long to forget himself entirely." If his Emile "just once" preferred to be someone other than himself—"were this other Socrates, were it Cato"—then "everything has failed." Freud was even more emphatic: among adults, role-playing was a repudiation of reality—and thus akin to delusion.[55] Throughout the twentieth century, many psychologists have posited a "unitary" or "coherent" self as the ideal.[56] In his classic *Childhood and Society* (1950), for example, Erik Erikson explained that teenagers naturally engage in a "search for and insistence on identity." Those who lack a coherent self experience "role confusion" and fail to achieve their proper "sex-linked identity."[57] Psychologists warned that the example of aggressive mothers or effeminate fathers would cause their children to become confused as to the proper gender role, precipitating "psychotic episodes" or even "schizophrenic psychosis."[58] In *Toys and Reasons* (1976), his final book, Erikson launched into a searing indictment of role-playing—the human capacity for "imagining different scenarios." He warned that such forms of "make believe" hijack a person's "self identity" and often lead to disaster, such as when Department of Defense officials, playing at "Game Theory," made plans for nuclear annihilation, or when soldiers at My Lai, regressing to childish rituals of "playing war" and "war games," "wasted" Vietnamese women and children. Because the imaginative fictions of the modern world were so enticing, Erikson wrote, there was "all the more desperate need for a 'real' identity."[59]

Such views have lost favor in recent decades.[60] Scholars in many disciplines now perceive the self as fluid and contingent, an open-ended process rather than a set pathway to a fixed destination.[61] Many psychologists regard a multiplicity of selves as sources of intellectual development and personal fulfillment. Some researchers have even found that people who assume many different role identities have a stronger sense of self, with higher levels of self-esteem and more success at coping with disappointment.[62] This new understanding of the self has important implications for theories of learning, most obviously by removing the chief objection to role-immersion pedagogies. The acquisition of multiple selves does not undermine our "unitary self" because no such thing exists. Our metaself negotiates among our many selves, including those playful (and sometimes not-so-playful) jesters who prod us to rethink who we are.

Multiple Selves and Critical Thinking

First-year student Ashley Bush balked after she read the name on the slip of paper she had pulled out of a hat: she was to be Emma Goldman in a game on woman suffrage and radical thought in the early twentieth century. "She seemed like a crazy lady," Ashley recalled. "I couldn't understand how one person could fight against the government and fight virtually alone." But Ashley warmed to the role; in the final session she startled classmates with a powerful defense of anarchism. In the previous game Ashley had made a similarly forceful appeal for adherence to Confucian tradition and order.

After the game, I interviewed her online. "Who was right?" I asked, "Confucius or Emma Goldman?"

"I am truly conflicted," she replied. "Both make sense, although they are seemingly opposite extremes."

"So the net result of taking contradictory roles is that you're confused?"

"Not confused," she replied. "Curious. I now have the knowledge to look at our society through the lenses of other perspectives. Not just what I have been taught to *believe*, but to take a step back and see that I can think for myself."

During the interview, I noticed that Ashley Bush's full Gmail chat address included "Walker." Until that moment, I hadn't realized that this first-year student, who had introduced herself to the class as a dog lover from Colorado, was the granddaughter of a past president of the United States and niece of the current one. Had I known, I might not have allowed her to play a role that potentially exposed her to public embarrassment: (tabloid headline: "Prez's Niece Nixes Government"). But by taking a role at odds with her family's conservatism, she had come to realize the value of looking at the world through the eyes—the ideas—of people different from herself.

A few weeks later, I reinterviewed Isabella (aka Huldah) and pressed her on a similar point. Didn't the fact that she had gone through a major life change suggest that she had been brainwashed?

"How can that be?" she asked. "I was forced to drop my presuppositions, ignore my social location, and get into a character I couldn't originally endorse. More the opposite of brainwashing."[63]

She added that she had decided against going to seminary. "I didn't want to immerse myself in a program that would wash over my questions or ignore problems in the text. I am a believer. I go to church every week, sometimes more than once a week. I lead a discussion group for young women on Christianity, Christian traditions, social issues, and the Bible. But I don't claim any authority. It is easier for me to admit that I don't know the answer. I like the way my faith feels: friendlier, more understanding of others' questions and beliefs."

But did the fact that she had abandoned seminary—a goal she once cherished—suggest that she had lost her faith?

"Not at all," she replied. "I was definitely going through an identity crisis and my faith was shaken in such a way that it changed shape, but I didn't stop believing. I wouldn't say that I lost myself during this process, nor did I lose my faith, but everything changed. I allowed myself to see the problems in the text, which made the text real, demystified in a way."

> MC: Do you mind that people who read this will know that you had a crisis of faith?
>
> ISABELLA: Not at all.
>
> MC: You have confidence in your uncertainty?
>
> ISABELLA: Quite. I am sure I know very little.

Fareeda, a devout Muslim, came to appreciate a great Jewish leader; Joshua, a committed Zionist, grew to admire a Palestinian nationalist; Victoria, a pacifist, perceived the limitations in her personal philosophy; Ashley, daughter of a famously conservative family, found admirable qualities in Emma Goldman; and Isabella, a devoted Christian, acquired less certainty but more faith. All were changed in fundamental ways by role-immersion games. By internalizing different selves and ideas, these students asked more questions about who they were and what they believed. Critical thinking of the most fundamental sort had become embedded in their very being.[64] They did not have to be told to think critically; the new occupants within forced them to do so. Their brains had not been washed of knowledge; their selves had become open to it.[65]

When we identify with other people, whether by reading novels, watching plays, or engaging in role-immersion games, we enlarge our cognitive universe. We gain access to more information and new ideas. But something else occurs, too. We find strangers less strange. When our self contains multitudes, as Chapter 5 shows, we connect more readily with others, confident that we can cope with new perspectives and ideas that may challenge our sense of who we are.[66]

CHAPTER 5

Overcoming the Silence of the Students

Free Speech in New York, 403 B.C.E.

As I settled into my seat in the back of the room, I pulled out the class roster for the first session of a game set in Athens in 403 B.C.E. The previous year Athens had surrendered to Sparta, a calamitous end to three decades of war. The Spartan army installed a group of dictators, soon known as the Thirty Tyrants, who butchered hundreds, perhaps thousands, of Athenian democrats. But some democrats eluded the death squads and fled to the mountains north of Athens. There they raised an army and resumed the war against Sparta and the Thirty Tyrants. Sparta eventually wearied of the insurgency and withdrew its garrison. The Thirty fled Athens and the insurgents restored the democracy. The game began with the first meeting of the Athenian Assembly.

Beth, a moderate, strode to the podium.

"The Thirty Tyrants have inflicted great pain on all of us here—here amidst the rubble of our once-magnificent city," she said, gesturing vaguely toward the windows.[1]

She looked up from her notes. A classmate took a sip from a bottle of Poland Spring water. Another chewed on a pen. Both regarded Beth closely.

"But now that the Thirty Tyrants are dead or gone," Beth continued, "we should banish them from our hearts and minds. We must not rekindle old hatreds."

She scanned her notes, turned a few pages, and read aloud: "I therefore propose to you, citizens of Athens, that we pass a reconciliation agreement. No Athenian shall ever again speak of the past wrongs of those who supported the Thirty. We must . . ."

"No!" Allison protested, "We must not forget those who died at the hands of the Thirty!"

Beth, taken aback, stared at her.

"Our dead martyrs demand vengeance," Allison said.

"But revenge is wrong!" another student piped up.

Another voice: "Revenge will lead to violence, and then to more violence."

"Not revenge, vengeance," Allison contended. She hunched forward, a strand of black hair tumbling across her eyes. "I ask you, Beth"—Allison's voice softened—"is memory bad? Is truth bad?"

"But sometimes the truth can hurt people," Beth answered.

"The truth is the truth," Allison declared.

"But talk of the past only stirs up trouble. We suffered enough under the Thirty Tyrants. Should we suffer again, under the memory of their rule?" Beth implored.

A half-dozen more joined in, and several students got up from their seats and walked to the podium, forming a line behind Beth.

"We must trust each other, not kill each other!" Beth's voice, pitched higher, pierced the room. The rhetorical flourishes were gone.

"That's right." Yet another student sprang to her feet, hands fluttering with excitement. "Let's say you've got two farmers who are neighbors. OK? One says to the other. 'Hey, last night I slept with your wife.' What would happen? A fight! The truth would lead to violence!"

"If you keep talking about the evil of the Thirty," Beth added, "we'll just keep killing each other. We've got to stop the hate and the hurt!"

More hands, more shouts, more debate.

Tucked in a back corner, scarcely noticed amidst the din, I recorded students' participation on the class roster. When I finished, every name had a check mark.

Except "Veronica's" (a pseudonym).

I spotted her at the far end of the table, her wide eyes moving from one speaker to the next, like a fawn that had wandered into a den of wolves.

After class, as students gathered their books and jabbered about Athens, Veronica at last spoke: "I thought the purpose of college was for everyone to help each other, not tear each other apart," she declared, loud enough for me to hear. She shot me an anxious look and left the room.

As Veronica slipped out the door, I consoled myself with the recollection of shy students who had found their voice in React-ing. Ting-Ting Kao, a soft-spoken student of that first Reacting class in 1996, came to mind. In the game set in Ming China—the one where Fiza and Purvi had taken charge of the class[2]—Ting-Ting was a member of the emperor's faction. During an early debate she alluded to her own Chinese background:

"You critics of the emperor don't understand," she almost whispered. "In China, when you talk to someone older than you, you lower yourself. When you speak to a parent, you lower yourself further. But when you speak to the emperor, then you must put yourself down, down, down on the ground." She was staring at the table, scarcely audible.

In the following weeks and months, Ting-Ting spoke more frequently and more assertively. In the final game, set in India on the eve of independence in 1945, Ting-Ting had been as-signed the role of Ali Jinnah, leader of the Muslim League. During the final session, most of the other factions—the Indian National Congress, Gandhi, Sikhs, and British mediators—had agreed on a constitution for an Indian federation. Except Ting-Ting, who rejected it. The Muslim minority, she insisted, had not received sufficient guarantees; their rights would be trampled by the Hindu majority. The debate became increasingly acrimo-nious. Ting-Ting, at the center of it all, strode to the podium.

"If you do not change the constitution," she threatened, "I will call on the Muslims of India to rise up and fight!"

A dozen students jumped to their feet, howling in protest. A civil war would plunge India into chaos; nearly all factions would lose. For twenty minutes, Ting-Ting stood at the podium, arguing, cajoling, brokering. At one point, a professor with an office nearby opened the door and poked his head in, face creased with concern:

"Is everything OK in here? I thought there was a riot."

"Not yet," someone replied.

In the end, Ting-Ting extracted the guarantees she felt the Muslims needed.

A few weeks after the India game, Ting-Ting ran for class office and was elected treasurer. During the summer between her junior and senior year, she worked as an intern in the government of the Republic of Georgia.

"How did you pull it off?" I asked when she returned. "I mean, you didn't speak Russian or Georgian, did you?"

"No," she said. "But I've got a voice."

Her words made me smile, but offered scant solace as I thought about Veronica. A few days later, I met with her privately. Veronica said that the class was so stressful she found it impossible to speak. I asked if she spoke in other classes. She did not answer directly but said that she preferred to listen and take notes. She disapproved of "show-offs" who monopolized class time.

For the remainder of the semester, when prodded by her faction to speak, she read her papers aloud. Occasionally she posed a question but otherwise contributed little. In the final session of "The Trial of Anne Hutchinson," she went to the podium and read her defense of Hutchinson's theology. Her ideas and research were excellent. After she had finished, Beth—now in the role of pastor of the Boston Church—began to pick it apart.

"When Anne said that she had a revelation, wasn't she acting just like Abraham?"

"Well, yeah," Veronica said, her voice falling in instantaneous capitulation.

"And there haven't been any prophets in a long time, have there?"

"Well, no." Veronica slumped against the podium. I winced.

Another barrage of questions, each sharper than the last.

Finally Beth asked: "Isn't it arrogant of Anne to think that she's a prophet like Abraham? Isn't that reason to banish her from Massachusetts?"

Veronica's eyes narrowed and her mouth tightened.

"No."

Her voice, though soft, had bite. "That's not right. That's not what she means. That's not what she said. You're twisting her words."

Jaws dropped. Beth stared. Veronica then reiterated the main ideas of her speech, but now she spoke freely. She lacked Beth's poise, but her argument was compelling and everyone knew it. When she walked out after class, I raced to catch up with her.

"You did it," I said at last. "You were terrific."

She smiled tentatively and looked down. We continued walking. (I've learned that often you teach best by shutting up.)

"That wasn't me," she finally said. "Not really. It was like this other person began speaking and I was standing beside her."

"Did it feel good?" I asked.

"When I walked away from the podium, I was shaking. I still am. I'm not sure that I like it. I don't think so."

We walked some more.

"You know," she continued, "I never speak in class. Any class. Not real speaking, I mean."

"Why this time?"

She took a few more steps, stopped, and looked at me.

"They were trying to hurt Anne. I couldn't let them do that."

The Silence of the Students

Words can wound; debate can hurt. The democratic Athenians understood this, which is why, at the first meeting of the restored Assembly in 403 B.C.E., they passed a law prohibiting public discussion of the city's recent past. No one was allowed to "remember the past wrongs" of those who had abetted the Thirty. Athenians took the law seriously, executing a citizen who filed a lawsuit against a supporter of the tyrants. The Reconciliation Agreement, and the trial of Socrates four years later, showed that in democratic Athens, certain subjects were off limits.

A culture of reconciliation also prevails in our colleges and universities. In 2009 the dean of Yale College banned a T-shirt containing F. Scott Fitzgerald's famous quotation, "I think of all Harvard men as sissies," after some students complained that "sissies" constituted a homophobic slur.[3] In 2011, Harvard officials pressured first-year students to sign an oath promising to act with "civility" and "inclusiveness" and to affirm that "kindness holds a place on par with intellectual attainment."[4] In 2012 the Foundation for Individual Rights in Education, a civil libertarian group, reported that 65 percent of a sample of

392 colleges had "campus speech codes" that violated the Constitution's right to free speech.[5]

The campus culture of reconciliation is so pervasive that it mostly goes unnoticed. The point became awkwardly evident to me when my wife and I took our daughter on a college-hunting trip through New England. During our tour of Wesleyan College, our energetic student guide touted the school's diversity. He ticked off various clubs and associations for all races, religions, and ethnic groups, as well as for all sexual orientations, including separate groups for gays and lesbians. "And I almost forgot," he added, "we have a really active asexual movement on campus." Toward the end of the tour, someone pointed to a large Victorian building with white columns and asked what it was. "Oh that," the guide said, his voice falling. "It's a fraternity. Where the conservative kids live." "But that's ok," he said, hastily recovering a bright tone. "That's where they do their thing so the rest of us don't have to deal with them."

What, I wondered, was my daughter to make of these words? I had hoped she would regard college as a place to grow intellectually by bumping against different people and ideas, but the guide was making the opposite point. A diverse student body ensured that everyone could find a comfortable niche among like-minded peers.[6]

Fraternities and sororities have long channeled students into homogeneous groups, but in recent decades the sorting trend has become more sophisticated and well-nigh universal. Even before they arrive on campus, about 80 percent of entering freshmen log onto college-run websites and choose simpatico roommates. Very quickly, such students form "self-selected cliques where their views are reinforced," observed NYU sociology professor Dalton Conley.[7] When students arrive on campus, moreover, they are invited to join countless clubs and associations based on religious, ethnic, political, sexual, or racial identity. When I ask why they join such groups, invariably students say that they like being among people who immediately "accept you for who you are."

Within companionable peer groups there is plenty of talk but little of the intellectual friction that stimulates learning. "Our antagonist is our helper," Edmund Burke wrote, adding: "He that wrestles with us strengthens our nerves and sharpens our skill." John Stuart Mill pointed out that often we don't understand our own thoughts because they rattle around our brains untested and unchallenged. "He who knows only his own side of the case," Mill noted, "knows little of that."[8] "Conflict is the gadfly of thought," John Dewey added. "It shocks us out of sheep-like passivity."[9]

Our students, having herded themselves into peaceable pastures, graze free from contentious words. Intellectual disputes, such as they are, rumble safely in the distance: "Whatever." When anthropology professor Cathy Small (pretending to be an undergraduate student) lived for a year in a college dorm and surveyed students' conversations, she discovered that only 5 percent of these touched on academics, and *all* concerned administrative details (when is the midterm?) or the personality or attractiveness of the instructor. "I never once overheard what I would term a political or philosophical discussion," she reported.[10]

In 2010 the American Association of Colleges and Universities found that only 35.6 percent of the students and 18.5 percent of the faculty strongly agreed that it was "safe to hold unpopular positions on campus."[11] A detailed survey of student attitudes at Grinnell College revealed that a majority of students refused to discuss sensitive issues with anyone whose views differed from their own. Nearly half went further: unless they knew in *advance* the views of the person with whom they were talking, they would not discuss *any* sensitive subject. Many said that they had a "right" to express their views without being challenged. Eighty-four percent of the first-year class thought it more important that students felt "comfortable" in college than that they "learned to deal with" uncomfortable ideas. "Promising our students that we will make them comfortable may simply confirm them in their view that they have the right not to be challenged," the authors concluded.[12]

Not only do students smilingly evade contentious discussion among friends, they don't say much in class either. Small reported that on those rare occasions when professors generated discussion, students dropped the subject the moment they walked out of the classroom.[13] Another scholar, intent on determining which techniques were most effective at eliciting classroom discussion, conducted a major research project at a large public university in the Northeast (she did not disclose its name). After asking students, faculty, and administrators to identify the teachers who were best at stimulating discussions, she came up with a list of twenty master instructors. Her researchers then tape-recorded a random set of these teachers' small, upper-level classes. Evaluators then listened to the tapes, noting when students spoke, for how long, and under what circumstances.

The data produced an awkward revelation. These master teachers talked nearly 98 percent of the time: in an eighty-minute class, students spoke for *only two minutes*. And the "student speech" was rarely substantive. "Will this be on the final?" was a characteristic utterance. The great majority of students said nothing. Indeed, the student response was so poor that the researchers couldn't recommend any effective strategies for stimulating discussion. The author concluded that even "very good" teachers should improve their "discussion-leading" skills and students should work on their "participation skills."[14] But people learn skills only when they need them, and today's students understand that they don't need to speak much to make it through college.

The problem is not confined to large public universities. In 2001 Suzanne Garfinkle (née Feigelson), newly graduated from Amherst, published an essay entitled "The Silent Classroom" in the *Amherst* magazine. She wrote that as a freshman she had been eager to express herself and debate big ideas. But the first lesson she learned at Amherst was to shut up. "There is a phenomenon at Amherst that students stop talking in class about midway through freshman year," she wrote. She told of a classmate who insisted that she had come to Amherst believing she had something to say: "But I don't think that anymore," her friend reported, "I feel broken." By their sophomore year, Garfinkle noted, most students learned that "it's not cool to talk in class." Upper-class students conveyed their disdain for the enthusiastic first-years with brutal effectiveness.[15]

Garfinkle's words echoed those of Henry Adams over a century earlier. The first professor in the nation to teach a history seminar, Adams had encouraged his students to ask questions. The problem, he reported, was that he couldn't get them to talk at all. His attempts to elicit discussion were "stifled" by the students themselves, who did not want to "risk criticism from their fellows."[16] A modern scholar on education arrived at much the same conclusion, after admitting that for decades researchers in the field had studied the classroom chiefly from the instructors' perspective: it turned out that a professor's personality or teaching technique had little impact on class discussions. The "chilly climates of college classrooms," the scholar noted, seem to be "created by the students themselves."[17] *Why* they did so, he did not say. So I tracked Garfinkle down to explore the matter further.

In the ten years since leaving Amherst, Garfinkle had completed a medical degree, finished a psychiatry residency at Columbia, and was now Director of the Academy for Medicine and the Humanities at Mount Sinai Hospital. She remained intrigued by the classroom dynamics she had experienced a decade earlier. When students arrived at college, she suggested, many continue to struggle with the challenges of adolescence. To become adults they must build an identity separate from their parents; yet students often regard professors in "some loose way" as surrogate parents. Students therefore distance themselves from professors and become "hypersensitive" toward their peers. Garfinkle regarded her eagerness to impress professors at Amherst as evidence that she had remained bound to "parental objects" and had yet to establish new ties to "peer objects." The seniors in the back row, shaking their heads at the callow freshmen up front, were forging the bonds that would help their generation build the future.[18]

Garfinkle's insight deepens the analysis of subversive play in previous chapters. If young people are drawn to fraternity initiations, beer pong, and *World of Warcraft,* part of the reason is that such activities effect their break from parents (and professors) and simultaneously strengthen ties to peers. Instructors who seek to promote discussions must often row hard against a strong undertow of student resistance.[19]

Harvard political theorist Michael Sandel, whose online course attracted 70,000 registrants, insists that teaching is, "above all," about "commanding attention and holding it."[20] Masterful teachers have devised myriad ways to "connect" with students—humor, story-telling, charisma and multimedia productions worthy of Hollywood. But when masterful faculty dominate the classroom, students contentedly slip into mute passivity. When roused from their star-struck stupor, such students may find it difficult to speak. The best teachers manage to draw students into meaningful discussions, or perhaps even exploit the pedagogical potential of "generative silence."[21] Nearly always this entails hard work; and often even the most skillful efforts fall short, as Henry Adams found out. Little wonder that many professors prefer lectures over small seminars. It's less work than trying to overcome the silence of the students.

"Students *Are* the Class"

When engaged in role-immersion games, students speak.

Evaluations of my first Reacting class confirmed this. One question on the standard assessment form—What could be done to encourage discussion?—stumped the students:

"What does this mean?" one student scribbled on the form. "Students are the class."

"The problem wasn't to get us to speak, it was to get us to shut up," another wrote.

"We didn't need encouragement," added a third. "Tranquilizers were more in order."

Speaking occurs spontaneously because Reacting reverses the psychological dynamics of Garfinkle's "silent classroom." As the professor recedes to the back of the room, student leaders fill the void. They exhort members of their faction to work harder—and to help the team by adding their voices. Students' hypersensitivity to each other helps ensure that the debates are interactive rather than grade-grubbing performances for the instructor.

Often students become so wrapped up in the social matrix of the game that they tune out everything else. Once I arranged for two separate videographers to tape four sessions of a Reacting class. (Experience had shown that a single cameraman could not follow animated disputes among multiple speakers.) A third member of the film crew handled a sound boom. Six months later, when I showed an edited version of the video to the class, several students were startled to see themselves on screen: they had no recollection of being taped.[22]

A major study has confirmed that students become better speakers in Reacting classes. It compared the "before and after" speaking skills of first-year students in a dozen Reacting seminars to students in nearly as many "regular" first-year seminars at three different colleges in the Northeast. On each campus, student subjects met individually with researchers who recorded an impromptu three- to five-minute speech on a topic such as gun control. The process was repeated at the end of the semester, but with each student speaking on a different issue. Other researchers, listening to the recordings, blindly scored the tape-recorded speeches according to a standard twenty-point rubric.

At the outset of the semester, the students in the non-Reacting and Reacting seminars had almost identical scores—slightly over seventeen. By the end of the semester, the scores of students in regular seminars had increased an insignificant 0.2, while those of the Reacting students had increased by 1.6 points, a significant improvement. The middling students in the Reacting classes, by the end of the semester, spoke nearly as well as the stronger students in the regular seminars.[23]

Few activities elicit more anxiety than public speaking.[24] Most of us are self-conscious—of our appearance, voice, intellect, clothing, opinions. A cottage industry of self-help books has emerged to alleviate such anxieties. Some provide technical guidance: speak slowly and clearly, eliminate nervous movements, and so on. Others provide psychological counseling: imagine your audience is naked. But Reacting teaches the exact opposite. Public speaking is not about you and your performance. A speaker's job is to touch an audience—to connect with it—not to impress it.

An illustration surfaced during the question and answer session after a talk I gave at Eastern Michigan University in 2010. A professor asked if shy students could handle Reacting classes. I invited Reacting students in the audience to come on stage and field this and similar questions. Three students toward the front exchanged sheepish glances and elbowed each other, so I pointed at them and waved them onto the stage. A young woman in the group shook her head vigorously, but the others grabbed her hand and all three climbed the stairs to join me at the podium.

I then asked them, "How *do* shy students handle Reacting?" The first two explained that the course had given them practice and confidence in speaking. The third—who had resisted coming up—now moved to the lectern, looked up at the spotlights, blinked, and spoke with a simple and direct eloquence. When she finished, I commented that these unusually articulate students could hardly reveal much about the anxieties of shy students. Then the last young woman touched my elbow and leaned toward the mic. "Actually," she said, her voice reverberating through the auditorium, "I'm shaking like a leaf."

Afterwards, we chatted. Her name was Jessica Howell, a first-year student majoring in special education and early education at Eastern Michigan University. She divulged that she often stuttered in public. When I had encouraged her group to come onto the stage, she said that a voice inside her head sounded an alarm: "This is a bad idea. You will look dumb. You will twitch. Someone will hurt you." She quickly surveyed the stage and saw that there would be no way to escape if it went badly.

But as she was leaving the podium, she realized she hadn't stuttered. She credited Reacting. "I learned how to take questions on the spot from people who opposed me," she added.

And she realized that what she had to say was more important than how she said it: "I got used to people actually listening to what I'm saying and taking something from it." The challenge was to say something worthwhile, to give her listeners real substance, rather than worry about how the words came out of her mouth. After debating her peers all semester, she had found that addressing an auditorium filled with professors "wasn't so bad at all."

Speaking in a Foreign Language

Stuttering is one constraint on self-expression; another is speaking in a foreign language—especially in a class composed of one's peers. Probably no American college has a greater challenge in this respect than Queens College in City University of New York (CUNY), 70 percent of whose students are immigrants or the children of immigrants. Its faculty have struggled for years to promote discussion in classes with so many non-native English speakers. Several years ago veteran professors Ann Davison and Susan Lantz Goldhaber tried an experiment: they assigned first-year ESL students to take a morning ESL course and also, in the same groups, a Reacting seminar the same afternoon. In the morning, students worked in their Reacting factions and polished their papers; in the afternoon, they debated their positions and ideas in Reacting games.

As students focused on persuading peers, their inhibitions evaporated. To Davison and Goldhaber, these classes perfectly exemplified Lev Vygotsky's "Zone of Proximal Development," an educational ideal that helps students lose their shyness and "linguistic self-consciousness." "At the end of each session," Davison and Goldhaber observed, the students behaved "like a theater troupe after a successful performance, leaving in integrated groups, laughing and kidding each other casually in English." Davison and Goldhaber had tried many approaches to teaching English skills but with this arrangement (and Reacting) the results were "fabulous."[25]

Barbara Gombach, project manager of the Carnegie Corporation of New York, went to see the Reacting initiative at Queens College for herself. In a class playing *New York and the American Revolution,* a Korean student, leader of the Loyalist faction in the New York colonial Assembly, caught her attention. While others plunged into a debate on whether New York should join the radicals in Philadelphia or remain loyal to the Crown, the Korean student was animated but edgy. He stepped forward, obviously intent on speaking, but the words failed to come and he stepped back. The debate swirled elsewhere. After a few minutes, he again stepped forward. Another Loyalist nodded to him encouragingly and the class fell silent; but again he faltered. On his third try, his agitation was visible. Then, as the hubbub mounted, he opened his mouth and nearly shouted. The English words tumbled out with such fluency that he seemed startled by them. "Other players listened and responded," Gombach noted, and then the student smiled. "He was no longer a frustrated spectator: he was in the game," Gombach recalled. A shiver went down her spine, for the student's trial resonated with her own struggles with oral expression in a second language, and she recognized that "mysterious moment when the brain shifts from translating conscious thoughts from one language to another and instead expresses itself in the new language."[26]

When Reacting Students Are Silent

Reacting faculty routinely report unprecedented levels of student attendance, engagement, and participation. But not always. Sometimes the magic fails. Sometimes students, bound by an implicit pact against eager-beaver participation, stare sullenly at the gamemaster. Sometimes students who are accustomed to sitting and taking notes are baffled by the expectation that they go to the front of the room and address their peers. Sometimes students cannot get over their aversion to public speaking. If, say, a third of the class succumbs to this mindset, an entire faction may fall silent. As a consequence, some issues will not be fully debated and the game may grind to a halt.

A special problem concerns slackers. Students who fail to study the texts on which "their" positions are based cannot give speeches on them. No one can "fake" a sermon in defense of Anne Hutchinson's theology. Slackers, of course, undermine "normal" classes: latecomers interrupt lecturers, as do snorers in the back row; but most lecturers have learned to shrug off such nuisances. And usually the problem goes away—often literally. (Then, as college dropouts, slackers become the nation's problem—as disengaged citizens or, worse, as those who are mindlessly doctrinaire.)

But slackers can ruin a Reacting game. In July 2013, for example, Jennifer Popiel, a history professor at St. Louis University, posted a message on the online discussion site for Reacting faculty. Over the past five years she had taught fifteen

Reacting games. Apart from a single "so-so" game, she regarded all as good or even wonderful teaching experiences. But she had just finished a disastrous summer session. The first game did not go well—with a few exceptions, the students hadn't done much work—but the next game, *The Trial of Galileo*, plunged over a cliff. This occurred during its second phase, after Popiel had folded Galileo's *Dialogue on the Two Chief World Systems* (1632) into the game. At this point, conservatives in the Holy Office (Inquisition) were supposed to criticize the text on scientific and religious grounds, and Galileo's supporters were to defend it. But few of the students were prepared. Most had apparently not read Galileo's masterpiece. "Why don't you speak up and defend your ideas?" Popiel asked, with mounting frustration. The students simply sat there, mute and confused.

Popiel was dumbfounded. Two years earlier a class playing the Galileo game had been one of her most memorable teaching experiences.[27] But the recent class had let her down. "How could they not see how fun this is when it's done well?" she asked. "I was heartsick. I blamed myself. I should have found a way to get them to see why this matters." Other Reacting faculty on the website offered consolation. Sometimes, they suggested, summer classes are clogged with slackers who had flunked courses during the year. Sometimes a strange convergence of psychological dynamics undermines a Reacting game. Other faculty reported similar tales of a class that failed to achieve "lift-off." Like Popiel, however, they had come to crave the magic of a super-charged role-immersion game.

Reacting faculty and game designers are constantly searching for ways to motivate slackers or minimize the consequences of their disinterest. For example, Kamran Swanson, a philosopher at Harold Washington Community College in Chicago, tweaked Reacting role sheets to provide more specific guidance: "For the second game session, you must write a paper and prepare a speech attacking Darwin's reliance on deduction; to do so, you must include at least three citations from the second chapter of Darwin's *Origin* and two from Francis Bacon's *New Method.*" Since he added this type of guidance, his Reacting classes run smoothly, with only a handful of disengaged students. Hundreds of Reacting teachers like Popiel and Swanson are addressing such issues. Role-immersion pedagogy has by no means solved all of its challenges; but while traditional pedagogies have evolved in ways that accommodate student disengagement, Reacting cannot do so.

Speaking in Someone Else's Voice

When Veronica at last raised her voice to defend Anne Hutchinson, she recalled that "[i]t was like this other person began speaking and I was standing beside her." By setting their own selves aside, students in role-immersion games find it easier to focus on "their" message and audience. Their anxieties subside.

Another illustration of this phenomenon was described by "Robin" (a pseudonym), a student at Greenfield Community College in Massachusetts and an assistant manager of an organic food store. At the outset of Lisa Cox's history course, Robin was terrified of public speaking. When she learned that the course consisted entirely of role-immersion games that featured public speaking, she was appalled. "Oh God," she thought, "what have I got myself into?" Some students dropped the class immediately. Robin decided to give it a try.

She found the first game challenging, but the semester took an alarming turn when, during a game set during the Second Crusade, Cox assigned Robin the role of King Louis VII of France. She would lead the French faction against a daunting "Patriarch Fulcher of Jerusalem," played by an older student who had served two tours of duty in Iraq. If anyone could speak authoritatively on foreign crusades, it was he. Robin expected to get slaughtered.

As she studied her role, however, she grew increasingly fond of King Louis. Unlike Crusaders who coveted power or sought plunder, Louis simply wanted to liberate the Holy Land. His task was all the more difficult because he was being sabotaged by another crusader: his wife, Eleanor of Aquitane (who eventually had the marriage annulled and married Henry II of England). Robin sympathized with the French king and appreciated the challenges he confronted.

Her first goal was to persuade the war council in Acre in 1148 to grant "Louis" command of the crusading army. During the ensuing debate, Robin-Louis decided to hold "her" main arguments until the end of class, when they would have more effect. But time ran short and the vote was held before she could offer rebuttals. Fulcher was chosen to lead the crusade.

"I was angry that I didn't push to delay the vote to the next class session, that I didn't speak up," Robin recalled. "I felt that I lost the game right there. I felt terrible that Louis VII was never going to win, and that the crusade would fail," she

recounted. After she left the classroom in frustration, she tele-
phoned her boyfriend. ("You've spent too much time on this,"
he told her.)

That weekend, though, she threw herself into her next "victory objective": persuading the crusaders to attack the Muslim
stronghold at Damascus. She suspected that "Fulcher" had
worked out a deal with the Muslim ruler to spare the city. Robin
prepared several strong political arguments, and added another
based on geography: Damascus, despite its fortifications, was
more vulnerable than it seemed.

On the day of the big debate, she was nervous about going
"toe-to-toe" against the Iraq veteran—yet she forced herself to
walk to the podium. She began somewhat hesitantly, but as she
unrolled a big map of the region, her words began to flow. Several students nodded. Suddenly she was struck by how easy it
was. She would just let Louis speak. His arguments were so
strong she had little difficulty advancing them with conviction.

When the vote came, "Robin-Louis" prevailed by two votes.
"I was excited for Louis," she noted. "I did my character justice.
I know that sounds corny, but it's true," she explained. "I did
redeem myself, my character."[28]

A Silent Generation

Robin mentioned that after appealing to classmates to support
Louis, she found it easier to approach strangers—in other
classes and also at the store where she worked. As she grew
more confident of her own social skills, however, she became
more conscious of the isolation of her friends. She realized
that many stayed home all day playing video games—racking

up months on the *World of Warcraft* counters. Six took prescription drugs for anxiety and depression. She suspected that they remained in their rooms because they didn't know how to talk to people.

I first became aware of how common such concerns were among young people in 2010, when I asked students in my lecture class on recent American history to indicate their chief fear for the future anonymously on three-by-five cards. (I sought to compare their anxieties to those of young adults on the eve of World War II.) One card included something new: "I worry that with the Internet we've lost the ability to communicate." At the beginning of the next class, I read the card aloud and asked if anyone could explain it.

Emily Arsen, a first-year student, raised her hand. She said that although everyone she knew loved social media, most were unsettled about the superficiality of these interactions. She and her friends found it much easier to click and tap on an electronic device than to talk, especially to strangers. "Our generation is uncomfortable around real people; we're even afraid of the phone," she said.[29]

I asked if anyone agreed. In a class of one hundred Barnard and Columbia students, all but three raised their hands. After class, a dozen stayed to discuss Emily's points. Andrew Edwards, a student in his late twenties who had worked as a reporter for Dow Jones, explained how a group of young graduate students, journalists, and computer scientists on his block in Brooklyn had grown weary of their superficial interactions during neighborhood parties. He proposed that they gather for a potluck dinner every Sunday. Nearly everybody agreed enthusiastically. He set the tone for the first dinner by reading a passage from Rachel Carson's *The Sea Around Us* as an invocation. Then came the food and discussion.

But to everyone's surprise, the conversation repeatedly careened into head-on collisions. A young woman who had been silent during a clever riff on feminism burst into tears and fled into the kitchen. The next week a conversation on religion triggered another emotional blowup. Soon the kitchen became the regular place of refuge for those whose feelings had been battered by the dinner conversation. "We were all sort of flabbergasted," Andrew recalled. "We had no idea we were treading in such depths until we were in trouble."

The group eventually concluded that they conversed during the dinners much as they presented themselves in parties and bars or in their online personas. This was a mistake. "You assume that people are as cool as they pretend to be," Andrew explained. "You don't realize the minefield that real people actually are."[30]

Andrew's hip New York professionals bore little resemblance to Robin's homebound *World of Warcraft* warriors, but both groups were clueless about flesh-and-blood interactions. They were comfortable in their online worlds; and they were accustomed to minimal conversations amidst the din of parties. "But we wanted more from people," Andrew noted. Emily, too, reported that while she and her friends were fully wedded to social media—"we cannot remember a world without it"—they sensed they might be missing a deeper level of connection. Worse, many doubted they possessed the social skills to initiate it.[31]

Employers share the students' misgivings. Surveys repeatedly show that employers are dissatisfied with the communication skills of college graduates. Employers also deplore grads' inability to work in teams, another manifestation of underdeveloped interpersonal skills.[32]

Nearly everyone complains, too, of the poverty of contemporary political debate. During the past three decades the proportion of young adults with college degrees has risen steadily, as has the proportion of college-educated members of Congress. Yet political discourse often seems as if it were scripted by the cast of *Jersey Shore*. We select our President much as we choose the next *American Idol*, though often with a lower voter turnout. We focus on candidates' appearance, personality, and character—their "selves"—because we don't know how to debate issues. Like students within their homogeneous peer groups, American citizens increasingly inhabit intellectually gated communities. We listen only to commentators, comedians, and news organizations who uphold "our" opinions, and when TV networks present opposing viewpoints, partisans shout each other down. What our elections show, mostly, is that we have lost the ability to engage in meaningful debate.

Students can learn to speak and influence the world around them. Shy Veronica, when confronted by Beth's prosecutorial acumen, rose in defense of Anne Hutchinson; the Korean student at Queens College, struggling to find the right English words, passionately denounced the rabble-rousing radicals in the New York Assembly in 1776; Robin, challenged by the authority of an Iraq veteran, persuasively asserted "her" views. These and countless other students have learned through role-immersion games that their words can change the world. Words can wound; they can also nurture and protect.

We hope that college students will find their voices; we pray that some will speak truth to power. But they will never do so unless they believe that they can prevail. This requires that they speak effectively and persuasively—that they connect with their audiences. Role-immersion games help show them how.

CHAPTER 6

Learning by Failing

"I've Never Failed at Anything"

"I'm not going to lose," "Madeline" (a pseudonym) declared. Two weeks earlier, she had been excited to be selected first grand secretary of the Emperor Wanli. But before lunch her meeting with the Ming empire's top literati had gone badly. Now she was worried she might lose the game.

"The odds are against you," I said. "In history the emperor lost and his critics won."

"Still," she said, " I'm not going to lose."

She set her jaw and fidgeted with the straps on her book bag.

"I've never failed at anything," she added, voice wavering.

Then her eyes moistened and her face scrunched. Within a few seconds she was in tears.

Bewildered, I pulled open a desk drawer, fumbling for tissues.

She pushed the tears from her eyes with her fingers and smiled apologetically. I held out some tissues and she took them. But her body convulsed and again she was sobbing. I made a show of rearranging the clutter on my desk. Eventually the sobs subsided.

"What I said before wasn't the truth," she said softly, staring at her book bag.

"Once, I failed."

I held my breath.

"I was wait-listed at Yale."

My shoulders relaxed. I smiled.

But the muscles around her mouth twitched. Again, her face started to disintegrate. I was too astonished to say anything.

During the next three weeks, Madeline proved to be an exemplary first grand secretary. She disarmed critics with exquisite deference, cajoled and persuaded the undecided "academicians," and infused her papers with a deep understanding of Ming policies and Confucian precepts. The final game session was a victory lap: her faction won easily. Through it all, she exhibited extraordinary mastery.

After the final class, Madeline congratulated her teammates, tossed the book bag over her shoulder, and strode triumphantly toward the door. She turned toward me, chin up, and flashed a smile—an "I-never-lose" smile.

But we both knew her swagger was a sham.

Surely Madeline's fear of failure was extreme. But more and more students seem consumed with such anxieties. I first caught wind of this in the 1990s. During the preceding decade, about three-fourths of the students in my large lecture class, when asked to indicate their concerns about the future on anonymous three-by-five cards, identified nuclear war, global warming, or some other national or international problem. The remaining one-fourth mentioned personal issues: finding a job, getting into graduate school, attaining happiness.

But by the first decade of the twenty-first century, a majority of the cards focused on personal matters, and about three-fourths cited fear of failure. Often an oddly personal tone resonated in their comments:

"I fear that I'll wake up at seventy, old, bored, useless, and realize I pissed away my life."

"I'm worried about being poor and living with my parents in New Jersey for the rest of my life."

"I worry that I'll prove the naysayers right and not achieve the goals I've set."

"I worry that I won't make my parents proud."

"I am scared I will not take the necessary risks in life to be successful."

Within several decades, my students had shifted from being mostly concerned about the fate of the nation to being worried about what would happen to them *personally*.

These responses paralleled a trend tracked by the UCLA School of Education, which since 1966 has annually surveyed hundreds of thousands of first-year college students. During the early years of the survey, a third of the respondents said that "being very well-off financially" was "essential" or "very important"; during the mid-1970s the percentage seeking wealth rose steadily; by 2011 over three-fourths of entering college students aspired to be "very well-off financially." In other words, most students nowadays define success in the most unforgiving way imaginable: making lots of money. If you seek to become a good person or a superb dentist, your failings won't be instantly evident to others. But if you strive for wealth and drive around town in a battered jalopy, everyone knows you're a loser. Perhaps this is why 76 percent of the students in the 2011 survey also reported a strong "drive to achieve"—the highest percentage ever. When failure is so visible, you'd better win.[1]

Other studies have shown that self-esteem among college students has been rising sharply since the mid-1980s.[2] So has narcissism, as measured by the extent to which students agree with statements such as "I am a born leader," "I will be a success," "I have a natural talent for influencing people." In 2006, the median narcissism score for college students was 30 percent higher than in 1986.[3] Narcissism, MIT sociologist Sherry Turkle observed, often signals a sense of self that is "so fragile" that it needs constant support.[4] In recent years, various studies have spotlighted the risk-averse behavior of young adults, who are twice as likely to live at home as their parents and considerably less likely to have a driver's license. The "App Generation," as psychologists Howard Gardner and Katie Davis term it, float passively on a sea of informational guidance, fearful of diving into life and swimming off on their own.[5]

More so than their parents, college students today seem to be brimming with self-esteem, a "drive to achieve" (which they equate with "being very well-off financially") and an inflated sense of self that often approaches narcissism. Many also harbor deep anxieties about failure.

The Unbearable Lightness of Success

Many scholars and pundits blame "achievement-besotted" parents for steering their children into activities and schools that ceaselessly affirm their children's talents, intelligence, and other excellences. Teachers and coaches withhold criticism (and failing grades) that might undermine children's self-esteem (and unloose parental criticism of teacher incompetence and retrograde pedagogy.)[6]

Whatever the reasons, many college students overestimate their academic abilities. The 2011 survey, cited earlier, also reported that 71 percent of first-year college students regarded themselves as above-average, the highest percentage in the forty-five-year history of the survey. Beleaguered faculty often cave in to student demands for high grades. The gentleman's C of yesteryear has been inflated by a grade or two. Failing a course now requires almost willful negligence. In a recent survey, one-third of college students said that they deserved a B or higher simply *for coming to class*.[7]

Over 200 colleges have gone further still, offering "positive-psychology" classes to help students find the success they think they deserve. Harvard's introductory positive-psychology course—dubbed "The Happiness Course"—was until recently the most popular at the university.[8] Many colleges have established "student success" bureaucracies, including Offices of College Success, Centers for Student Success, Deans of Student Success, and "Student Success" courses. Virtually every conference on higher education now includes multiple panels and lectures that feature "success" in their titles. Such initiatives suggest that the purpose of college is not to teach students anything in particular but to condition them for success, because success builds self-esteem and self-esteem boosts happiness.

By its own standards, the "success movement" has been just that, as evidenced by Americans' rising self-esteem scores since the mid-1980s. More college students feel better about themselves than ever before. But the 2011 UCLA survey of nearly 200,000 students noted that the record highs in self-esteem and "drive to achieve" coincided with the lowest levels of emotional health ever.[9] Students were feeling better about themselves yet they were also ten times more likely to be depressed and three times more likely to commit suicide than their parents at the same age.[10]

The self-esteem movement apparently suffered from a fatal flaw. When someone compliments us, we often feel a flush of happiness and satisfaction; but if we've done little to warrant the praise, we doubt its sincerity. Many young people suspect that their inflated GPAs, like the ribbons and trophies gathering dust in their closets, are little more than confidence-building scams. Their happiness and self-esteem bob upon a churning sea of doubt and anxiety. "There is not nearly as much benefit as we hoped," declared Roy Baumeister, a psychology professor who had long promoted the self-esteem movement: "It's been one of the biggest disappointments of my career."[11]

In 2012 a Harvard senior observed that his classmates resolutely refused to discuss failure. "Many Harvard students have never seriously failed at anything in their life," he noted, partly because such talk exposed their weakness and insecurity.[12] Psychologist Jean Twenge concluded that young Americans were "more miserable" than their parents because their happiness and self-esteem rested upon a foundation of sand. She found that on "the first blush of criticism" many students simply "crumbled."[13] University of Utah neuropsychologist Sam Goldstein compared college students to bubbles: seemingly happy and confident but liable to burst when they encounter adversity.[14] In 2010 Linda Bips, a psychologist and professor at Muhlenberg College who had counseled students since the 1980s, observed that more students nowadays lack resilience. After failing a test, breaking up with a girlfriend, or being cut from a team, many are unable to "function and persevere." When confronted with even the possibility of failure, many are paralyzed. Bips dismissed the argument that college nowadays is inherently more stressful than in the 1980s. For young adults, she insisted, stress is an existential constant. "What I do think is that many students are often not prepared to be young 'adults' with all the responsibilities of life," she observed. Bips called on professors—and parents—to impose greater challenges and expect students to meet them. "We have to step back and let them fail and pick themselves up and move forward."[15]

Pushing Students to the Edge—and Over It

Amanda Houle, standing on a chair, struggled to get the attention of her classmates, many of whom were yelling at each other. How, she wondered, had she ended up in such a predicament? Assigned to be a disciple of Gandhi, she thought she had brokered a compromise between the Indian National Congress (INC) and the Muslim League. But when Hindu radicals distorted the arrangement to ensure that their voting majority would control the new government, the Muslim League angrily withdrew from the pact. "We knew Hindu radicals would dominate this allegedly united India," fumed Sarah, a leader of the Muslim League. "That's why we Muslims must form Pakistan! Muslims and Hindus cannot coexist in the same state. Violence is inevitable." In the game, tensions escalated into bloody riots; thousands died, Gandhi among them.[16] Pandemonium raged.

Amanda knew that with Gandhi dead, his dream of a united India would die as well. Now, while balancing on a chair, she searched "within" to find Gandhi's voice. She recalled the previous evening, when she and her teammates were sitting on the floor of her dorm room, eating popcorn and scouring Gandhi's writings. Now the words came:

"Either we defer to the unholy weapon of armed strength or we assert our historic greatness as a nation empowered by the sacred force of nonviolence," she called out. Faces looked up at her. "No power on earth can stop the onward march of a peaceful and godly people!" she added.

Another Gandhi adherent seated near Amanda dejectedly held her head in her hands. "It won't work," she muttered. "Indians can't get along." Then Amanda felt a cold hand touching hers, and she turned to see another member of the INC climbing unsteadily on a chair.

"We cannot forsake Gandhi's dream," the INC leader called out.

An instant later, a third teammate grabbed a chair and pulled herself up. "We must greet our antagonists with spiritual nonviolence. Violence begets more violence," she said.

The other students, jolted by the spectacle of their three classmates standing on chairs, fell silent. Amanda's heart leapt. Perhaps the peoples of India would listen. Perhaps a united India could emerge from the chaos. Perhaps Gandhi's dream would be realized.

But it was too late. The British governors, desperate to put an end to the violence, announced that they had divided the subcontinent into India and Pakistan, two nations that would long remain bitter enemies. Amanda had failed and she knew it. The class ended and she was supposed to go to calculus. Instead she ran to a bathroom, hurried into a stall, locked the door, and wept.

I learned of this episode several months later at a training workshop at Trinity College in Hartford. A professor had asked if students were sometimes overcome by the stress of a Reacting class. I referred the query to the veteran students who were helping run the workshop: I asked if any had ever cried because of Reacting.

To my surprise, Amanda raised her hand and described the tearful aftermath of her India class. Then Rivka Friedman, a senior, also raised her hand. "I cried once," she declared.

I was flabbergasted. Rivka was a natural leader, steady and unflappable.

"I was Lafayette during the French Revolution," she told the group. "I had spent a month winning over the undecideds, crushing rebellions, building alliances, defeating foreign invasions. And in a few moments it all collapsed. My France, my faction, my goals. I felt completely and totally helpless. When I left the class, I burst into tears. I was furious with myself. I never cry. Never!"

These remarks unsettled me. If such capable students were reduced to tears, what of those who lacked their ability and competence? Several weeks later, when I put this question to Amanda and Rivka, they offered reassurances. Apart from those twenty minutes when her hopes for France were dashed, Rivka said she loved "every minute" of Reacting. I was not persuaded, and my doubt must have shown. Amanda looked at me carefully and said in a quiet but firm voice, "It's not a bad thing to care so much about something that you weep over it."

Part of my anxiety over Amanda's and Rivka's tears stemmed from the fact that the deck had been stacked against them. During the middle phase of the French Revolution, the center party is unavoidably squeezed between increasingly radical extremes: Lafayette and the constitutional monarchists will inevitably be attacked from all sides. And when everyone plays the India game well, no one can win: the historical situation was probably insoluble.

Because Reacting games are designed to replicate historical reality, the outcomes will often be unfair. Students may work hard, write superb papers, make persuasive arguments— and still lose; and sometimes students may bungle their way to victory. Just as in life: plenty of CEOs, politicians, and college professors succeed because of serendipitous circumstances or just dumb luck.

If Reacting games are to provide a credible approximation of the past, they must reflect its hard realities, or so I assumed. And for a time I accepted the assurances of Amanda, Rivka, and other students who insisted that the stress had not diminished the experience. But my complacency would soon be shattered. I never saw it coming.

On Not Being Master of Your Destiny

It happened during a meeting with Steven Stroessner, a top-notch psychologist hired six years earlier to assess the impact of Reacting on students. The data for this three-college study, which involved before and after tests of students in Reacting and those in "regular" first-year seminars, had only recently attained statistical significance. During the meeting Stroessner first described some of the positive effects of Reacting, such as improvement in public speaking. Then he added that the data had produced some "interesting" results. These were so odd, in fact, that he initially assumed there had been an error in coding the data. He went back to the original forms and rechecked them. The numbers were correct.

The most "interesting" of the results concerned "locus of control"—a measure of attitudes concerning students' sense of control over their lives. Stroessner's interviewers had asked students to indicate the extent to which they agreed with statements such as

"I have found that what will happen will happen."

"Many times I feel that I have little influence over the things that happen to me."

He then pointed to the "before and after" columns for Barnard students. Those who had enrolled in regular first-year seminars showed no change in their responses, but those who had taken a Reacting seminar experienced a "significantly lowered" locus of control. Students who had believed that they could influence "the things that happen to me" felt significantly less confident on that score after taking Reacting. Then Stroessner showed that the same pattern held for Smith and Trinity Colleges. Unlike students in regular first-year seminars, students who had taken a single Reacting class were less likely to believe that they were in control of their lives.

I recalled Rivka's words—that she "felt completely and totally helpless"—and Amanda's despair over the fact that her India was "spinning out of control." These exemplary students entered college believing that they were masters of their destiny. Despite doing everything in their power to prevail, they had experienced crushing defeat. Stroessner's data showed that such students had come to believe the fatalistic injunction, "what will happen will happen." No wonder they had been reduced to tears.

It got worse. Stroessner mentioned that numerous studies showed that people who lacked control over their lives were often plagued by depression.[17]

But then he showed several pages of data showing that the Reacting students' self-esteem increased significantly at all three colleges. Stroessner explained that, nearly always, scores for "locus of control" and self-esteem moved in the same direction. People who think they are being buffeted by forces over which they have no control often feel inadequate or worthless, while those who believe they are masters of their destiny usually feel good about themselves. Reacting had produced an anomaly—a rare instance in which people acknowledged that they were in less control of their lives but nevertheless felt better about themselves.[18]

Puzzled, Stroessner reexamined the original focus group interviews. He found that often Reacting students had said that they had "learned to cope" with unexpected changes during Reacting games and that they eventually enjoyed "surviving and even thriving" in such an environment.[19] Role-immersion games, it seemed, had taught students not only how to deal with failure but also to profit from it.

Teaching Students That the Self Can Change

These results fit into an emerging learning paradigm that has all but eclipsed the "self-esteem movement" of the 1970s and 1980s. Columbia psychologist Carol Dweck has argued that the capacity to learn depends on the extent to which people regard the "self" as changeable. Those who believe that the self is fixed do not learn as readily as those who believe that intelligence and character are capable of fundamental change.[20]

The former category of students, whom I call Solid Selves,[21] concentrate on pursuits at which they excel and avoid those they find difficult. After Solid Selves perform poorly on math tests, for example, they may conclude that they are "no good" in math and shun it. This insulates them from failure and spares pointless labor: Why struggle with something you can't do well?

By contrast, Malleable Selves regard failure as evidence of poor effort or mistaken strategy rather than innate incapacity. When Malleable Selves fail math exams, they may chastise themselves for not studying harder or for neglecting to check their answers, but they assume that they *can* learn math. This outlook encourages them to explore new fields and helps them summon up the effort to do better. Even if they fail, Malleable Selves may appreciate that they have improved and learned: in the process of struggling, their self has grown and changed.[22]

Students at highly selective colleges almost inevitably come to believe in the Solid Self. For as long as most can remember, their intellectual "gifts" have been touted by parents and confirmed by standardized tests. They have been funneled into accelerated tracks, enrichment programs, and special schools. Their high scores on the Scholastic Aptitude Test purportedly prove not that they have learned more than other students but that they have greater aptitude. By the time such students receive acceptance letters from selective colleges, they often believe that their "achievements" are a product of their inherent smarts. How, then, can they possibly fail?

When they get to college, however, brainy Solid Selves find themselves surrounded by equally (or more) gifted classmates. Their chances of failure increase. Fearing that their Solid Self will be exposed as deficient, many pursue a low-risk strategy. They seek easy courses or stick to subjects they've nailed in the past; they say little in class, lest some gaffe reveal a fault line in their Solid Self. But when they butcher an exam or get dumped by a girlfriend, their Solid Self crumbles. Many make a beeline to the overburdened mental health facilities on campus.

A variant of the same reasoning also applies to so-so students at less selective schools. For as long as they can remember, these students have received mediocre or poor grades; they conclude that academics are not "their thing" and define their sense of self according to some other standard: athletic prowess, popularity, mastery of video games. When parents or teachers complain that they are not doing well in school, these students shrug it off: that is not who they are, so they channel their energies into those activities—often subversive play— that affirm and uphold their Solid Self. With a little luck (and prudent selection of easy courses and majors), they may even graduate without compromising their status as Beer Pong champion or Most-Friended Person on Facebook.

Dweck maintains that Solid Selves will not learn much until they think like hardworking Malleable Selves. Solid Selves must acknowledge that "natural aptitude"—in *anything*—is overrated. Even if you lack ability, you can do much to improve your performance. "Hard working is what gets the job done," she insists.[23] The first task of any good teacher, then, is to persuade students that their "self" *can* change.

Researchers have confirmed the educational advantages of believing in the malleability of the self, but a team led by Jennifer Crocker at the University of Michigan discovered a significant hole in Dweck's model. After asking questions that sorted college-age subjects into Malleable and Solid Selves, Crocker's researchers then asked how important they regarded academic achievement. All were then told that they would be given an exceptionally difficult word association test. If they wished, they could listen to "distracting music" during the test. As Dweck's model predicted, Solid Selves usually requested the distraction: this provided them with an excuse if they did poorly. ("How could I do well? I was listening to distracting music.") And as predicted, most Malleable Selves declined the distraction: they preferred to concentrate on solving the difficult problem.

But one group did not behave as Dweck predicted. Malleable Selves who had indicated deep concern about academics also requested the distracting music. They acted, in other words, like Solid Selves—sacrificing the chance to learn and excel in order to protect their self from naked failure. But why? By their previous responses, these Malleable Selves had shown that they understood and appreciated the benefits of difficult challenges. But when placed in a learning situation that might imperil their academic self-esteem, these students went into psychological lockdown mode.

Crocker and her researchers concluded that teaching students that the self can change and grow is not enough. Educators must also persuade students to stop obsessing about their self: "A glib way of putting it is to say, 'Get over yourself,'" Crocker concluded.[24]

But the "self" is the one thing most of us cannot get over. Deborah Stipek, dean of education at Stanford University, described how she kept a box of Kleenex in her office for graduate students who have "made straight A's all their lives" and who crumble the first time they receive the "tough feedback" they need to develop skills in graduate school.[25] Even tenured scholars at major universities can be crippled by fear of failure: many search endlessly for "one more" confirmatory citation or data set. Why risk exposing your "self" to the humiliation of an inadequately supported thesis? Better to leave the magnum opus unfinished.

If such anxieties plague even tenured professors, how can students thrust themselves into unfamiliar and psychologically perilous situations? How can they be persuaded not to retreat, turtle-like, into the protective shell of their Solid Self?

For her part, Dweck encouraged students to regard setbacks as "informative and challenging." But she didn't go so far as to set students up to lose. "I am certainly not advocating early failure as a training regime for our young," she adds.[26]

But what about for college students?

On Being Beheaded and Shot Down in the Street

Amelia Vanderlaan, a first-year student in a Reacting class at Smith College, almost immediately found herself in trouble. Assigned to be a follower of Socrates in the Athens game, she tumbled into a heated argument with a radical democrat who made noises about ostracizing her—a procedural device to prevent Athenian politicians from getting too big for their *chitons*.

Amelia appealed to her professor for guidance. "Better come up with a plan," he said, intentionally unhelpful. (One way to empower students is to refrain from telling them what to do.) So she researched Athenian precedents relating to ostracism, crafted a thoughtful speech in her own defense, and brokered some backroom deals. (She discovered that negotiations were most productive during meals.) She also adopted a less confrontational tone. Her work paid off: she avoided ostracism and her faction won the game.

During the final game of the semester, she was assigned the role of Thomas Cromwell, chief minister to the king in *Henry VIII and the Reformation Parliament*. As Cromwell, Amelia held "midnight-meetings by clock towers, spent hours poring over sixteenth century political documents and economic reports, and had too many conversations to keep track of." For four weeks, she held the realm together.

Then it all went bad. Amelia-Cromwell's enemies engineered "her" arrest on charges of treason. That evening she stayed up all night studying Tudor law and spent most of the next day politicking. But in the final session Amelia-Cromwell was voted guilty and beheaded.

"It sucked," Amelia recalled. For a few weeks, she tried to figure out where she had gone wrong; but eventually she made her peace with failure.

> "Down the home stretch of the game, it seemed I had done everything right. But I learned that sometimes your best isn't good enough. Or at least that your best isn't perfect. I know I gave everything I had to that class, and regardless I never got the A. But in the end that didn't matter because I tried harder than anyone else.

David W. Cohen, chair of the mathematics department at Smith College, was similarly thrust into the maws of failure during his introduction to Reacting at a faculty training workshop in Northampton, Massachusetts, in 2004. He had been assigned the role of Georges Danton, leader of a Paris section in revolutionary France in 1791. Because the legislative majority in the National Assembly had established a constitutional monarchy, the radical sections of Paris had become irrelevant, the fall of the Bastille a distant memory.

Stifled during the first day of the legislative debates, Cohen and other section leaders (all of them professors) plotted an uprising. They hoped to take control of the National Assembly or intimidate it into renouncing the monarchy. Conspiring in secret, they perfected their Rousseauean rhetoric and practiced revolutionary songs. When the sections finally trooped into the National Assembly, Cohen-Danton in the van, they sang lustily, "We'll win, we'll win; we'll string up the aristocrats by the lampposts." But Lafayette, commander of the National Guard, imposed martial law and demanded they disperse. When Cohen-Danton refused, Lafayette ordered the guardsmen to fire. As gamemaster, I rolled two dice, consulted a table, and proclaimed the outcome: the crowd had been decimated and fled the scene, leaving behind one hundred dead and many more wounded (including one of the professors—a section leader who was now barred from speaking in the next session). The rising of the sections had failed; the National Assembly could continue its deliberations in peace. We then recessed for dinner.

Cohen hurried toward me. "What have you done?" he demanded, horror-stricken. "The crowd had all its ducks in a row. After being ignored so long, we were preparing for a triumphant victory. And then to be shot down?" He was upset and made no attempt to conceal it.

"It happened in history," I said, "the Champs de Mars massacre."

"But this is terrible," he said. "If I got so frustrated, what about students? Aren't they demoralized and discouraged?" he asked, concern etched in his face. "Is this any way to treat them?"

"Citizen," I asked, measuring my words, "do you think revolution is easy?"

He looked at me searchingly. Then he nodded slightly, turned, and walked away.

A decade later I asked Cohen if he remembered the incident.

"Oh, yes," he replied. "At that moment I realized how emotionally I had become involved in the game, which came as a shock. I don't get emotionally involved when I watch or play sports. I shy away from crowds and mass entertainments, and I'm suspicious of all emotional displays. And yet I had been crushed by what had just happened. I realized that Reacting had an emotional dimension that no other form of teaching approached."

Cohen decided to teach a Reacting class the next year and continued every year until he retired.[27] And as gamemaster, Cohen dutifully led his students to the brink of failure—and then gave them a nudge.[28]

Destabilizing the Self versus Shoring It Up

Participants in role-immersion games are often surprised by the intensity of their emotional response to failure. Amelia brooded for weeks over her demise as Cromwell. Amanda, to explain her tears, wrote an essay, "Reacting to 'Reacting'" that was published in *Change*, an influential educational journal.[29] Rivka recalled that losing the game "sucked the life out of me." Cohen, who prided himself on emotional detachment, had been "crushed" by what transpired among a group of faculty playing a game. Failure had sent a shockwave to the core of their selves.

In this sense Reacting is analogous to the Socratic interrogation, which culminated in Socrates's demolishing his interlocutors, inflicting a fatal wound to their self that would ostensibly enable their rebirth as truth-seeking philosophers.[30] Reacting similarly lures students into situations fraught with failure, enticing them to give speeches while standing on chairs, to sing songs as they march into gunfire, to adhere to the whims of a capricious English monarch. Sometimes they win; but if they play a couple of games, sooner or later they will fail.

Unlike a Socratic interrogation, though, the jolt to the self in Reacting is diffused through a cluster of identities. On the one hand, Amanda regarded her defeat as a personal failure: she had made a spectacle of herself, haranguing her peers while standing on a chair, "red-faced and breathless" as her "ex-boyfriend's new shiny-haired girlfriend" looked on. However, Amanda also shared her burden with her Gandhian self. "Up on that chair," she recalled, "I felt like it was part me and part Gandhi."[31] Amanda hadn't failed: Amanda-Gandhi had done so.

Amelia's identification with Cromwell similarly mitigated her failure: "Cromwell exerted himself in every way he could to get things done, and so did I," she recalled. She took comfort from the fact that Cromwell had it worse than she did: his head, after being chopped off, was boiled in a vat and stuck on a pike.

Several students mentioned how failure during Reacting games had "shaken" their sense of self. The experience of playing a Reacting game demonstrated that the self was not fixed: their *own* self had been destabilized and acquired more complexity. New selves were layered upon their "normal" self, as Amanda became Amanda-Gandhi and Amelia became Amelia-Cromwell. These students had not been *taught* the advantages of becoming a Malleable Self: their self had *become* Malleable. In the process, they learned to see failure in a positive light. "There was something enjoyable even about that pain of losing," Amanda recalled. "It was the kind of loss that makes you cry and that you still feel good about years later," she added.

The testimony of a handful of students—and one veteran mathematics professor—hardly proves that role-immersion games convince students that their self can change and grow. But Stroessner's before-and-after study included a component that examined exactly this issue. The questionnaire asked students to indicate the extent to which they agreed with standard statements pertaining to the malleability of the self, such as, "No matter how much intelligence you have, you can always change it quite a bit" (belief in Malleable Self), and "You can't teach an old dog new tricks" (belief in Solid Self).[32] After taking Reacting, statistically significant numbers of students at three colleges were more likely to agree that you *can* improve your intelligence and that an old dog *can* learn new tricks. Reacting students were becoming Malleable Selves. Students in the regular first-year seminars experienced no such shift in their thinking.[33]

This observation dovetailed with the other main conclusions of Stroessner's study—and all of these results focused on the self. Reacting students were more likely to believe that they were less in control of what happened in their lives; that their self could grow and adapt in ways they hadn't thought possible; and that, though they might fail, they felt better about themselves. The psychological dynamic is summarized in the accompanying table.

Much of the emotional impact of Reacting is likely triggered by failure, or by the prospect of failure, which heightens the emotional intensity of the experience while complicating the self and rendering it more malleable.

Significant psychological effects associated with taking a first-year seminar (FYS) at Bard, Trinity, and Smith Colleges: Control versus Reacting		
Psychological category	Students who took non-Reacting FYS (control)	Students who took Reacting FYS
Locus of control	No change	Lowered sense of control
Belief in Solid Self versus Malleable Self	No change	Stronger belief in the malleability of the self
Self-esteem	No change	Higher self-esteem

Note: All results are statistically significant.

Failure and Flow

The notion that failure can be a positive experience is almost wholly alien to the culture of success that prevails in education.[34] The influential psychologist Mihaly Csikszentmihalyi, for example, has encouraged educators to replicate conditions that lead to "flow," a state of intense concentration, achievement, and contentment. The concert violinist—a favorite example— achieves flow as she transcends technical challenges and becomes lost in the music. Because passive pedagogical modes can rarely induce the intense dynamics that characterize flow, Csikszentmihalyi's views have served as the psychological justification for many active-learning pedagogies. Some psychologists, after observing Reacting classes, have described them as vivid illustrations of flow. Students appear to "lose themselves" in the experience, utterly absorbed in the discussions and debates, intent on solving problems rather than earning extrinsic rewards.[35]

But one aspect of the flow paradigm does not seem to apply. Csikszentmihalyi contended that flow grows out of positive thoughts and energy.[36] He cited countless athletes, entrepreneurs, and artists who report that while in flow, they are unmindful of "irrelevant thoughts, worries, distractions."[37] Elite cyclists, for example, while pushing their bodies through intense pain, are infused with an exhilaration that "nothing can go wrong and there's nothing that will be able to stop you or get in your way."[38] Teachers are thus advised to calibrate challenges to ensure that they do not surpass students' skill levels. The teacher who "over-challenged" students risked inflicting failure on them, which would lead to discouragement.[39] If a violinist attempted music that was too difficult, she would become anxious and self-conscious and flow would evaporate.[40]

But failure is the elephant in the concert hall, and in all of the practice rooms leading up to it. The prospect of failure elicits the surge of adrenaline that explains why live performances surpass the more perfect results of recording studios. We concentrate harder and work more intensely because we can still feel the sharp sting of previous failures. Lance Armstrong likely experienced flow when "clamped" to the pedals of his bike while putting himself through grueling twelve-hour training sessions, as some psychologists proposed,[41] but we now know that his fear of failure was so intense (and secret) that he risked everything by continually taking banned steroids. In *Ball Four*, an irreverently candid account of baseball, Jim Bouton confessed that all the time he was pitching two World Series wins, one thought ran through his head: "Please don't let me embarrass myself out there." Bouton concluded, "Maybe there is a power to negative thinking."[42]

Video game designers have learned to make sure that winning is difficult—if not impossible. Once players win a game, they grow bored with it and try something else.[43] Well-intentioned teachers, seeking to create positive classroom experiences, often err in creating activities with little or no risk of failure. Designing pedagogies and courses to ensure that students succeed only ensures that they will be bored.[44] José Antonio Bowen, president of Goucher College and author of *Teaching Naked*, adds that failure encourages students to contemplate

change. "We need more planned failure in the college experience," he notes.[45]

Obviously, there is more to teaching than grading harshly.
Indeed the fear of academic failure is sometimes so intense that
students are crippled by it.[46] In Reacting classes, too, most students feel vulnerable when they first give a speech or advance
an argument. But flubbing a speech, getting the facts wrong
during a debate, or losing a game is different from failing a
course, being dumped by a girlfriend, or being fired by a boss.
Reacting games are games, an ideal mechanism for experiencing failure.[47]

Failure teaches a difficult truth. Life is hard and often unfair; much of what happens is beyond our control. Parents and
educators evade this unsettling reality because we worry that if
young people work and fail they will become discouraged and
give up. So we spin a protective cocoon: we preach that hard work
leads to good grades, a college degree, a successful career, and
happiness in life.

But students know better. They've seen hard-working
parents get laid off. They know that bad things happen to good
people. Thus when students encounter failure in a role-immersion
game—even undeserved failure—they often take solace from
it. To be sure, many immediately complain about losing: "It
wasn't fair! I deserved to win!" To which Reacting faculty reply, as did gamemaster Cohen: "You're right. It wasn't fair.
That's life." I can recall no student ever challenging this assertion. Most seem to be relieved by the vivid illustration that
failure is not an indictment of their self but an unavoidable step
in our existential journey.

Aftermath: Winning by Losing

I encouraged Madeline, the student who told me that she never failed at anything, to take the continuation Reacting seminar the next semester. "No thanks," she said instantly. "Too risky."

Four months later, toward the end of her freshman year, she stopped by my office. She said she was applying to transfer and asked if I would write a recommendation. I agreed instantly—she had worked hard and done well—but I did ask if she were unhappy or discontented.

"Not in the least," she replied. "I'm not even sure I will leave."

At first I was puzzled. Then it dawned on me. "What schools are you applying to?"

"Only one."

I didn't need to ask. Madeline coped with failure the Solid-Self way: by expunging it. Then she could say, with complete honesty, "I've never failed at anything."

After college, Amanda, the Gandhi adherent, enrolled in law school with some trepidation. The atmosphere was intensely competitive and she knew that some students had higher LSAT scores. But she persisted—"I just work as hard as I can"—and it paid off in her being elected editor-in-chief of the law review. After graduation, she clerked with a federal judge in Manhattan and then was hired by one of Manhattan's most prestigious law firms.

Amanda said that some days she feels good about herself, such as when she's developed an important point in a case. "But never do I feel secure," she added. Reacting, she thought, had not taken away her fear of failure: "It just makes you realize you can survive it."

When I contacted Rivka in 2010, she told me that she had always been "pretty adept at shaping and projecting" an image of competence and success. But partly she was driven by a fear of failure—a fear, more specifically, that if she failed her admirers would "think less of me." As an "overachieving woman at a school for overachieving women, failure and lack of control seemed anathema," she recalled.

Thus her defeat as Lafayette came as a shock. But it also provided her first real-life lesson that even when you work hard sometimes you fail miserably. "This was one of the first times I realized that even when you do everything right, you might not win," she added. This failure—which led to one of the few times she had ever cried—proved to be liberating.

After college, Rivka found that the world seemed to get larger.

> "As I dip my toe into more and more projects, I realize I cannot control all the outcomes. Nowadays, my answer to a lot of tough questions is "I'll do my best and hope for the best." Most of the time, I do get my way, and I do succeed.[48]

"I'm still plenty stubborn and persistent," she added. "And occasionally, I still have a sense of entitlement about success.

But when I fail, I'm no longer shattered by the experience. I just try a bit harder."

Amelia graduated from Smith in 2009. When I tracked her down in 2010, she reported that her beheading as Thomas Cromwell had caused her to "redefine failure." "Now," she wrote, "I don't see things as single battles with wins and losses."

> I've learned that sometimes, when things aren't going the way you want them to, you can shift your vantage point and make a defeat a first step toward something bigger. It's only through being tenacious that one can succeed.

Amelia had learned to work hard, take risks, and stick her neck out—even when there's a chance someone's going to lop it off. The proof is that this self-described "average" student won one of the nation's most prestigious Fulbright fellowships. As I was interviewing her online, she was preparing to teach a class at Sinop University in Turkey, overlooking the Black Sea.

She mentioned that before her flight to Istanbul, she first stopped at Smith College during registration week. As first-year students stood in line to sign up for classes, she intercepted them and urged them to enroll in Reacting.

I asked why.

"Students are scared of the writing and public speaking," she explained. "They have a hard time believing that in Reacting you enjoy writing five-page papers at 2 A.M."

Why, I meant, did she take it upon herself to recruit for the course?

"Reacting did so much for me," she replied. "I can only hope it will impact students half as much," she added.

If she could become a Malleable Self, so could others. They just need a little push and, with any luck at all, they will fail, too.

CHAPTER 7

Building Community and Global Citizenship

The Loneliness of the First-Year Student

"I hate you."

We were in the school cafeteria and she was sitting to my right, at the end of the table. The three students opposite me, members of Governor Winthrop's faction in *The Trial of Anne Hutchinson*, exchanged glances. They had waved me over as I was walking through the student cafeteria on the way to the faculty dining room. As I approached, they urged me to join them. I sat down and they peppered me with questions: "How did individual Puritans determine whether God had chosen them to be among His saints?" "How did they know a revelation was truly the word of God?" Soon we were lost in conversation.

I had been only dimly aware of the student at the end of the table. Now I looked at her carefully. She was not smiling.

"Do I know you?" I asked hesitantly. I am not good with faces.

She ignored my question: "My second week in college, Katy and I were in our dorm room"—I glanced at Katy, leader of the Winthrop faction. Katy stared at her pizza.

"There's a knock on the door," her roommate continued. "I answer it. They're Athenians, they say, come to see Katy. Next thing, they're hanging out. 'Athens this, Socrates that'—all night! Next night, same thing. Then they show up on the weekend."

I smiled tentatively: she was dead-panning a joke.

"October comes and they're gone," she said. "Then some Confucians show up. More of the same. Then November and it's the Puritans. I can't even eat a meal without them."

She looked me in the eye: "And now you."

I gulped. There would be no punch line. She was angry.

"You stole my roommate," she declared. She stood, picked up her tray, and walked away.[1]

I thought of Katy's roommate as I read Tom Wolfe's *I Am Charlotte Simmons*, a novel that chronicled a first-year student's loneliness. The heroine is independent, smart, and studious. But Charlotte Simmons agonizes about being left alone in her dorm room—"sitting at her desk, staring out the window at the uplit library tower while loneliness *scoured* out all semblance of hope, ambition, or simple planning. Charlotte Simmons!— removed from all family, all friends, every familiar terrain, every

worn and homely object. . . . Did a single other student at Du-
pont feel as lonely as she had felt?"[2] She is inexorably drawn to
the boozy campus social scene—wild frat parties, raucous sporting events, and hookups. By the end of her first year, Charlotte
is plagued with depression.

Many academics have dismissed Wolfe's novel as a carica-
ture of college life, but Wolfe's journalistic instincts were spot
on. In 2004, the year of Wolfe's novel, two sociologists settled
into a residence hall at a large public university in the Midwest.
Almost immediately they encountered scenes that could have
been lifted from Wolfe's novel. Late one Friday evening the
dorm was "totally dead," a researcher reported in her field notes.
Most students had been "swept up onto the party pathway"
that defined the social life at the university. Only two students
remained behind. "I just can't imagine how awful it would be
to live in this residence hall if not a partier," the sociologist
wrote. Lonely students later told researchers that they had no
choice but to "make forays" into the party scene. "I tried so
hard to fit in with what everybody else was doing here," one
explained. "I don't like the way I am right now," the student
added. "Growing up to me isn't going out and getting smashed
and sleeping around."[3]

Pervasive binge drinking and other student-created subversive play worlds are facts of collegiate social life (see Chapter 2).
And mental health researchers have confirmed the high incidence of depression on college campuses. In 2007 the National
College Health Assessment found that 43.2 percent of 20,500
student respondents on thirty-nine college campuses were "so
depressed" they had difficulty functioning at some point during

the previous year.[4] A 2011 survey of over 200,000 students reported that the emotional health of college freshmen, which had been declining for a quarter century, had reached its lowest point ever.[5] About half of the nation's colleges and universities run a 24-hour-a-day suicide or crisis hotline. Social anxieties top the list of student concerns.[6]

LONELINESS IN COLLEGE

When they first come to college, students think it will be easy to make friends. Unlike high school, where many different types of students cross paths in the same hallways, college students are often presorted according to academic and economic backgrounds. College brochures assure them that the campus is filled with others much like themselves. Why, then, can't they make friends?

As an academic adviser over the past quarter century, I've talked with dozens of students who were transferring into my college or out of it. All explained their decision on academic grounds; but they also conceded that they had few friends. A new school, they imagined, would provide a tighter social mesh. Sociologists who followed one hundred randomly selected Hamilton College students over eight years concluded that friendship was "virtually a prerequisite for success in college."[7] When researchers at another large university in the Midwest asked sixty students to identify the most important part of college, most said that it was making friends; only four listed academics as more important. "To survive," one student explained, "you have to make friends fast! Otherwise, you'll be out there all alone. You'll crash and burn."[8]

When students fail to establish strong social connections, they cling all the more tightly to parents, which makes it even more difficult to make and keep friends on campus. Helicopter parents contribute to the problem by hovering over their children. The University of Vermont has hired "parent bouncers" to prod parents to leave after delivering their children to campus.[9] A survey of over 9,000 college students found that 70 percent communicated with a parent or guardian "very often"—on the average, about 13 times a week; and 40 percent of first-year students had asked parents to intervene on their behalf to solve a problem at college.[10]

Weekends are especially trying for lonely students. Many head home, disconcerted by the prospect of evenings alone in their dorm room. The term "suitcase college" has been around for years, but during the past decade the phenomenon has reached astounding proportions. By Friday evening, and even Thursday, university dorms that held thousands of students become ghost towns. Student newspapers report that "our campus becomes empty each weekend" or complain that "by Saturday, nary a soul is to be seen walking across campus." One newspaper observed that no one knows what they're missing on the weekends because no one is around to chronicle it.[11] At one large campus of the University of Wisconsin, administrators conducted a census on a randomly selected weekend twice a year: in both semesters in 2008, nearly two-thirds of the students were gone.[12] As more students head home on the weekends, they find it easier to reconnect with high school friends who have made the same homeward migration; those left in the dorms become lonelier still.

Sometimes such students seek solace in Facebook, where they find statistical proof that, their own anxieties notwithstanding, they have an astounding (and precise) number of friends. Their feverish compulsion to maintain contact with virtual friends—"I'm doing laundry now. What are you doing?"—underscores the intensity of their fear of loneliness. And while social media may attenuate some anxieties, it also breeds new ones: "Why do other people have more friends/accomplishments/interesting experiences?"[13] MIT sociologist Sherry Turkle, initially a proponent of online socialization, has concluded that "we are so enmeshed in our connections that we neglect each other."[14] As novelist Richard Powers observed, the web is "more efficiently lonely" than the neighborhood it replaced, for its solitude is "bigger and faster."[15]

As lonely students anxiously stalk virtual "friends" or add more thinly gilded bricks to their Facebook wall, pop-up ads from the University of Phoenix repeatedly appear along the right-hand side of their Facebook screen. When students click on the link, a counselor (or perhaps a bot) urges them to apply. Phoenix promises to "provide a sense of community and support"—and it assigns students to online teams (like their friendship networks!).[16] Plenty of students take the bait. They tell worried parents that they have not really dropped out of college because—frankly—they didn't spend much time on campus anyway.

Loneliness and Retention

Many scholars contend that the main reason why one in four college freshmen fails to return the next year is that they fail to find a comfortable social niche: they're lonely.[17] Since the 1970s

Alexander Astin, an education professor at UCLA, has collected questionnaires from nearly ten million students. He found that the student's peer group was the "single most potent source of influence" during college. Those students who failed to make friends were far more likely to drop out than students who became ensconced in a social network. Scores of other studies have confirmed this conclusion.[18]

Vincent Tinto, an education professor at Syracuse University, argued that universities consisted of two separate systems—one social, the other academic. Students who failed to connect with both felt that they didn't "belong" and were more likely to drop out.[19] Richard Light, an education professor at Harvard who supervised intensive interviews of some 1,600 undergraduates, found that the most obvious "warning flag" of impending difficulties was a student's "isolation from the rest of the college community."

> These are the students most likely to feel lonely when they get to campus. Such students may not integrate quickly or easily into their new community. For many, their academic work as well as their social life and sense of being grounded will suffer. When this happens, it illustrates how strong the connections are between academic performance and outside-of-class activities.[20]

Many studies have confirmed that students often drop out because they are lonely.[21]

Conversely, students who live on campus, join fraternities and sororities, and belong to sports teams or organizations such as ROTC, are far more likely to remain in college than students who do not belong to such groups.[22]

The student's peer group was "the single most potent source of influence on growth and development," Astin added.[23] He urged college educators to focus less on what they do—as professors and administrators—and more on what students do; and students, he noted, are preoccupied with building and maintaining social networks.

The Response: Failing to Build Community on Campus

Because attrition threatens the financial health of their institution, college presidents often identify community building as their highest priority. In recent decades they have committed more resources than ever to this task.[24]

The traditional approach has been to expand the "student life" bureaucracy. In addition to hiring more administrators, staffers, counselors, and mental health professionals, most colleges have established elaborate freshman orientation programs and have spent more on residential life services, including dorm parties and college-wide amusements and events. Often these activities are imaginative and well-conceived, but participation rates remain disappointingly low.[25] The loneliest students often fail to show up; and almost universally students complain that their campus is "dead." Administrators at Harvard were so desperate to address student complaints of an "inadequate social life" (in Cambridge!) that the school hired a "fun czar" and opened a college-run pub near the freshman dormitories—beers for a dollar—despite the fact that only two of its nearly 1,700 first-year students were old enough to drink legally.[26]

Yet despite the razzle-dazzle of planned campus activities, retention rates nationwide have not improved.

Many administrators, intent on doing *anything* to build community, have endorsed more radical nostrums. When top administrators at the University of Northern Colorado distributed a memorandum asking, "How do we create a sense of community on campus?" one suggestion was succinct: "Provide a big place for students to hang out."[27] During the economic boom a few years ago, one of the most popular ways to build community was with bricks and mortar. A new breed of architect emerged to satisfy this demand. Specializing in "the psychological effects of architecture," these professionals advise legislators and college trustees that students fail to socialize because the old dining halls are dingy and uninviting, the student centers impede traffic flow, and the dorms lack cozy nooks and attractive amenities. Architects prescribe designs for new spaces to help "self-conscious" students "overcome their anxiety and connect with peers." Architect Herb S. Newman's website, for example, claims that his designs "nurture students by engaging them in interaction with one another through path, portal, entry, and space."[28]

Over the past decade or so, colleges have spent immense sums to "build" community with bricks. But a weekend visit to nearly any large state university will confirm that this approach has largely failed. Visitors will likely find a magnificent new student center, often boasting distinctive architecture, inviting arcades and lounges, and state-of-the-art exercise facilities and game rooms—all nearly empty. Yet as the sun goes down perhaps only a few blocks away, thousands of students will jam themselves contentedly—yea, blissfully—into ramshackle apartments and dilapidated fraternities that diligent inspectors would have condemned a half-century ago. Students crave social interaction; they don't much care about the design or decor of the place in which they find it.

Bureaucratic Community: First-Year Seminars

The persistent problem of retention has spawned another administrative effort to build community: "first-year seminars" and "learning communities." About 95 percent of four-year institutions offer first-year seminars, small classes (ranging from 15 to 25 students) that often include an orientation program on time management, study skills, and admonitions on the usual pitfalls of college life. Some last several weeks; occasionally, they encompass a semester or even a full year. The social element of the course is often as important as the curriculum. Many activities are designed to promote socialization, ranging from trust-building exercises and pizza parties to team-building games and outings.

"Learning communities" aim for a similar convergence of intellectual and social pursuits. First-year students apply to theme-based dorms, and members of that community will together enroll in a couple of courses. Some studies show that students in learning communities are more likely to persist and graduate from college.[29]

But if learning communities improve retention, they may do so at the cost of undermining meaningful diversity. Because most learning communities are based on themes, they inevitably sort students into homogeneous groups. Ohio State University, for example, offers learning communities such as engineering; sports and wellness; African American; Spanish language and culture; and so on. Sometimes colleges devise learning community themes that will not so obviously segregate ethnic, racial, and social groups. The University of Kentucky has a GREEN community, whose students "live with other people who value their same beliefs in protecting and saving natural resources"; an arts community, "for majors in fine arts or creative writing"; a CREED community, whose participants "share a common interest in exploring various aspects of spirituality"; an ROTC community, whose cadets "will live together in Blanding Tower and build strong relationships with fellow cadets, mentors, and leader"; and a "new economy incubator" community, for "savvy" business and engineering students.[30]

But it makes little sense to promote diversity as a goal of higher education when we channel students into homogeneous learning communities. Students in the GREEN community might feel more comfortable with those who share their passion for the environment, but they would probably learn more by living with engineers and ROTC cadets—and vice versa. We learn by exploring what we do not know. That's hard to do when you're surrounded by people whose views mirror your own.

Although administrators recognize such objections, the main goal of the program is to improve retention by reducing loneliness. And this is most easily accomplished by drawing students into a companionable social web. This imperative to facilitate social interaction forces administrators to promote homogeneous groupings. As the proponents of MIT's "Chocolate City" learning community explain: "People group together by whom they get along with. If we say that any two people can live next door to each other, then we are evading the obvious. Yes, any two people can live next to each other, but not any two will be neighbors."[31] Randomly assigning students to learning communities merely replicates the anomie of the dorms—and the resulting high drop-out rates.

Fraternities and sororities have long understood this principle, a reason why they spend so much time and effort scrutinizing potential "brothers" and "sisters." To ensure compatibility, they select pledges much like themselves. Administratively engineered learning communities, mandated to reduce loneliness, necessarily adhere to similar principles. Colleges thus attempt to foster community by grouping like-minded people within the same spaces—appealing spaces, if the architects have their way.

But while research shows that fraternity and sorority members find college more enjoyable and are more likely to graduate, their academic performance is generally poorer than that of nonfrat peers. Fraternity members and athletes are so focused on their subversive play they have little time or energy for academics. On the whole they derive less academic benefit from college.[32]

Despite four decades of earnest administrative efforts and increasing expenditures on recreational facilities, retention rates have shown little improvement.[33] Studies suggest that students are lonelier and more depressed than ever. What should be done, then, to build real communities that promote academic purposes? Probably much less than we're doing now.

How to Build Community without Really Trying

Like millions of first-year students, Katy and her roommate ("I hate you!") had expected that their friendship dyad would be the foundation of their college social network. But when Katy enrolled in a class featuring role-immersion games, she was thrown into one randomly assigned faction after another. Each faction swiftly became a microcommunity. Katy's roommate, enrolled in regular classes, made few friends. This is not un-usual. Few seniors can remember the names of students they met in freshman courses. Yet in 2012, when I separately asked three students from the first Reacting class in 1996 to list the names of students from that course, two remembered five names, and the other, four. It wasn't all that hard, because they had remained in contact—sixteen years later.[34]

In the early years of Reacting, I had no idea how frequently Reacting factions met outside class to discuss strategy, prepare papers and speeches, and gossip about the game and the other players. After my encounter with Katy's angry roommate, I added a question to the course evaluation forms: "How much time did you spend meeting with other students outside of class?" Calculating the average proved impossible because so many re-spondents ignored the numerical options and instead scribbled in comments: "Almost all the time," "Constantly," "More than you would believe." "What you don't understand," one student explained, "is that after midnight a whole Reacting world comes alive in the dorms."

"Comes alive?" What did that mean? How, I wondered, does a community spontaneously generate itself?

Some clues appeared during a discussion among Barnard first-year-seminar faculty in 2007. The issue was whether the college should continue to provide each instructor with several hundred dollars for a dinner for their class. Seven or eight professors described their heroic attempts to make the dinners special: some invited students to their homes and cooked distinctive meals; others planned an excursion to a museum with dinner afterwards. Yet each story had the same result: only a handful of students showed up. The no-shows usually sent email apologies: they were swamped with jobs and coursework. The faculty voted to eliminate the dinners—and the stipend. None of the Reacting instructors offered comment.[35]

While leaving the meeting, I was approached by Rebecca Stanton, a professor of Russian literature. She mentioned that her Reacting class had held a dinner on their own a few weeks earlier, and that every student attended. I nodded and we continued walking. Then I remembered that she had taught her Reacting class the previous semester. How, I asked, had she had a class dinner? "This was a reunion dinner," she said.

She explained that after the first game, set in ancient Athens, her students decided to hold their own celebratory dinner at a Greek restaurant. Then they organized dinners after each of the two remaining games, followed by the reunion dinner a month after the last meeting of the class.

But something didn't make sense. If students were "always" overwhelmed with jobs and courses and other commitments, how did Stanton's students repeatedly manage to organize, fund, and attend their own dinners? I asked Stanton if I could explore this with her students; she agreed and invited her students to contact me online.

Anna Scaife, then a sophomore, logged in first.

She explained that it all began when her classmates "sort of organized it together."

> We had just finished the Athens game, and the democrats' attempt to convict Socrates had failed. The game was pretty intense. Someone proposed a dinner as a joke. But then we all decided that some non-game-related time was probably a good idea, to prevent bitter feelings from settling.

After Anna logged off, Reni Calister logged on. She reiterated Anna's main points: Feelings had been "frayed," but students had come to regard themselves as a community. Because the class was fun, they figured that the dinner would be fun, too.

"I'm confused," I typed. "You say that Reacting was fun and created a close community. If so, why did you need to soothe frayed feelings?"

"Not every class was tense, but most every class was fun," she replied. "The tensions did not inspire hatred, only some bruised feelings, and they were remedied fairly quickly. Besides, throughout the semester, the games forced us to meet, work with, and in most cases, trust each and every member of the class."

"So you had three dinners during the semester and another after it ended?"

"Yes," she replied. "And we just had another reunion dinner last week."

"Wait a minute," I typed. "A year after the class?"

"Yes."

"Why?"

"Because we missed each other," she wrote. "It seems silly, but we really love one another."

"If I write that, no one will believe it," I replied.

"Ha ha," she replied. "I hope they do."

She typed those words in 2009. In February 2014 some of Stanton's students held their *sixth* anniversary dinner, this time at the same Greek restaurant of their first back in 2007.

This story did not surprise or especially impress other Reacting professors. Nancy Reagin, a history professor at Pace University, mentioned that after playing *Henry VIII and the Reformation Parliament,* her class organized a baby shower for Anne Boleyn. The students sent invitations, decorated the dorm, baked a cake, dressed up in costumes, and brought along dates and friends.

"Let me tell you a story," Reagin added. A year earlier she and her husband, also a history professor at Pace, were teaching two different Reacting classes, though both began with *The Trial of Anne Hutchinson.* Many students in both classes had been assigned to the same dorm floors as part of a learning community. This meant that two "John Winthrops" and "John Cottons"—along with their factions—were living in close proximity. Eventually the pro-Winthrop groups formed a super outside-of-class faction, as did the pro-Hutchinson group.

After the second week, Reagin received an email from the resident assistant: "Can you please pour some cold water on these students? All they talk about is this game." The dorm, the resident advisor (RA) wrote, was becoming "obsessed" with it:

when something happened in one class, it was immediately transmitted to the other and then dissected and debated, far into the night. The Reacting students, with one exception, enjoyed the nonstop socialization. "But it's driving everyone else on the floor nuts," the RA reported.

After *The Trial of Anne Hutchinson,* Reagin's class moved on to the Henry VIII game, while her husband's class played *Patriots and Loyalists: The Revolution in New York City, 1775–1776.* This reduced the volume of Reacting chatter, but the class remained the focus of social life in the dorm. Now students endlessly debated, gossiped, and strategized Tudor religion and politics. Reagin was pleased that some socially awkward students got caught up in the interaction, especially the class-related website.

"You will not believe the number of postings our class had over three weeks," Reagin added. "Wait a second," she said, as she logged onto the site, access to which was restricted to the twenty-four students in the class. "Over the course of three weeks, we had 618 posts and 13,998 hits."

"Excuse me?" I blurted. I had been typing her words, phone wedged between my neck and shoulder, and thought I misheard.

"I said 13,998 hits," she reiterated.

Pause.

"700 hits per student?" I pressed.

"I said you wouldn't believe it," Reagin repeated.

The causal dynamics warrant closer examination. Stanton did not knit her class into a community. She didn't learn of the first dinner until she overheard students chatting about it before class the next day. Her surprise showed. The students misinterpreted her reaction. At that moment (as they reported to me) they were horrified by their "mistake": They had held a class event and forgotten to invite the professor!

Stanton and Reagin did not "create" student communities: rather, they pushed students into complex and intellectually demanding competitions that students transformed into vibrant subversive play worlds. The students reached out to members of their factions, knowing that if they failed to coalesce as a team they would do poorly. Probably they would lose the game (and the tiny grade bonus that sometimes accompanies winning); worse, they would be left vulnerable. Lacking someone to cheer them on as they gave a speech and the benefit of outside-of-class sessions during which ideas are tested and strategies debated, students would stumble at the podium, misinterpret a key text, or build an argument on a misunderstood historical fact, errors their better-organized foes would gleefully exploit. Students banded together because otherwise they would likely fail. And when factions were reshuffled at the start of the second game, former foes became teammates, and former allies, opponents. The class itself became a complex and emotionally rich web of social relationships.

Ann Engar, a professor in the Honors College at the University of Utah, provided a graphic illustration of this phenomenon. At the beginning her conventional humanities seminar, Engar asked students to list all of their friends and acquaintances in the class. A researcher mapped the resulting social network, with each student identified as a dot with lines to indicate ties to other students (see the left-hand portion of the accompanying figure). About a dozen students each had six or

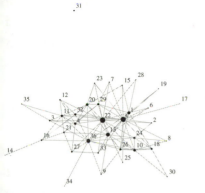

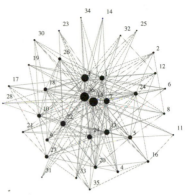

Friends and acquaintances before Reacting.

Friends and acquaintances after Reacting.

Ann Engar administered the questionnaire to her class at the University of Utah, a campus of 32,000 students, many of them commuters. The data was mapped by Professor Jeff Webb, associate director of the Leap Program. Each number refers to a particular student. Thus, student 35 had two friends before taking the Reacting seminar and six after playing the game, while student 15 had three friends before Reacting, and over twenty afterwards, represented by a proportionally larger dot.

seven "friends or acquaintances" in the class; another dozen students listed only one or two friends or acquaintances.

Then Engar's class played a Reacting game, after which she repeated the questionnaire and had it compiled and mapped (see the right-hand side of the figure). In just four weeks, the social network had become far denser: all of the students who had previously identified no friends or acquaintances in the class now listed at least two; some students listed fifteen or more. Further research revealed that six of the students been in the same class the previous semester, and they accounted for most of the large initial friendship clustering. Indeed, they had formed something of a clique. But during the Reacting game, the class as a whole formed ties that bore no relation to sex, race, or living arrangements. The authors of the study concluded that a single Reacting game "eliminated social isolation" and helped students connect across existing clique boundaries without creating new cliques. The class network became "simultaneously denser and more inclusive."[36]

We often imagine that a close community is one in which people share common experiences and fundamental values. We think that by encouraging students with similar interests to live in close proximity, they will come to know and understand each other better. Friendships will ensue and these friends will coalesce as a community.

But this interpretation of community formation is deeply flawed. Few people were more similar or lived in closer proximity than the Puritans of seventeenth-century Massachusetts. Yet the Puritans were famously litigious. Often their animosities turned lethal, as evidenced by the witchcraft trials that ripped apart scores of villages. Puritans put aside their (minimal) differences and banded together only when imperiled by external forces, such as the threat of Indian attack or the prospect of London's interference in local matters.

Edward Shils, a sociologist who specialized in the study of "primary groups"—the intense communities that matter to us most—arrived at a similar insight during World War II, when he was a young intelligence officer. He interviewed captured German soldiers to determine why they continued to fight when their cause was lost. He discovered that they cared little about German nationalism or Nazi ideology. What held them together were the bonds forged in battle. Each man needed the others in his platoon; their collective survival demanded individual sacrifice. Shils concluded that our closest social groups grow out of mutual dependency. We reach out to others when we need them.[37]

Students playing role-immersion games do not share a trench or face an enemy, but they repeatedly expose themselves to visible failure and defeat. Reports of bruised egos and "frayed feelings" prove that the competition generates emotional sparks. Players quickly learn that success in large measure depends on their ability to cooperate. Together, they struggle: sometimes they win a key debate or even the game, and sometimes they lose. They laugh, they fight, and sometimes they cry. They become a community. And they look forward to renewing their bonds of friendship when they return to college the next year.[38]

Professors must sometimes shut up to create space for students to speak. So, too, administrators and faculty should ease off on attempts to "build" community for students. If we give students challenges that exceed their individual abilities, and if we invite them to inhabit intriguing subversive play worlds, students will build communities on their own.

Bill Gates envisions that in the future, bricks-and-mortar colleges will have little purpose "except for the parties."[39] Gates's prediction is an extrapolation of the past two centuries, when fraternity and tailgate parties—and similar subversive play worlds—have in large measure defined campus social life. If our bricks-and-mortar colleges are to survive, however, the college classroom must itself become the focal point of intellectually vital communities. Many professors and administrators are proposing inventive and clever strategies to achieve this goal. Role-immersion games are one way to make it happen.

Creating Citizens of the World Community

We must do more than build vital campus communities. We must broaden our concept of community to encompass peoples throughout the world. College graduates—and future citizens—will inevitably inhabit a global environment.

One way to prepare students for a global community is to send them abroad to study. But only one in ten full-time American students spends a semester abroad, and most of these go to English-speaking nations whose culture often resembles that of the United States. Many colleges require students to take one or more courses on a people or culture outside the United States. But which people or country? College should prepare students for global problems and opportunities, but no one can say which nations and cultures will matter to them in the future.[40]

Classicist Martha Nussbaum recognized that the task of global education was not to impart information about particular peoples and cultures but to "develop sympathetic understanding" of them all.[41] Students (and their teachers) must cease to "define themselves primarily in terms of local group loyalties and identities" and instead become citizens of the world. "Only a human identity that transcends these divisions shows us why we should look at one another with respect across them," she added.[42]

Students who take a course on the "untouchables" of India, for example, may learn to sympathize with *dalits*. But compassionate concern is not the same as identifying with others. A century ago many British civil servants pitied the untouchables and worked to improve their lives, but few British put themselves in the shoes of *dalits*, nor will many college students reading historical or sociological accounts of the subject.

How, then, can students attain a "human identity"?

In 2002, when first-year student Sarabeth Berman walked into the Pnyx (the Athenian Assembly) during her Reacting class at Barnard, she loved it. She enjoyed its raucous evocation of Athenian democracy, where speakers stood at the front of the room and appealed for support for various laws. She regarded this world as a metaphor for college: an "ultrademocratic space" where students could engage in free-wheeling discussions of big ideas.

But the second game, set in Ming China, threw her for a loop. When I interviewed her a decade later, she remembered being stunned by the weirdness of this "incredibly serene and quiet world" shrouded by Confucian decorum and politeness:

> As a first-year student, who was already struggling to understand the culture of college and the new expectations that come with college, I entered a new sphere during that game, where another student—the emperor—controlled everything: "he" sat at the head of the table. We couldn't say or do anything without "his" permission. We couldn't even look directly at "him." I was entirely frustrated. I found it claustrophobic. I remember flipping through the *Analects,* trying to find texts to support my points, but feeling incapable of saying what I wanted to say when I wanted to say it. And the "emperor" lived three doors

down from me in the dorm! What I remember most was a sincere sense of discomfort.

After she graduated in 2006, Sarabeth, talented in performance and dance, went to Beijing to work as a manager for a contemporary dance company. She didn't speak Chinese and few of her coworkers spoke English.

I have always been someone who felt comfortable in my skin. Here, I was stripped of my greatest protection, my ability to communicate. I didn't know the rules of when to speak and when it was OK to voice my opinion. But I felt comfortable being uncomfortable, because I had been uncomfortable in much the same way before—when I was in Ming China in Reacting.

"Wait a minute," I said. "While you were in that office in Beijing, you actually thought 'This is like my class at Barnard in 2002?'"

"Oh, certainly," Sarabeth replied. "I thought of that game often. It was the first interaction I really had with Chinese culture. Plus a major issue in the office—and in the game—was the tension between the traditional ways of doing things and new ways of approaching things."

"Sarabeth," I replied, "I'm not sure anyone is going to believe that Reacting prepared you to live and work in China."

"Remember," she typed, "I engaged with Reacting almost every semester at Barnard.[43] I gained a lot of experience learning about new cultures, trying to figure out the customs and motivations of my classmates or other game players. But mostly, I learned to be comfortable with discomfort. Reacting threw me into so many uncomfortable moments: I landed in France during the French Revolution. I stood with my fist in the air as a Sikh who wanted an independent Sikhistan. These games prepared me for a world of unknowns."

Sarabeth is now a vice-president of Teach for China, an affiliate of Teach for America. It recruits outstanding college graduates from the United States and China to teach in rural China, where some 200 million children lack access to education. "As global citizens," she noted, "this is a problem we cannot ignore."

Professors may regard the creation of campus and global communities as irrelevant to their professional concerns. Their job is not to help students find friends or land jobs in China. But real learning obliges students to wrestle with unfamiliar structures of thought. Often students resist: "Why don't you just give us the answer?" they plead, preferring to gather factoids rather than contort their minds to accommodate the unknown. The intensely social character of role-immersion games, however, helps lure students away from their customary social networks. As they socialize with different students, and in unfamiliar contexts, their sense of self undergoes a metamorphosis. Sometimes this is disorienting and even painful. But when they share the experience with others, they often find it manageable and even intriguing.[44]

We often neglect the social dimension in higher education. Many of us recall the "eureka" moment when, while working alone at a cubicle in the library or feverishly ransacking the stack of books on our desks, an original idea surfaced, almost to our amazement. We want our students to experience such moments of solitary discovery, as indeed they should. But education also has a social component, as learning researchers have repeatedly found.[45] A group, even one composed of people with uneven abilities, often generates creative insights that help solve difficult problems. Role-immersion games enlarge our social universe, which opens us up to new ideas and people.

We reach out to others because we need them; and we internalize the ideas of other societies and cultures because we acknowledge the insufficiency of our own. Doing so is not a sign of personal weakness or cultural inferiority; on the contrary, it affirms our belief that we can find meaning in the ensuing complexity. That conviction is perhaps the main prerequisite for learning.

CHAPTER 8

Inculcating Morality and Empathy (!)

The Morality of Slavery

"Slavery is a positive good."

James, standing, clutched the pages of his speech with both hands. His classmates, seated around him in a large half circle, fell silent. Behind him, through an expanse of windows, the hills of Ypsilanti, Michigan, sloped toward the Huron River.[1]

"These laborers fuel the engine of commerce," he declared, and then listed the economic benefits of slavery. He gestured toward a book "allegedly written by Frederick Douglass" that had appeared in print just last year. Whether Douglass had written the book credited to him, or whether the stories it related were true, James had no idea. He *did* know that the Constitution of the United States, by basing representation on the number of free persons "and all other persons," acknowledged the legality of *unfree* persons. Slavery was the law of the land. Those who demanded its abolition waged war on the Constitution. "The institution of slavery is not unnatural and it is not immoral," he concluded.

James set the speech down and scanned his classmates.

"Senator Calhoun, I have a question," a black student interjected, peering through wire-rimmed glasses. He fixed James with a wry smile, a blue pen in his clenched fist.

"Why do you believe it is good to whip the slaves, even though they're human, just like you?" He clicked the pen twice and lifted his head.

"I didn't say it was good," James answered softly. "I said it was sometimes necessary."

"So if you were in their shoes, would you welcome the whip?" He chewed the end of the pen, his smile gone.

"I can't really speak on that," James replied. "I'm not in their shoes." He then reiterated the points of his speech. The black student, still chewing on the pen, gazed at James for a time but said no more.

Then James Tatum (aka John C. Calhoun), a freshman at Eastern Michigan University, sat down. He, too, was black.

Teaching Morality in College

The debate in which James Tatum defended slavery may seem pointless. Why should students devote large chunks of class time on an issue that had seemingly been resolved 150 years ago? For that matter, should colleges make it their business to "teach" morality?

Most colleges, according to their mission statements, profess to do exactly that.[2] Denison University seeks to inspire students to become "discerning moral agents and active citizens." Dartmouth promises to "prepare students for a lifetime of responsible leadership" and to "encourage a culture of integrity." The University of South Dakota claims to be "deeply committed" to teaching "ethical conduct" and "moral responsibility."[3] When Harvard embarked on its curricular revision in 2004, its leaders declared, "We remain cognizant of our responsibility to educate morally responsible citizens and leaders."[4]

But colleges seldom deliver on such grandiloquent promises. A few months after vowing to educate "morally responsible citizens and leaders," Harvard eliminated its moral reasoning requirement. "I have almost never heard discussions among professors about making students better people," observed Harry Lewis, a Harvard dean and longtime faculty member.[5] Shortly afterwards *New York Times* columnist David Brooks concluded that young adults received guidance in all aspects of their lives "except the most important, which is character building." On such matters, most universities leave students alone.[6]

Many professors, including me, regard the academic world as a place to advance knowledge rather than build character. In 2008 Stanley Fish, noted professor of English, summarized the views of many when he declared that college faculty were "competent in a subject, not in a ministry."[7] Professors were not only unprepared to build character or to offer guidance on moral matters, they were uninterested in doing so. "It is not the business of the humanities to save us," he concluded. The task of college professors was to pursue and teach subjects that interested them. "They don't do anything, if by 'do' is meant bring about effects in the world," Fish added.[8]

The professors I know admired Fish's candor but were appalled that he said such things publicly. If colleges (and their highest-paid professors!) do not build character, promote morality, or instill citizenship, why should legislators and trustees shell out vast sums for the enterprise? If a college education merely exposes students to faculty who are absorbed in their own "moments of aesthetic wonderment"—as Fish mischievously put it—why should society foot the bill?[9]

Some colleges consequently require students to take courses on moral reasoning and ethics. Derek Bok, after surveying scores of scholarly studies, concluded that the results of ethics courses were "moderately encouraging": students who took them did slightly better on tests of moral reasoning than students who did not.[10] But even if colleges can teach students to think about moral issues more logically, there is no evidence that this will induce them to *behave* morally. This became evident several years ago when a cheating scandal rocked the graduate journalism program at Columbia University: the cheating occurred in the course on professional ethics.

The problem of cheating is doubtless universal: underwear embroidered with hundreds of Confucian analects in tiny characters was worn by candidates taking exams for positions in the sixteenth-century Ming bureaucracy. Technology has only intensified this time-honored proclivity. During an exam in my large lecture class a few years ago, several students asked to use the bathroom. More followed. A student in the front of the room, boiling over with exasperation, caught my attention. I walked over and asked if anything was wrong. He scribbled on a page from his exam booklet, ripped it out, and thrust it at me: "They're using BlackBerries." My TAs and I flushed the students from the bathrooms; when the whistle-blowing student turned in his exam, he gave me a hard stare. Seventy percent of college students cheat.

Columbia University now advises faculty to confiscate cell phones and other electronic devices and prohibits students from leaving the exam room. The problem is hardly unique to my university. Recent studies show that over two-thirds of college students admit to plagiarizing papers or cheating on exams.[11]

Some contend that today's students are simply more honest than their predecessors about admitting to their cheating. One reason for their candor is that many students regard cheating as a "trivial matter" that harms no one.[12] This evades the obvious fact that, by raising the curve for the entire class, cheaters lower the grades of honest students. This pain was evident in the face of the student who alerted me to the cheating during my exam. When students blithely claim that their cheating is inconsequential, they not only betray a moral laxity but also exhibit a failure of empathy: they don't care much about their classmates. If a tree falls on a bunch of people in the woods and I don't hear their screams, what's the problem?

Morality 101: What Adam Smith Really Said

If the young are moving toward a more pragmatic, individual-istic sensibility, they have learned it from society. And many regard Adam Smith as the original guru of greed, for in *The Wealth of Nations* (1776) he proclaimed that self-interest was the engine of economic progress:

> It is not from the benevolence of the butcher, the brewer, or the baker that we expect our dinner, but from their regard to their own interest. We address ourselves, not to their humanity but to their self-love, and never talk to them of our own necessities but of their advantages.[13]

Smith insisted that those who pursue self-interest in a free market build a dynamic economy that redounds to the benefit of all.

In 2005, Federal Reserve Chairman Alan Greenspan trav-eled to Kirkcaldy, Scotland, Smith's birthplace, to deliver the Adam Smith Memorial Lecture. On that occasion Greenspan observed that prior to *The Wealth of Nations* the selfish pursuit of profit and wealth had been perceived as "unseemly." "[One] could hardly imagine that today's awesome array of interna-tional transactions would produce the relative economic sta-bility that we experience daily if they were not led by some international version of Smith's invisible hand," Greenspan de-clared. Greenspan briefly referred to Smith's *Theory of Moral Sentiments*—this in the forty-third paragraph of a forty-six-paragraph speech—noting that it delved into "the roots of human motivation."[14]

But Greenspan distorted Smith's intellectual biography. Smith published *The Theory of Moral Sentiments* in 1759, long before *The Wealth of Nations,* and he spent his final years adding several major sections to *Moral Sentiments*. Smith labored on *Moral Sentiments* for decades because it filled a gaping hole in *The Wealth of Nations*. The benefits of a free economy resulted from individual initiative and effort: in the race for wealth a person should run "as hard as he can" in order to "outstrip all his competitors." But "if he should justle, or throw down any of them," the race was ruined and the benefits of free markets evaporated. The rise of market-rigging monopolists and financiers in the 1770s and 1780s intensified Smith's anxieties on this score.[15] The obvious remedy was for the state to punish those who cheated. But as the economy grew in size and power, the state would be obliged to appropriate even greater powers to regulate it. And if the state became a Hobbesian leviathan, it would inevitably constrain markets. In the absence of a large regulatory state, how could markets be protected from crooks and cheats?

The Theory of Moral Sentiments provided the answer. In its opening sentences Smith maintained that, despite man's natural selfishness, there were "evidently some principles in his nature" that inclined man towards empathy:

It is by changing places in fancy with the sufferer, that we come either to conceive or to be affected by what he feels. . . . When we see a stroke aimed and just ready to fall upon the leg or arm of another person, we naturally shrink and draw back our own leg or our own arm; and when it does fall, we feel it in some measure, and are hurt by it as well as the sufferer.[16]

Most businessmen do not engage in fraud or deceit because they empathize with those who would be harmed by such actions. There was "scarce any man" who failed to behave with "tolerable decency" toward his fellow man, and it was a good thing, for without it " the very existence of human society" would be imperiled.[17]

The financial collapse of 2008–2009 showed how even Greenspan's "awesome array" of financial products could turn rotten if people behaved immorally. Blame tended to fasten upon supersized villains such as Bernie Madoff and the Enron executives, but moral culpability for the economic debacle was widespread. Millions of applicants for mortgages and credit cards misstated their assets and employment history; "liar's loans" became a standard implement of commerce. Tens of thousands of realtors sold homes they knew buyers could not afford. The sharpest minds in elite investment firms concocted deceitful financial products. Brokers ground up the bad mortgages like sausages, rebranded them as prime, and sold them to unwary and distant investors. Credit-rating agents and accountants vouched for the worthiness of securities that reeked. Insurance executives never bothered to set aside sufficient funds to insure the investments for which they collected huge premiums (and bonuses). Politicians grabbed with both hands for a piece of the action while government regulators, nurturing visions of lucrative postretirement consultancies, looked the other way. Tens of millions failed to behave with "tolerable decency." The result, foreseen by Smith, was calamity. Our society was in moral meltdown before the financial one hit home.

The moral failing was not the work of the nation's poor, struggling to feed their families, but of mostly well-to-do college graduates who longed for gaudy McMansions, larger flat-screen TVs, and more exotic vacations. Many of the worst offenders had been educated in the nation's most selective schools. ("Why does everyone at Harvard concentrate in economics?" the *Harvard Crimson* asked in June 2008.) The "morally responsible leaders and citizens" alluded to in college mission statements were nowhere to be found.

To blame higher education for the financial collapse of 2008–2009 is absurd. A liberal arts education encourages students to examine their lives in the light of the finest humanistic discourse. The problem was not that college grads didn't know enough but that they didn't feel more. When realtors sold houses buyers could not afford, or when securities brokers ripped off distant investors, they did so oblivious to the pain such actions would cause. Many of the cheaters were loving parents, community-minded citizens, and generous philanthropists. But they had not learned, as Adam Smith insisted, how to "change places" with others.

The Decline in Empathy among College Students

The moral meltdown hardly surprised those who had been tracking the attitudes of college students during the previous

half-century. The proportion of entering college students seeking to become "very well-off financially" had been rising steadily
since the late 1960s, yet those seeking to acquire "a meaningful
philosophy of life" had fallen sharply: from 1966 through 1969,
five college students in six agreed on the importance of a
"meaningful philosophy of life," but since the mid-1980s fewer
than half concurred.[18] Over these decades, too, a growing proportion of college students reported a stronger drive to achieve
and rising levels of narcissism.[19]

If Adam Smith were right, however, these changes would
have no impact on moral behavior. Empathy, he insisted, was
a human constant: everyone winced when he saw someone
else being hit with a hammer. And because human beings are
naturally empathetic, a basic degree of morality—"tolerable
decency"—would always prevail. Yet a recent analysis of seventy-
two studies of empathy among college students from 1979
through 2008, based on a standard empathy index, found that
empathy levels have declined sharply. Fewer students agree
with statements such as "When I see someone being taken advantage of, I feel kind of protective toward them" and "Before
criticizing somebody, I try to imagine how I would feel if I
were in his or her place."[20] Psychologists Howard Gardner and
Katie Davis found a similar trend. They analyzed fictional stories by seventh- and eighth-graders in the early 1990s and compared them to those written by a similar group in recent years.
Of the stories written by students in the early 1990s, 32 percent
featured characters who differed from the student writer, but
none of the stories by the sample of recent seventh- and eighth-
graders included a character who differed from the author.

"This decline in 'character play,'" Gardner and Davis concluded, "indicates that today's students may be less inclined—less able?—to assume the perspective of characters who are different from them."[21]

The convergence of these social trends—rising levels of self-esteem, narcissism, and greed; and declining levels of empathy—seriously undermine social coherence, as Smith predicted. Commentators have become increasingly uneasy over the rising incidence of bullying, the pervasive use of vile epithets online, and the growing popularity of reality TV, which mocks drunken drivers, overweight brides, unsuccessful suitors, inept cooks, off-tune singers, and all of the other "weakest links" of society. We do not feel "the hurt of the sufferer," as Adam Smith put it; we put that loser in front of a camera and laugh.

Portraits of a "narcissism epidemic" and a "decline in empathy" may be overdrawn. Previous generations of Americans showed precious little empathy for blacks who were disenfranchised or lynched, for Japanese-Americans who were interned, or for women and gays who were subjected to coarse jokes and physical abuse. Nor is it true that most college-educated people nowadays engage in online bullying or smirk at the suffering of overwrought bridezillas. Longitudinal analyses indicate that well over a third of college students still seek a meaningful philosophy of life, express no desire for great wealth, and exhibit no symptoms of narcissism. And this has been true for decades.

But even small attitudinal shifts can have dire social consequences: if one driver in a hundred ignores stop lights, driving becomes impossibly dangerous. The significant decline in empathy for another third of college students is cause for concern.

Society is bound by a tissue of trust; when it tears, everyone suffers.

Inculcating "Moral Responsibility" and "Ethical Conduct"

But how can colleges inculcate "ethical conduct," "integrity," "tolerance for others," or any of the other moral blandishments that adorn their mission statements?

Not only are faculty disinclined and unprepared to undertake such work, as Fish trenchantly observed, few students, parents, or legislators want professors to exchange their lecterns for pulpits. Such concerns loomed large during the culture wars of the 1980s and 1990s, as conservatives complained that the predominantly Democratic professoriate inculcated liberal values. The debate finally died out for the simple reason that opinion polls (and voting trends) showed that college graduates were much more conservative than their professors.[22] Perhaps liberal faculty had refrained from promoting liberalism in the classroom. More likely, students paid them little heed. Rousseau, who understood the psychology of immorality as well as anyone, recognized that by preaching virtue, "you make your students love every vice; you instill these vices by forbidding them."[23] The lesson is simple. When professors preach, students tune out.

Martha Nussbaum addressed this pedagogical challenge in a creative way. To cultivate "habits of empathy and conjecture," she recommended that professors assign novels and poems by American minorities and peoples from other parts of the world. Students reading these works would no longer regard such peoples as "forbiddingly alien and other." Students would learn to "think what it might be like to be in the shoes of a person different from oneself"—much as Adam Smith proposed.[24]

Literary works *can* create an empathetic bond. Perhaps the most consequential example was Harriet Beecher Stowe's *Uncle Tom's Cabin* (1851–1852), which encouraged white Northerners to imagine the plight of slaves. But this signal moment in the moral education of the nation also illuminates the chief weakness of this pedagogical turn. White Southerners complained that Stowe's view of slavery was preposterous, derived from a handful of abolitionist tracts and a few brief visits to the South; her rendering of slavery was as fictitious as the characters she invented. (To this day, references to her stereotypical "Uncle Tom" intermittently surface, nearly always to the detriment of enlightened race relations.) To oblige students to read any work of art, especially texts chosen for their moral force, is to undertake political advocacy. To base a pedagogy on such literary works is akin to preaching.[25]

Nussbaum, well aware of this danger, insists that faculty pose "critical questions" about such works. But small group discussions, as Harvard dean Harry Lewis observed, are rarely the "best forum" for raising difficult moral issues,

> as the requirement for quick answers encourages rote pieties and snappy argumentation and discourages deep thought. Just as in any other subject area, asking known questions, about the value of diversity, for example, is likely to elicit safe and reliable answers.[26]

How, then, are students to learn the intellectual foundations of ethical issues while acquiring the empathetic capacity to see why such issues matter? How do you explore contentious issues in ways that go beyond reflexive pieties?

On Becoming John C. Calhoun and Moammar Gadhafi

When James Tatum—aka John Calhoun—told his black friends that he had volunteered to take the role of the staunchest defender of slavery, they were shocked. Why would an African American *choose* to articulate such ideas? James explained that he wanted to understand slavery—to *really* understand it, which meant getting inside the heads of slaveholders. If he could figure out what made Calhoun tick, he would move closer to the eye of the hurricane of this nation's legacy of troubled race relations.

But after he had volunteered for the role, another factor influenced his thinking. James is competitive by nature: he plans a career in politics. He had lost the previous Reacting games and was determined to win this one. After receiving the description of Calhoun's views and objectives, James studied Calhoun's speeches and writings. Quickly he saw that Calhoun's position possessed intellectual merit. Not only did slavery surface repeatedly in the Bible, but it was intrinsic to the great civilizations of ancient Greece and Rome. Most important was the U.S. Constitution's endorsement of slavery: therein lay a moral dilemma that defied easy rebuttal. James would argue that people who lived in society must abide by its laws, and slavery was the law of the land. No society could function if people obeyed only the laws of which they approved.

But James realized that his classmates would reject this argument out of hand. Everyone knew that slavery was wrong, and Frederick Douglass's narrative, assigned with the game, had driven home this point with force. To win the game, James had to persuade classmates to put aside their own beliefs. But how? He finally happened upon a strategy. By showing his own ability to identify with the foremost defender of slavery, he was challenging his classmates to do likewise; they, too, could learn to "think what it might be like to be in the shoes of a person different from oneself"—as Nussbaum put it.

But James's rhetorical task was made more difficult by the structure of the game. As he advanced Calhoun's arguments, and prodded classmates to relinquish modern beliefs, other students criticized those arguments: "So if you were in the [slave's] shoes, would you welcome the whip?"

James's reply was careful: "I can't really speak on that. I'm not in their shoes."

This delicious irony ratcheted up the stakes of the unspoken debate, especially among black classmates. James was suggesting that students who unthinkingly opposed slavery were akin to the slaveholders who unthinkingly supported it. James dared classmates to examine slavery from the slave-owners' perspective. If they did, then some of them would agree with Calhoun's position, and James could win the game.

This dynamic recurs in many Reacting games, most of which revolve around a moral dilemma. Is it fair for uneducated Athenian citizens to wield as much power as large landowners who are trained in managing businesses and vast estates? Is it morally right for Galileo, who lacked training in spiritual

matters, to propound scientific hypotheses that undermine biblical faith and thereby consign countless souls to hell? Should
Nelson Mandela compromise fundamental rights in order to
reach an accord with white racists who rule South Africa?

Reacting students report that although they usually empathize with their historical figures, they do not always agree with
them. While James came to understand Calhoun's reasoning,
he was bewildered by Calhoun's inability to empathize with
slaves. James eventually loathed just about everything Calhoun
said and stood for. Indeed, the process of identifying with Calhoun helped James "shore up the arguments against the wrongs
Calhoun had advocated."

Reacting students, in papers, classroom debates, and
outside-of-class faction meetings, scrutinize such matters endlessly. They challenge peers to empathize with those who think
differently from themselves, which imparts a distinctive edgi-
ness to role-immersion games. In the spring of 2011, for example, a student in my class was playing Louis XVI, trapped in the
Tuileries Palace in Paris during the French Revolution.

"Now I know how Moammar Gadhafi feels," she said, re-
ferring to the thousands of Libyans who were then converging
in Tripoli to drive the dictator from power.

"Do you feel badly for him?" I asked.

"As a matter of fact, I do, a little," she said sheepishly.

The next week, after NATO announced plans to take Gadhafi out with unmanned drones, the student grabbed me after
class. "I know he was a terrible person but can this be moral?"

Why, I wondered, had that question not occurred to me?
But, then, I hadn't put myself in the shoes of a beleaguered
autocrat.

Empathy, some philosophers contend, is "noncognitive" and thus incompatible with moral reasoning.[27] When we see the video of Saddam Hussein, noose around his neck, being taunted by his executioners, we instinctively put ourselves in his place. Our empathetic inclination may short-circuit our cognitive operations. Plato's Socrates denounced role-playing for exactly this reason: it had the "terrible power" to corrupt "even the best characters." Skilled actors, poets, and storytellers elicited powerful emotional responses. But justice, he insisted, emerges from reason. If we are undone by the suffering of others, how can we think clearly?[28]

Philosophical abstractions notwithstanding, however, moral behavior is a matter of the self. It is one thing to ask, "What is justice?" and another to *do* something about it, such as when we resolve to treat others as they would treat us. When one acts, one's self becomes entangled in the action. Our behavior, for good or ill, is inescapably self-involved and self-interested. And when we have internalized multiple selves—when we examine slavery from the perspective of both slave and master—our moral understanding is deeper. That's why, according to most definitions, a good judge tempers legal reasoning with compassion. "Empathy and fellow feeling form the very basis of morality, as philosophers such as Mencius and Immanuel Kant have maintained," observed ethicist Sisela Bok. "Without some rudimentary perception of the needs and feelings of others, there can be no beginnings of felt responsibility toward them."[29]

Stronger evidence of the link between role-immersion games and empathy comes from the Stroessner study, cited in previous chapters. Stroessner's interview consisted of 94 statements drawn from eight different psychosocial indices.

The responses to most of these eight types of questions yielded no change in opinions over the course of the semester. The exceptions—noted in earlier chapters—pertained to self-esteem, locus of control, and attitudes on the malleability of the self. The final exception concerned empathy.

Stroessner's forms included statements such as "I cry at the end of sad movies," "I like to watch people open presents," and a dozen more statements drawn from psychologist Albert Mehrabian's Balanced Emotional Empathy Scale (BEES), a standard measure for determining the empathy of potential nurses, social workers, and foster parents. The BEES scores of both the Reacting and "regular class" students were nearly identical at the beginning of the semester: in psychological terms, they were equally empathetic. But by the end of the semester, the BEES scores of the control group had declined slightly while those of the Reacting students rose. This juxtaposition generated statistical significance. In other words, after taking Reacting, students were more likely to cry at the end of sad movies and otherwise respond positively to statements that have proven to be consistent indicators of empathy.[30]

People with high BEES scores are also more receptive to new ideas and learn more easily. Students surely can make better use of their compassionate concern than identifying with bloody autocrats like Moammar Gadhafi or racists like John C. Calhoun. But this habit of "changing places" with others—even those whose views are reprehensible—promotes critical analysis and understanding. By thinking differently, students learn to think better.[31]

BEES scores also correlate with a still wider variety of psychological predispositions and behaviors. People with high BEES scores also communicate more effectively and work better on teams. Psychologists have found that persons with higher BEES scores also have

- "higher scores on measures of moral judgment;"
- enhanced "altruism in behavior towards others;"
- greater capacity for coping with people of different backgrounds.[32]

Role-immersion games appear to create empathetic feelings and also encourage deep reflection on moral matters. But is it really plausible that a college course can "teach" these psychological predispositions?

A Late-Night Pacing

Reni Calister was distressed. A few nights earlier her friend, the first grand secretary of Ming China, had persuaded Reni to change her position and support the Emperor Wanli. This would likely result in the defeat of the Donglin, a secret society of high-level bureaucrats who had criticized the emperor's moral laxity.

But now, the night before the final session, Reni had second thoughts. She realized that while her friend was herself a fine person, the historical first grand secretary had been "pretty bad" in relation to Confucian moral standards. From the perspective of a sixteenth-century Confucian scholar, Reni had come to believe in the purist criticisms of the emperor's henchmen. Moreover, Reni had made many friends among the Donglin and she worried about betraying them.

"I was pacing around my room for hours trying to decide what was right," she wrote during a Gmail interview.

"That is not true," I typed. "You did not pace for hours."

"I literally paced for hours," she replied, "reading my two essays—one supporting my friends in the Donglin, the other supporting my friend, the grand secretary. I called my mom and dad. I talked to the first grand secretary. I ranted at my roommate. I emailed the professor several times. And in between the conversations and the rants and the emails, I was contemplating."

"What did your parents suggest?"

"They told me to go with my gut," she typed. "I felt so much for the first grand secretary. But I also empathized with my group [the Donglin] and knew I could not go against them. That's what was killing me morally. In retrospect, it all seems pretty absurd."

"So what did you do?"

"I stayed with the Donglin. What matters," Reni concluded, "is not what society tells us, but how we feel about other people."

I thanked her and apologized for encroaching on her study time, especially since final exams began the next day. "After exams," I typed, "maybe you could explain this last sentence a little more?"

"I can't talk about it just a little," she replied. "Since that game, I've written several papers about it for other courses."

"About moral dilemmas?"

"Yes."

As students in a Reacting class, James and Reni devoted a significant portion of their first year in college to moral issues with little evident applicability to their futures. Perhaps they would have made better use of their time focusing on courses in their major or cultivating skills for their careers.

But perhaps a few years from now, when James is devising company policies on equity or writing laws on race relations, and when Reni is analyzing security issues for NATO or revising lending policies for a bank, we all will benefit from the time they spent pacing in their dorm rooms, pondering antique moral dilemmas and imagining what it was like to walk in the shoes of people whose bones have long since turned to dust.

CHAPTER 9

Teaching Leadership through Teamwork

Leading of Necessity

"I will never forget the smell of burning bodies."

Beyond that, Mateso Mbala-Nkanga would say no more. She had been a young girl when troops from Rwanda and Sudan invaded mineral-rich Kinshasa and drove thousands of Congolese from their homes. Some of Mateso's friends were killed and others vanished. Mateso and her immediate family escaped through Gabon and eventually settled near Detroit. A decade later, Mateso enrolled at Eastern Michigan University.

During the first semester, her history professor assigned her the role of John Ross, principal chief of the Cherokee nation in a Reacting game set in 1835. The Cherokee were being driven from their homeland by Andrew Jackson and the legislature of Georgia. As Ross, Mateso had to prevent the Cherokee from being relocated west of the Mississippi.

"I was stressed," Mateso explained, "because it seriously hit home." This was "the exact same situation" that had driven her family from Africa. Back then, the military junta that ruled the Congo had failed to protect the Congolese, including the Nkanga. Now, Georgia land-grabbers, having won a state-sponsored lottery, were seizing Cherokee farms and homes in blatant violation of federal treaties. President Jackson sided with the Georgia legislature and prepared to crush the Indians. Some Cherokee leaders, believing resistance futile, urged negotiation for better terms for resettlement in the West. Mateso-Ross led those Cherokee who refused to cede their land and homes.

Mateso had never thought of herself as a leader. In the previous Reacting game, she had been an effective teammate, adept at smoothing over personal differences and promoting cohesion. As John Ross, however, she was called to lead "her people."

As she pondered her task, she realized that she knew something about leadership from taking care of younger siblings; and she had learned lessons in leadership from the previous Reacting game. She had seen, for example, how several slackers had fatally weakened their faction. Now, by the bad luck of the draw, two of these slackers were among her Cherokee faction.

At an initial meeting of her group, Mateso explained that everyone would have to contribute. Each person would be obliged to research, write, and speak on particular topics. She scheduled a meeting the next evening in her dorm to parcel out the first assignments. When the slackers failed to show, her concerns mounted.

At the next meeting of the class, she forced herself to be assertive: "I told them what they had to do and gave them a deadline for doing it," she recalled. When one of the slackers failed to complete a research paper in time for a pivotal debate, she refused to allow him to present it later, when the issue was moot. Mateso was uncomfortable about exercising her authority so forcefully, but over time she regarded her job as an honor.

Despite her best efforts, the tide turned against her faction. The Cherokee Council rejected Mateso-Ross's proposal to defy Jackson and instead accepted another faction's removal settlement. Mateso-Ross lost. As in history, the Cherokee, fatally divided, were obliged to set out along the Trail of Tears to the West.

But Mateso was proud of her team members. She recalled that they had made some solid arguments and even convinced some people on the other side. Although she still recognized the importance of teamwork, she acknowledged the need for assertiveness. She even learned to speak sternly and enforce limits on her younger siblings. And Reacting had taught her something she had never before considered: "I am a very good leader."

Fostering Leadership

In a survey of 312 college mission statements, 101 cited leadership as an essential skill.[1] Princeton's seven-sentence statement was typical. It asserted that Princeton prepared students for "positions of leadership" and helped them develop a "capacity for leadership."[2] Exactly how, though, was anyone's guess. Of the hundreds of courses in the Princeton catalogue, only five mentioned leadership—and undergraduates were barred from three of these.

Hundreds of colleges and universities have established leadership institutes and programs, although professors are often skeptical of such initiatives. "Most leadership books," one scholar sniffed, are nothing more than "ego exercises for the author."[3] Few scholars agree on what makes a good leader—and even whether leadership can be taught. "Leadership," James MacGregor Burns declared, "is one of the most observed and least understood phenomena on earth."[4] Derek Bok omitted "leadership" from the skills that should be taught in college simply because he knew of no program that succeeded in doing so.[5]

Yet leadership programs have found a ready constituency among students who imagine that by appending a "leadership studies" credential to their resumes, they can skip a few of the lower rungs of the hiring ladder. But such programs may teach students the wrong principles. Careerist students who gravitate to such programs may be so focused on *leading* that they fail to appreciate the importance of the lower-level group work that sustains any organization. Psychologists have found, for example, that students with high self-esteem and narcissism are less effective at working with others. "People who feel like they're unusually special end up alienating those around them," psychologist Jean Twenge observed: "They don't know how to work on teams."[6]

When high-profile CEOS, politicians, and generals credit college for their subsequent success as leaders, moreover, they often cite their experiences as officers of fraternities or captains of athletic teams. In such organizations, everyone starts at the bottom. Initiatory hazings teach potential "brothers," "sisters," and teammates that they must first suppress egoistic desires in order to become part of the group; they learn to lead by following and studying leaders. The problem with such activities is that they have little to do with the academic enterprise—except subvert it.

A Tale of Two Thrasybuli

Role-immersion games, however, use the social dynamics of subversive play for academic purposes. Consider the experiences of two students from the University of Minnesota at Bemidji.

In 1997 Kamran Swanson graduated from high school and enrolled in the Marines, where his interest in philosophy blossomed into a passion. At Guantanamo and elsewhere, he devoured Plato's *Republic*, even sneaking it into his shirt to read on duty. After completing a tour of duty in 2001, he left the Marines and registered at Bemidji State to pursue a degree in philosophy. In 2004, his senior year, he took a history of philosophy course taught by Brendan McManus that featured *The Threshold of Democracy*, the Reacting game set in ancient Athens.

The dominant student in the class was a man in his forties who played Thrasybulus, the general who initiated the democratic insurgency that drove the Spartan-installed Thirty Tyrants from Athens. Kamran was impressed with the man's forceful bearing, decisive manner, and mastery of logic and persuasion. The man shrewdly negotiated one-sided deals, and his faction won nearly every vote. Seemingly unstoppable, he sprinkled speeches with references to the "inevitable" democratic victory. Kamran, though still in awe of the man, sensed a simmering resentment.

Then "Thrasybulus" made a fatal mistake. He resolved to remove an opponent through an ostracism vote. If a majority in the Assembly agreed, broken pieces of pottery (slips of paper) would be distributed to all voting citizens, who would write the name of the person they sought to ostracize. The person whose name appeared on the most shards would be exiled for ten years. Ostracism was risky: in the fifth century B.C.E., the person *proposing* ostracism was the one most likely to be ostracized.

Heedless, "Thrasybulus" demanded an ostracism vote and got it, but when the "shards" were counted, he was himself ostracized and exiled. Astonished and outraged, the man cursed, denounced the class, stormed out of the room, and dropped the course. Kamran was dismayed. "He could have learned from the experience," he noted. "My guess is that he'd not had much experience working with teams."

But Kamran and his classmates learned plenty. "We continued to work hard to win," he observed, "but we were careful not to overreach." He and his peers had witnessed an indelible illustration of the dangers of power.

In the fall of 2007, Professor McManus featured the Athens game at the beginning of another philosophy class. "Who will take the role of Thrasybulus?" he asked. (Sometimes Reacting professors assign roles randomly; occasionally they seek volunteers.) Michael Meelhause, a first-year student, initially hesitated. In high school he had been a successful runner and cross-country skier, but others had been chosen to captain these teams. His exclusion was painfully evident his senior year when, as one of only three seniors on the ski team, the other two were elected co-captains: "This made me think that I just wasn't cut out to be a leader." He also doubted whether he could "move beyond his comfort zone" to speak forcefully in public.

Yet Thrasybulus intrigued him, so he raised his hand and got the role.

He grew into it quickly: "The more I researched the character, the more I was inspired by what Thrasybulus fought for, so I really saw myself as fighting to finish the job he started." While delivering his first speech—a plea to punish the supporters of the Thirty Tyrants—he got caught up in the moment and his voice rose to a climax: "Never forgive, never forget!" Inspired by his words, a majority of "Athenians" voted for his proposal—reversing history.

And Michael, at least, did *not* forget—as I learned when I interviewed him in 2011. "I kept the speech because it was really one of my first public speaking opportunities," he observed. It marked a turning point in his life. "I learned that I could inspire and persuade others and I learned to stand up for my beliefs," he recalled. "It really gave me confidence in my leadership abilities."

At the beginning of the last game of the semester, Michael again volunteered for a leadership role, this time as a British governor of India in 1945. He relished the opportunity to hone his newfound leadership skills. But soon he confronted a cluster of bewildering problems: Gandhi and the Indian National Congress demanded that the British turn the entire subcontinent over to them; the Muslim League insisted that "their" Muslim-majority provinces be transformed into a separate state of Pakistan; other minorities—ranging from the untouchables to the Sikhs to the independent princes of Hyderabad and Kashmir—called for guarantees the British governor could not enforce. The factions were ripping the country apart.

Michael resolved to save the day single-handedly through rhetorical brilliance, much as he had done as "Thrasybulus." The crucial moment came when he unveiled his masterpiece—a blueprint for a single federated government that would address everyone's needs. The main factions, however, were caught by surprise and denounced the plan. Tensions mounted and India "fell deeper into chaos."

"I was wrong," Michael confessed. "I failed to talk to the various groups before presenting the plan."

For a time Michael brooded over his failure: "I learned what it felt like to struggle as a leader. While I couldn't find a solution at the time, I learned to move beyond my mistakes to see where I could have gone in a different direction. I learned that in the future I needed to include others in the conversation and not just rely on myself."

His two roles together shaped Michael's views on leadership: As Thrasybulus he "gained the confidence to lead," but as governor general of India he learned that leadership was less about assertion than building consensus.

When "Good Leadership" Leads to Disaster

The first principle of good leadership is to reject all leadership maxims (perhaps even this one). I grasped this at the close of a weekend spent test-playing a Reacting game set in Rome after Caesar's assassination. I had been assigned the role of Cicero, leader of the senate faction that sought to restore the republic; my right-hand man (actually, a female professor from Bluefield College in Virginia) was Brutus, the most prominent of Caesar's assassins.

From watching scores of Reacting classes, I had learned that the chief ingredient for success was an effective team. During the first meeting of our faction, with the opening debate in the Roman senate just an hour away, my teammates were eager to refine our arguments in support of a republic. But I insisted that we first organize ourselves as a team. I wanted to ensure that we worked together effectively.

We succeeded. Our team was cohesive and harmonious. We gathered and shared information systematically. We formed several well-defined negotiating units. We devised procedures for making consensual decisions swiftly. But by the end of the weekend, as we were running for our lives toward the hills above Rome, our dreams of a republic as dead as Caesar, I sensed that something had gone wrong.

Exactly what, I learned during the postgame discussion. Many of Caesar's former allies had been amenable to working with the republican senators—especially if it would prevent rivals from seizing power; but they could not join with Brutus.

They had repeatedly demanded Brutus's arrest and execution—or at least his expulsion from the senate—but our commitment to the team caused us to dismiss such proposals out of hand. One by one, potential allies turned against us.

My team erred in deferring to my leadership. Someone should have demanded we sacrifice Brutus, much as generals sacrifice regiments to win battles. Despite my Reacting experience and commonsensical bromides ("All for one and one for all"), I was wrong, and someone should have called me on it. Our team was *too* harmonious, *too* respectful of experience and authority. But how can such counterintuitive principles be taught?

Most good leaders *do* learn that they cannot rely solely on their own judgment. Young George Washington, a wealthy planter and slave owner, was accustomed to giving orders and having them obeyed. During the French and Indian War, as a lieutenant colonel in his early twenties, Washington punished disobedient soldiers by having them locked in a dark room, bound in chains, and flogged. He even hanged two deserters, raising the gallows forty feet to ensure that his men understood who was boss.

But despite his "natural" bearing and self-assurance, young Washington was a mediocre leader. His early military record was full of mistakes and diplomatic gaffes. When the British attacked New York in the summer of 1776, Washington's blunders nearly resulted in the destruction of the patriot army, which barely escaped and fled across New Jersey to refuge beyond the Delaware River in Pennsylvania.

Historian David Hackett Fischer contends that these failures staggered the Virginia aristocrat. A shaken and humbled Washington now solicited the opinions of subordinates and encouraged frank discussions during war councils. He also listened to the views of ordinary citizens. From these conversations came the inspired *collective* decision to recross the Delaware and strike the Hessian garrison at Trenton. According to Fischer, Washington "created a community of open discourse and a spirit of mutual forbearance."[7] He had learned to lead through consensus and conciliation, a model suited to the emerging democracy.

Why Donald Trump Is Wrong

Authoritarian leaders rarely transform weak teams into good ones. Rather, good leaders grow out of effective teams and are sustained by them. Sometimes a team requires inspiration, such as when Michael urged Athenians to remember the democratic martyrs; and sometimes a team requires firm guidance, such as when Mateso prodded slackers to work harder. But sometimes teammates must press for a change in policy or blow the whistle on wrongdoers; teammates must become leaders and vice versa. Michael needed to be forewarned that Gandhi and other Indian leaders would regard British proposals with suspicion; and the arrogant "Thrasybulus" in Kamran's class needed someone to advise him that his high-handedness was alienating potential supporters. Likewise, as Cicero, I needed to be told that my inclusive concept of team, by harboring a notorious assassin, was misguided. Failure had resulted from the lack of strong two-way connections.

This bottom-up concept of leadership conflicts with contemporary American attitudes, summed up by Donald Trump: "I believe in bragging about yourself." High-flying CEOs, millionaire football coaches, and aspiring politicians often insist that leadership is synonymous with rare qualities of willfulness and foresight. Good leaders, they claim, are worth their weight in gold, which is how they should be paid. No wonder success-oriented students, awash in self-esteem, aspire to join the ranks of Donald Trump by adding "leadership" credits to their many-feathered careerist hats.

The celebration of transformative "great men" was once a historical commonplace. Such persons, biographers insisted, dictated the course of history. Some modern scholars of leadership have similarly insisted that leadership emerges from a rare convergence of traits such as intelligence and charisma. But if leadership is a product of innate capacities, the chances of learning it in college (or anywhere else) are slim. Other scholars insist that leaders emerge in response to an infinite number of contexts and situations; thus, the best preparation for future leaders is to expose them to many different leadership styles and skills.[8]

By the 1990s, however, scholars were gravitating to a less manipulative and more reciprocal notion of leadership: leaders and followers "influence one another."[9] In 2003, after concluding that "almost all leadership scholars" had embraced this view, James MacGregor Burns insisted that scholars had gone too far in "denying a distinct leadership function." He insisted that transformative leaders possessed a special capacity to *empower* people, to enable others to gain efficacy within their own lives.[10]

This subtle reformulation poses a difficult pedagogical challenge. If the essence of transformative leadership is improving how others think and act, how can students be expected to learn it? How can people be taught to work together effectively? The answer to these pedagogical questions, like most others, is to shift perspective from teacher to learner. Students learn how to work with others by working with others; they learn leadership by leading and by being led.[11] Role-immersion games do just that, by thrusting students into complicated situations that oblige them to work in teams—and sometimes to lead them.

This reciprocal conception of leadership—channeling individuals into effective collective action—has become the dominant ethos of the modern workplace. Unfortunately, this idea has little resonance within the pedagogical structures of higher education. In 2014, when *New York Times* columnist Thomas Friedman asked a senior executive at Google what he sought in potential employees, the executive declared that test scores and college GPAs were worthless. What mattered most, apart from demonstrable knowledge in technical subjects, was leadership: not "traditional leadership," the senior vice president explained, but "emergent leadership":

> What we care about is when faced with a problem and you're a member of a team, do you, at the appropriate time, step in and lead. And just as critically, do you step back and stop leading? do you let someone else?

Intellectual humility, he added, mattered far more than expertise in particular fields.[12]

Yet the older stereotype of leaders as a breed apart has deep intellectual roots in the academy. Students who attend the most selective schools, earn the best grades, and win highest honors expect to become leaders. Thus Princeton maintains that its graduates learn leadership simply by completing the university's requirements for a degree. This meritocratic assumption, like so many others in higher education, dates back to Plato. The rulers of the Socratic utopia were to be culled from among the best and the brightest; everyone else was compelled to listen to them. Our society adheres to a variant of this model: in most walks of life, economic and political elites call the shots, though, unlike Plato's philosopher-rulers, our politicians and CEOs are spared the burden of studying philosophy and eschewing material comfort.

But we need another model of leadership. Within work groups, research teams, local communities, and national politics, we need leaders who listen. We also need workers and citizens who speak up, and, when necessary, assume leadership roles themselves. Many may doubt that they have the right stuff to lead; but sometimes they have no choice. A reticent mother whose autistic child is being neglected may be obliged to launch a crusade to change school policy; a nose-to-the-grindstone researcher who devises a new procedure may have to take on the medical establishment. The health of our businesses, communities, and nation requires that we work in teams, sometimes suppressing our egoistic desires, and that sometimes we take the initiative on our own.

Back to the Future

Bard president Leon Botstein regrets that despite a half-century of curricular change and increased access to higher education,

> the encounter with the primary purpose of college—learning—seems not to have left many traces on our lives after college. . . . There is little empirical justification for the conceit of influence embedded in the rhetoric of liberal learning and general education.[13]

We have little evidence that the enormous public expenditure for higher education has strengthened our democracy, improved our communities, or benefitted our society. Indeed, much of the current furor over the cost of higher education is fueled by the judgment that while the *experience* of attending college—living away from parents and participating in the campus newspaper, athletics, or dramatic productions—is valuable, few academic courses leave much of an imprint on students afterwards.

But few individuals *as individuals* ever leave much of a mark on the world—or their communities. To affect the world, we must add our efforts to those of others. Too few college students acquire the teamwork and leadership skills that would enable them even to think in this transformative way, much less implement it after college.

Reacting students tell a different story. After playing the French Revolution game, Joe Hogan, a student at Grand Valley State University (Michigan), wrote that Reacting revealed to students "their own authentic capacity to effect real change in culture—to have a vision for the world and be bold enough to enact it."[14] The students featured in this chapter tell a similar tale; more important, their lives exemplify it.

Michael Meehlhause, having learned from his success as Thrasybulus and his failure as a governor general in India, subsequently ran for the student senate and was elected; he helped lead the fight to save the men's track team and then joined the delegation of Minnesota-wide student leaders that lobbied in St. Paul for more funding for higher education. By the time he was a senior, he was president of his class.

By then, too, Michael was working as a volunteer teaching assistant with Reacting classes, helping students "grow into their roles as leaders and speakers." He saw them flourish, moving from role-playing activism to participation in environmental groups, the college Democrats and Republicans, and other organizations. "Next, I hope to take what I've learned to the classroom as a social studies teacher where I hope to inspire other students to not only go to college but to try new things, move beyond their comfort zone, and find attributes they might not have thought they had," he explained.

After graduation Michael began his career in teaching—and he went into politics. In 2012, at twenty-three, he was elected to the Bemidji City Council, among the youngest elected municipal officials in the nation. Though his precocious political success was mostly a product of hard work and dedication to public service, he still credits Reacting. "That first speech in Athens," he recalled, "was like turning on a light switch."

Kamran likewise learned both the thrill and the power of leadership. "It is one thing to make an argument for the sake of expressing my views; it is another to change the world," he noted. "It sounds cheesy," he added, "but after Reacting I felt I could stand on my feet, look my opponent in the eye, and deliver a precise, point-by-point argument with clarity and without notes." "In other words," he said, "I felt well-armed and ready for graduate school."

He enrolled at the University of Chicago, completed a thesis on Spinoza and freedom, and was hired to teach philosophy at Harold Washington Community College in inner-city Chicago. During his second year, he included several Reacting games in his philosophy course, the first instructor at Harold Washington to do so. "I'm trying to create an environment that will encourage my students to change, and also to give them the tools so they can think about how they want to change," he noted. He is now completing a book on implementing Reacting in community colleges.

Mateso, who had doubted her capacity to lead, was named director of diversity for the Eastern Michigan University student government. For her birthday in 2013, she launched a successful campaign to raise funds for a women's support organization in South Kivu in Congo. Now she is making plans to return to Congo and open an orphanage for refugees from the civil war. "As much as I try to run away from it," she said, "I fear that I might just end up being a leader after all."

"In such an unstable country, that won't be easy," I replied.

"Yes," she said, "It will take a whole lot of leadership."

But when Mateso embarks on the great work of her life, she won't be a novice. Like other Reacting students, she will have had many centuries of experience—working on teams and leading them.

CHAPTER 10

Teaching the Past by Getting It Wrong?

The bill of his Mets hat, tilted upward, was twisted halfway around his head. "His name is Juan," Barbara Waldinger whispered, sitting next to me in the back row of her classroom at Queens College in New York City. Her students were midway through *The Trial of Anne Hutchinson*. Juan was John Winthrop, governor of the Massachusetts Bay Colony. I recalled the famous painting of Winthrop, hatless, wavy black hair spilling over a starched Elizabethan ruff. I wondered what the Puritan leader would have made of the young man who was now walking—no, loping—toward the front of the classroom.

As Juan neared the blackboard, he stopped and pivoted. Now facing his classmates, he moved closer, his yellow and gray Air

Jordans nearly touching the shoes of those in the front row. He scanned the room and spoke with a slight accent.

> Wasn't easy getting here. Not for any of us. Remember the Arbela, out there in the ocean? I told you we'd have to stick together. It didn't get any easier when we got here. Some got sick. Some died. . . . But we stuck together, right?

His splayed fingers reached toward one clump of students, as if to grab them. Then, releasing them with a twist of the wrist, he moved to the other side of the room and reached out to others.

> But Anne, nunh-uh. She says we don't have to stick together. Says that some of us are saved and some aren't, and she knows who. All her friends—right over there—they're saved. That's what *she* says. What about the rest of us? No way, no how. Says we're damned to hell.

"That's wrong!" a student called out. Her accent was eastern European, probably Russian. "That's ridiculous. *You're* driving us apart! You won't let the new immigrants into the church!" She gestured toward a group of students seated in the back row to my right.

Juan looked at her.

> I'm not on trial here. Anne is. She says our ministers don't know what they're talking about. How does she know?

Seems that God talks to her. That's what she says. Just her. He must whisper in her ear or something. You'd think He'd have better things to do. She says she's a prophet. You know, like Moses? Next thing she'll be walking in here with a big tablet.

The scattered chuckles throughout this monologue erupted into hoots. Juan smiled—the first acknowledgement that this was a performance—then he turned it off.

Well, that's OK. Everybody can say what they want. But don't you forget. We're all in danger. Around every corner, every tree. You're minding your business, right? Next thing you know you've got an arrow in your head. Look. We're just trying to survive. Some want to help out. That's good. That's real good. Those who don't, well, you just leave. And take Anne with you. Plenty of room out there in the woods.

Transition

Juan's was a masterful performance, an ingenious fusion of rap swagger and orthodox Puritan doctrine. To win the game, Juan had to persuade the indeterminates—students who, though obliged to represent different Puritan interests, were otherwise free to decide on the fate of Hutchinson. And Juan knew his audience. Over two-thirds of the students of Queens College are immigrants or the children of immigrants. Juan pleaded with his peers to band together in an alien environment.

Yet I grew increasingly uncomfortable with Juan's riff. The more he translated New England Puritanism into an idiom that resonated with his classmates, the less he evoked the Puritan world as I had learned it.

Had Juan brought history to life—or flat-out murdered it?

(Mis)Representing the Past

Some historians have charged Reacting with precisely this crime. They say that role-immersion games encourage students to *think* that they have stepped into the past and interacted with people in different times and places, but this is wrong. Historical understanding does not come from pretending to be a historical figure; it comes, if at all, through the rigorous study of the historian's craft. Reacting games do not teach history; they constitute an offense against the values of the historical profession.

"Juan Winthrop" could have served as Exhibit A in such an indictment.

But a case can be made for the defense. It was anticipated over a half-century ago by R. G. Collingwood, a philosopher of history at Oxford who explored the distinction between the actual past and the historian's renderings of it. Collingwood observed that if a historian were to claim, "I am Thomas Becket," he would be speaking nonsense. Becket, however, is knowable to us only through the words he left to posterity. Becket exists—the present tense is crucial—only when we bring his thoughts, as conveyed by his writings, into our minds. The historian, by studying Becket's thoughts and rethinking them, acquires the subjective essence of Becket. The process of "rethinking" the thoughts of Becket, Collingwood acknowledged, was complex: "I do not 'simply' become Becket, for a thinking mind is never 'simply' anything: it is its own activities of thought." But a rethought Becket was as close as we would ever get to the historical figure.[1]

Professional historians lampooned this thesis. Some criticized Collingwood for reducing historical analysis to an act of "clairvoyance." In 1970 David Hackett Fischer charged him with the fallacy of idealism.

> To require a historian to rethink Brutus's thought before he killed Caesar is to require him to become Brutus. And this he cannot do. . . . For Brutus did not merely think different things than Collingwood thought—he thought them differently. The whole idea is antihistorical, antiempirical, and absurd.[2]

Fischer's reasonable words reflected the positivist consensus of the historical profession—the conviction that more research and sophisticated analyses were bringing us ever closer to understanding the truth about the past. Collingwood had contrived to replace the hard work of historical research with a specious and intuitive empathy.

But even as Fischer was criticizing Collingwood, the positivist foundations of the discipline were giving way. A key (though oft-neglected) sapper in this work was the British philosopher Michael Oakeshott, a contemporary of Collingwood.

The past, Oakeshott wrote, was an infinitude of complexities and contingencies; at no time and place did it possess "unity or feeling or clear outline" or "over-all pattern or purpose."[3] The inhabitants of, say, Winthrop's Boston were continuously awash in sights and sounds. No one experienced "life in Puritan Boston" because no such thing existed.

The past, Oakeshott explained, comes into existence only when a historian writes it down. "To write history," he added, "is the only way of making it."[4] Historians operating from a positivist perspective may imagine that when they compile the pertinent facts and put them in logical order, they have written a truthful history. Oakeshott disagreed:

> No distinction whatever can be allowed between the raw material of history and history itself, save a distinction of relative coherence. There is no fact in history which is not a judgment, no event which is not an inference. There is nothing whatever outside the historian's experience.[5]

As an exercise in recapturing the real past, the historical enterprise was transparently absurd.[6]

Most historians were left speechless by Oakeshott's nihilism. A few, though, did speak up. Gertrude Himmelfarb declared that Oakeshott had illegitimated "almost the entire corpus of historical writing." His philosophy signaled "the death of the past and the futility of any meaningful writing about the past."[7] Little wonder, she remarked, that even

Oakeshott's admirers refused to follow his lead. Rather than abandon the writing of history, they simply ignored his challenge.

By then, however, the grounds of the debate were shifting. A new genre of criticism focused on the *mode* by which historians advanced their theses. Hayden White showed how historians inevitably used narrative structures that resonated with the cultural expectations of readers. Though clothed in the white-coated garb of scientific empiricism, historians performed "an essentially *poetic* act," using tools of "emplotment" to shape their materials into various literary tropes.[8] Others pointed out that the subjectivity of individual historians was further compounded by the subjectivity of those who read their texts (or listened to their lectures). The past itself is not only a hall of mirrors, but readers perceive this perceptual fun house through the distorted lenses of their own minds.[9]

In 2002, Cambridge historian Richard J. Evans declared that historical accounts were the "invention" of the historian and not "a true or objective representation of past reality, which was in essence irrecoverable."[10] The "real" people of the past must remain shadowy figures, hidden in the deep recesses of time, further enveloped in a fog of words and language. Historian Lynn Hunt summarized the views of many when she declared that historians cannot stand on any "unproblematic ground of truth." "History is 'out there' in some sense," she added, "but its thereness is not fixable."[11] "The perfect historian of the future," biographer-novelist Jay Parini observed in 2014, "will acknowledge the fact that he is a fiction-maker."[12]

The dispute between Winthrop and Anne Hutchinson illustrates this phenomenon. Most of the extant accounts of the trial were gathered by those who prevailed in the dispute. Winthrop himself may have authorized (or even written) the transcript that serves as the main source of trial testimony. Other primary sources are equally problematic. Seventeenth-century printers published unauthorized accounts of the trial that even the participants rejected as false. John Cotton complained of "a written Booke [that] goeth up and downe in England under my Name," but he knew nothing of the opinions it attributed to him. Thomas Shepard, a critic of Hutchinson, similarly lamented that a book purportedly consisting of his (Shepard's) words had been "published without my will or my privity." He insisted that it did not reflect his views.[13]

Charles Francis Adams (brother of Henry Adams), after compiling the major texts of the trial, flagged another problem. The theological disputes were couched in "a jargon which has become unintelligible."[14] "So far as the reader of to-day is concerned," Adams wrote in 1894, the Puritan theological controversies might "best be described by the single word impossible."[15] In recent years, Michael Winship (*Making Heretics: Militant Protestantism and Free Grace in Massachusetts, 1636–1641* [2002]) has perhaps offered the most sophisticated account of the trial, focusing on doctrinal differences among the disputants. But he recognized that his narrative rested upon uncertain footing.

One leaps from less-than-transparent source to less-than-transparent source, guided by one's accumulating assumptions, and tries not to look down at the dizzying gulf of archival blankness beneath. This is far from an ideal situation, but there is no dodging it.[16]

But if the truth about the past is so uncertain, so unknowable, how can anyone teach it?

Constitutional scholar Forrest McDonald insisted that as teachers, historians inevitably imposed a specious coherence and certainty upon their subject. It was "absurd" for historians to "deceive ourselves into believing that we can convey any real knowledge" of the past.[17]

Some scholars, especially those trained in literary theory, call on instructors to disavow any "truth" connection between historical sources and the events they purport to describe. They insist that the transcript of Hutchinson's trial—like any text—is significant in and of itself; its relation to what transpired in Boston in 1637 is unknowable. The new iconoclasts advocate pedagogies of deconstruction, decentering, and interdisciplinarity. Textual sources must be subverted; students must be "disoriented" and "discomforted."[18]

But Stanley Fish has identified the chief problem with this pedagogical turn. "The proponents of radical pedagogy must negotiate an impasse produced by one of their own first principles, the unavailability of a perspective that is not culturally determined." How can professors, while professing, subvert their own authority?[19]

Role-immersion games provide a way of addressing this perplexing problem. The nearly 500 pages of roles, rules, and advisories in *The Trial of Anne Hutchinson* reflect designer Michael Winship's theological interpretation of the dispute. But Juan, intent on winning the game, reshaped these materials—the historical texts—to fit his alternative narrative of immigrant survival in a hostile world. And other students in the class simultaneously rebutted Juan's interpretation. ("*That's ridiculous.*") The experience of playing the game deconstructed Winship's interpretation of the texts and interrogated the alternatives. Students were not told that the past is elusive and contested; they experienced it. In doing so, they discerned that the past is always, as Lynn Hunt explained, "a field of moral and political struggle in which we define ourselves in the present."[20] Many history majors couldn't make much sense of these words; but none of Juan's classmates needed to be convinced of the relevance of Puritan Boston to their lives.

When Anne Hutchinson Is Acquitted and the Monarchy Wins the French Revolution

Despite Juan's brilliant leadership, the members of his General Court voted to acquit Hutchinson. In history, however, Hutchinson was convicted and banished. Which leads to another issue: How can you teach history if you get it wrong?

Reacting instructors insist that Reacting games focus on the collision of big ideas as articulated in major texts. Most of the classroom debates and student papers in *The Trial of Anne Hutchinson,* for example, concern whether Hutchinson or Winthrop better understood God's intentions as reflected in the

Bible—and seventeenth-century Puritan commentaries on it. Although Juan eschewed the terminology of the Puritans, he outlined their position accurately: *She says our ministers don't know what they're talking about. How does she know? Seems that God talks to her.* The students' rendering of the theological debate was mostly on target. Because the final vote of the General Court occurred in the last few minutes of the game, the game exemplified error only briefly. That "error," and any others, were corrected in one or two "postmortem" sessions, when the instructor returned to the front of the room, explained what "really happened," and encouraged students to consider the issues in light of their own (real) beliefs.

Critics counter that the brevity of its errors hardly constitutes much of a defense of the pedagogy; and the postmortem discussions cannot repair errors induced by role-immersion games: if the most memorable learning comes from experiencing the games, then the students will remember false history.[21]

These criticisms are fair. Anthony Crider, chair of physics at Elon University (and member of the board of the Reacting Consortium), gave his class a quiz after playing *The Trial of Galileo*. He learned that many students believed that the universe has a center. That is, many ended up agreeing with the Aristotelian position (championed by conservatives in the Holy Office). They agreed with error: physicists have shown that the universe, being infinite, has no center.[22] Because Reacting classes are games (and not reenactments), students must have the chance to win—in essence, to change history. Competition is an indispensable element for transforming classes into subversive play worlds. In Reacting games, students compete with each other; often they also compete with the past, such as by attempting to acquit Anne Hutchinson.[23]

But if Reacting games inherently subvert historical understanding, historians—in their role as pedagogues—necessarily impose their own distortions on the historical record. In my lectures and narrative accounts, I try to tell the story of the past as succinctly as possible. Yet my college text, *The American Nation,* has over 1,000 pages. Like most college instructors, I spin a thread that binds events in tight causal sequences: one thing leads to another and another. I omit extraneous materials lest they obscure the narrative's overall arc. If I fail to tell the story clearly and concisely, students will not remember it correctly.

But history does not cohere. None of it had to turn out the way it did. If, during Louis XVI's flight from Paris, his carriage driver had not recklessly clipped a wheel, breaking an axle, the king might have escaped from France and crushed the revolution. Causal chains are paper figments of the historian's imagination. History is a smorgasbord of plausible "what-ifs," some of which depend on mere serendipity, and others, on the efforts of extraordinary individuals. Describing "what happened" and why ignores the contingency of the past. It paints a picture with broad, clear strokes; but the clarity of that picture is why it is wrong.[24]

Students *prefer* this clear rendering of the past, anchored to hard facts and dates. Thus when Michelle Laughran distributed the role sheets for the French Revolution game to her Western Civ class at Saint Joseph's College of Maine, many students were confused. Raven Riendeau, a first-year student who "liked to deal in facts," was initially boggled by the prospect of diverging from what really happened. While playing the game she discovered that every decision, even one as small as her choice of friends, could "drastically" alter the course of the revolution. What she learned from Reacting, mostly, was that "history is messy."[25] Which is perhaps the most important lesson of all.

If historians distort the past by making it too tidy, they often impose a more subtle distortion in seeking relevance. All historians know that the past is a forest of complexities that can dead-end in thickets of antiquarian irrelevance. Good historians resist this temptation by highlighting themes of larger significance, such as the rise of industrialism, the persistence of patriarchy, the confluence of peoples across borderlands. Historical studies of this type confer larger meanings and contemporary significance on the past.

In so doing, however, we often reduce individuals to mere flotsam and jetsam upon heaving seas of causal absolutes. Particular individuals may swim against the currents or be borne up by them, but their own exertions matter little. Students often regard the future fatalistically. If history is driven by titanic forces, why bother to vote, work on a political campaign, or help out in a soup kitchen? But this fatalism is wrong. No universalizing force dictates the future. For better or for worse, individuals influence what happens. This became evident to "Rosalind" (a pseudonym), a "nontraditional" student in Justin Burnette's class at Pikes Peak Community College. A mother who worked as a nurse, Rosalind was masterfully leading her faction to victory when a family emergency caused her to miss a crucial session. Deprived of her leadership, her faction lost. When she learned of the failure, she was flabbergasted. "I wouldn't think one person would make that much of a difference," she told Burnette. A few weeks later she told him she was considering a career in politics. Role-immersion games teach students that they can alter the "course" of human events. This truth—so hard to learn from history books and lectures—provides an antidote to the apathy that so often deadens our classrooms—and poisons our democracy.

Juan's class, to be sure, did not accurately represent the past. But Juan and his classmates were always conscious of the artifice. The real John Winthrop did not wear a Mets hat. In playing the game, however, Juan and his classmates gained a deeper understanding of the contingency of history. More, they learned that the past is never dead. It says something new to every generation.

Plato's War against Homer—and Movie History

Most historians charged with teaching undergraduates pay little attention to the abstract musings of the philosophers of history. Instructors confront more pressing problems every day: getting students to pass exams (or to graduate from college) bearing few hideously evident scars of historical ignorance. This is no easy task. Students often fail to read the required texts; many skip class or send text messages during it. When upbraided by teachers, students often complain that "the past is past" or insist that since history is dead we might as well let it rest in peace. Historians have become inured to such complaints; their common lament is that students care only about the present.

This is untrue, as can easily be confirmed by the enduring popular appeal of historical movies. In the early twentieth century, D. W. Griffith experimented with various genres in his two-reelers, each of which cost a few thousand dollars to produce. But when he embarked on a momentous and extravagantly expensive new type of movie—a twelve-reeler that eventually cost $110,000—he bet on history and his hunch paid off. *The Birth of a Nation* (1915), a racist rendering of Reconstruction, was the first box-office smash.[26] In 1917 Cecil B. de Mille, following in Griffith's footsteps, made *Joan the Woman,* a film about Joan of Arc. Producers balked at the expense of this and other "costume dramas," but de Mille insisted that audiences craved engagement with the past. When financial backers expressed doubts, he held a contest among moviegoers, placing ballot boxes in the theaters. Then he filmed the "winner": *The Ten Commandments* (1923).[27] Despite the success of that film, producers remained skeptical. "You can never make a nickel on a Civil War picture," Louis B. Mayer declared. Then David O. Selznick proved him wrong, spending a record $4.5 million on *Gone with the Wind* (1939), which made $160 million during the next fifty years, or, in current dollars, about $1 billion. The appeal of history persists: a new historical blockbuster hits the movie theaters nearly every year. How many people would have paid any attention to James Cameron's *Titanic* if the movie had been set on a fictional ocean liner?

Why do people flock to historical films but grumble about history classes?

"You will actually see what happened," Griffith boasted of *The Birth of a Nation.* Most modern filmmakers—and their publicity departments—use more cautious language: their films are "based on a true story." Yet directors proceed to "prove" the historical accuracy of their inventions by spending extravagant sums to make the costumes and sets *look* like the past. By the time the lights dim and the opening scenes appear, audiences quickly understand that they have left the present: they are "there"—within a wondrously evocative rendering of the past.

Humans have always longed to connect *directly* to the past. The figures on the walls of the caves at Lascaux, the hieroglyphic chronicles of ancient pharaohs, the stories of the Bible and the *Mahabharata*—nearly all of man's early cultural productions were attempts to evoke the past in a vivid way. In Western civilization, a key figure in this story is Homer, the poet (or poets) who wove folk legends into the epic tales of the *Iliad* and *Odyssey.* Stoic philosophers routinely invoked his words to clinch nearly any argument; his works came to constitute what one scholar has called the "national soul" of the Greeks.[28]

Homer transported audiences to the past by means of a "you are there" modality. In the climax of the *Iliad,* for example, when Hector lies dying at the feet of Achilles, the Homeric orator declaims in Hector's voice:

I beg you by your life, by your parents,
don't let the Achaean dogs devour me!

Then the orator, taking the part of Achilles, replies:

You swine, don't babble about my parents!
I'm so angry that I could carve you up
and eat you raw, for the harm you have done.[29]

Much like actors in Hollywood history, Homer's orators themselves represented figures from the past, speaking in the present tense. Audiences lapped it up.

Plato's goal was to supplant Homer as the educator of Greece. ("In Plato," one scholar observed, "Homer is always there, a named and unnamed presence, antagonist and inspirer."[30])

Plato's struggle with Homer was seemingly a clash between rationalist philosophy and poetic art, but this dichotomy is misleading. Plato's prose was infused with a dramatic power and genius that surpassed Homer's. Their opposition lay not in literary style or philosophy, but in the *mode* of conveying meaning.

THE PLATONIC ATTACK ON *MIMESIS*

Plato's Socrates denounced *mimesis*—the assimilation of "oneself to another person in speech or manner"—and banned it from his ideal state: "So if we are visited in our state by someone who has the skill to transform himself into all sorts of characters and represent all sorts of things . . . [we] shall tell him that he and his kind have no place in our city."[31]

This statement, so baffling to students, is central to the Socratic worldview, which is why Plato devised multiple arguments in its defense. He first insisted that representations are false. Poets like Homer "have no grasp of truth but merely produce a superficial likeness of any subject they treat."[32] Socrates then insisted that when actors took on many roles, audiences, enthralled by the performances, did so, too. But a shoemaker who imagined himself to be a warrior would do neither job well. This was particularly pertinent to the ruling elite. Because their task was to rule, rulers should do nothing but rule: they should never imitate (through *mimesis)* actions of any other kind.[33] But Plato, who disdained material things, could hardly justify censorship on grounds of utility. This argument, like the "falseness" of literary representation, was little more than a smoke screen to conceal a far more compelling danger.

Namely, that *mimesis* was psychologically *too* potent. Socrates noted that *mimetic* poets and orators gave "rare pleasure," especially to "children and nurses and the general public." Socrates even confessed that as a boy he had come to love and respect Homer's stories; and he assumed (correctly) that Glaucon, his acolyte, remained fascinated by them.[34] Athenians, Socrates insisted, had become besotted with Homeric representation: they crowded round to see orators and actors bring to life Achilles or the Trojan women, and to hear celebrated rhetoricians passionately profess the innocence of some scoundrel in the law courts. The Greeks had become suckers for the reality shows of their day.

In his ideal state Socrates was obliged to extirpate *mimesis* because it had "a terrible power to corrupt even the best characters." He ranked as the highest excellence of his utopia its suppression of poets and actors because *mimesis* inflicts a "cumulative psychological damage" on audiences. Reason, he added, appeals to our best self, while representation appeals to the "lower elements of the mind." No well-ordered state could depend on citizens who had been so debauched.[35]

Plato's argument against *mimesis* has long reverberated within the classrooms of higher education. Scholars of literature do not write plays or novels; musicologists do not perform or sing; nor do historians act out scenes from the past. To put it more precisely, when English professors write novels, they usually describe themselves as novelists, much as academic musicians usually distinguish between their scholarly analyses and performances. Most scholars, when engaged as instructors, assume a staunchly rationalist, *antimimetic* disposition toward their subjects. Their task is to analyze the representations of others, not to produce their own. The achievements of the academic enterprise are in large measure a product of its critical perspective, its dissecting acumen.

But the indisputable benefits of scholarly analysis come at a cost. When we seek distance to gain perspective, we lose empathy. After something has been dissected, it ends up dead. That's why our scholarly analyses of poetry, music, religion, music—and history itself—sometimes seem lifeless. Critical detachment can be dull.

Plato's Socrates unintentionally illustrated this phenomenon. He insisted that Homer could have avoided the error of *mimesis* by narrating the *Iliad* from the vantage point of the third person, sticking to the facts and employing the past tense. To explain what he meant, Plato's Socrates rewrote several paragraphs at the beginning of the *Iliad,* including Chryses's appeal for release of his daughter.

> The passage would have run as follows (I'm not a poet, so I shall give it in prose)—The priest came and prayed that the gods would allow the Achaeans to capture Troy and return in safety, and begged the Achaeans to show their respect for the gods by releasing his daughter in exchange for the ransom.[36]

These lines are among the dullest Plato ever wrote.[37]

Plato understood, as perhaps his teacher did not, that scholarly detachment is an ineffective pedagogy. To ensure that his ideas endured, Plato eschewed factual historical narration in the manner of Thucydides. Instead Plato channeled the spirit and words of Socrates and had him "speak" directly to readers in the first person, present tense (like Homer!). Future generations, by reading the "actual" words of Socrates, would rethink his thoughts and become questing philosophers in his image. Plato, in short, had anticipated the historical methodology of Collingwood—and D. W. Griffith and Cecil B. DeMille. Plato's readers would imaginatively identify with Socrates.

Plato's was perhaps the most audacious gamble in the history of ideas—to advance objective rationalism through *mimetic* impersonation—and it is some measure of Plato's literary genius that it worked. Countless generations of rationalist philosophers have committed themselves to their life's work after reading Plato's representation of Socrates in the *Apology*, which concludes:

The hour of departure has arrived, and we go our ways—
I to die, and you to live. Which is better, God only
knows.

Homer wrote no better lines, nor in a more powerful *mimetic* idiom.[38]

But while Plato used the pedagogical power of *mimesis* to advance his rationalist goals, *mimetic* pedagogy nowadays is thought to be so strange that few professors can imagine what it might look like, much less embrace it in their own teaching.

History in the Present Tense

Noelle Pilchak, an interior design major at Michigan State University, didn't have high hopes when she signed up for Carl Anderson's course on ancient Rome. "I'd taken history classes before and they usually tended to be dry," she explained. "I enrolled only because I needed some credits." When Anderson announced that the last month of the course would be occupied with a Reacting game set in Rome after the assassination of Caesar, she had doubts. "In a lot of classes—especially history—I'm passive," she observed. (In fact, she said she had never before spoken in a history class.) She didn't believe that she or her classmates would have much to say about ancient Rome. "In an undergrad course, about two-thirds of the students are generally there for the credit," she figured. "I didn't think we were going to put enough of an effort in to make this sort of thing work. I pictured a lot of awkward silences." Then she was assigned the role of Cleopatra.

The first minutes of the initial game session confirmed her fears, as students in leadership roles were unsure of themselves. But within half an hour, and to her "pleasant surprise," students took charge of the class and threw themselves into their roles. After that session, Noelle became intrigued by the complex challenges that confronted Cleopatra. She did extra reading and research; soon she was hooked. Several times she felt as if she really were Cleopatra.

Once was when "Marcus Antonius" and "Gaius Octavius" asked her to join their conspiracy against the senate. "They wanted my forces to leave Egypt and march with them," Noelle wrote, unconsciously assuming her Cleopatra self. In return they promised her a seat in the senate. From that position of power, she might connive to have her son by Caesar elevated as the new emperor. "But I did more research and found that they were lying," Noelle-Cleopatra explained. "I couldn't take a seat in the senate because I was a woman and a foreigner."

In the end she worked out a deal with another set of conspirators and persuaded Lepidus, commander of a nearby legion, to join them. In the final session, as armies were gathering near Rome, Lepidus strode into the senate and denounced Cleopatra and the other conspirators. Noelle's heart pounded, her hands became sweaty, and time seemed to stop. "In that second, we all actually felt our stomachs drop, like we were personally going to be executed," she wrote. It reminded her of the final minutes at an MSU basketball game as the team was surging from behind and the fans were going wild. "You are kind of suspended outside of reality," she explained.

In those moments, Noelle's history class dissolved, and she inhabited a compelling subversive play world, one that was nearly 2,000 years old.

It is one thing for a sober Oxford don such as R. G. Collingwood to rethink the thoughts of figures in the past and thereby bring them to life. But can one justify an undergraduate's doing so?

The alternative, it seems, is for students to ignore the past entirely. The sad fact is that most Americans have forgotten much of the history that has been drummed into their heads from the third grade onward, or they recall history only as disjointed factoids whose utility is confined to various trivial pursuits. The lessons taught by diligent and even inspiring history teachers fade (even if their jokes and personas remain vivid). Insofar as history lives in the minds of most people, it has been conjured up by Hollywood directors like Oliver Stone and Martin Scorsese, who feature the *mimetic* representations of Brad Pitt, Tom Hanks, Russell Crowe, and all the rest. Rarely does historical understanding inform our lives—or public discourse.

Professional historians, by eschewing *mimesis,* have made it easy for media conglomerates to monopolize its motivational power through movies, television shows, and video games. Some professors have appropriated the *mimetic* appeal of Hollywood history films by showing them in class.

Subversive play worlds built upon historical representation exploit the pedagogical power Plato's Socrates found so unsettling. Its "natural magic" takes hold of student's imaginations and doesn't let go.

I had been teaching Reacting for only a couple of years when I received a postcard from a former student, a member of Winthrop's faction, who had been visiting friends in Boston. After walking up Beacon Hill, she happened upon King's Chapel Cemetery and spotted the burial site of Governor Winthrop. "When I saw his tombstone," she wrote, "I felt a shiver go down my spine. I thought I knew him."

A year or two later, I received a postcard of the ruins of ancient Athens from Amanda Houle, a former student who had been vacationing in Greece.

> After dragging my family through Athens in the sweltering heat, attempting to use a map that I couldn't decipher and a language unintelligible to me, I finally landed at my intended destination: the ancient *agora*. I searched until I found the small marble plaque marking the spot where Socrates is thought to have held discussions with his pupils. Staring at the worn stone, I found tears streaming down my face.
>
> When my mother pressed me for an explanation, all I could say was that, standing in the dust and ruins, some part of me was surprised not to find him there. In my mind, the *agora* exists as a bustling and exciting place where Socrates can still be heard in the early morning, speaking on matters of justice.[39]

Through the *mimetic* power of role-immersion games, Amanda, Juan, Raven, Noelle, and nearly all of the students in this book have brought the past to life. All unconsciously spoke in the first person and used the present tense when discussing the historical figures they represented. For these students, history exists as an active force in their imaginations.

Did Amanda really know the man for whom she wept? Perhaps not. But in her he lives.

CHAPTER 11

The Strange World outside the Box

When Barnard president Judith Shapiro asked me to explain Reacting to her science advisory panel, a group of esteemed scientists and physicians, it seemed like a good idea. But as I walked to the podium, I wasn't so sure. During the preceding thirty minutes I had watched in mounting horror as these formidable scientists grilled a tenured scientist about his new course. What would they make of a historian's proposal to teach science through role-immersion games?

As I stood at the podium, perspiration trickling down my neck, I outlined the general concept of Reacting. When I saw the same stony eyes that had scrutinized the science professor, I swallowed hard. I explained how *The Trial of Galileo* pitted

Aristotelian motion physics against Galileo's alternative "world system." Then I described Galileo's difficulties in proving that the Earth moved given the data available to scientists in the seventeenth century.

After I sat down, everyone turned to an older woman with strikingly pure white hair.

"This story is familiar to us all," she declared. "The moment when we learned that what they taught us in graduate school was wrong. No one taught us that science changes."

Maureen Strafford, a professor at Tufts Medical School, nodded in agreement. Then she explained how, as a medical student, she had been taught not to administer painkillers to infants after heart surgery. Standard practice held that such drugs might delay recovery or prove addictive; moreover, the undeveloped neurological system of infants left them less susceptible to pain. After Strafford began making the rounds as a young physician, however, she was struck by nurses' accounts of the struggles of infants following heart surgery. The defining moment of her career came when she chose to advocate postoperative pediatric pain management. Like Galileo, she confronted staunch opposition from the scientific establishment. After Strafford finished speaking, other members of the panel chimed in with similar stories. They had been taught plenty of scientific information in college and graduate school, they said, but no one explained how new "truths" managed to supersede existing ones.

Nearly forgotten, I raised my hand and gingerly suggested that Reacting might be a good way to introduce English and art history majors to science, perhaps as an alternative to introductory chemistry or biology. The panelists struck this down cold. "Science majors need this program more than nonscientists," the white-haired woman said. "They need to learn to think outside the box."

That phrase resurfaced several months later. I had emailed a foundation official about Reacting, and he suggested we chat after a lecture he would be giving in Manhattan. I agreed and instantly hatched plans to ambush him with a grant request. During the lecture he rehashed the familiar critique of higher education: student disengagement, poor retention rates, discouraging test results, employer dissatisfaction with grads—the whole litany. Then he said, "We need to think outside the box."

I snapped to attention. Immediately dollars swam through my head like floaters during an eye exam. How many zeroes, I wondered, should I tack onto my grant request?

Afterwards I hurried to the podium to introduce myself. We adjourned to a coffee shop and soon were chatting amiably. When I said that I agreed wholeheartedly with what he had said, he raised his cup in salute. But as I launched into my description of Reacting, he stiffened, set the cup down, and looked at me carefully. When I explained that Reacting classes were configured as games, run by students, his brow furrowed.

"I wasn't thinking of anything quite like that," he said.

I spoke more rapidly, rattling off anecdotes and summarizing studies touching on the points raised in his speech.

As I caught my breath, he said, "This all seems very strange."

"But once you get out of the box," I replied, exasperation tumbling out with my words, "you're in a strange place. If everything looks familiar, you're still in the box."

He lifted his cup and studied it. There would be no grant.

Delineations of the Box: General Education

American higher education is an impressive edifice, a workshop that has produced much of the knowledge revolution of the past century. Though located at hundreds of separate institutions, the workshop's chief structural element is everywhere the same: the academic department, a box of considerable strength—and rigidity.

Departments have promoted knowledge chiefly by embracing specialization. In 1936, when Harvard President James Bryant Conant declared that knowledge advanced "because of specialization" he was stating the obvious. But the specialization of Conant's era was rank dilettantism compared to what was to come. Specialized scholarly organizations and professional journals popped up everywhere. In 1983, for example, Philip Curtin, president of the American Historical Association, citing the "proliferation of knowledge," noted that eighty-five specialized organizations had affiliated with the AHA. During the next thirty years, the number of AHA affiliates would increase fifty percent.

Specialization necessarily narrowed scholars' intellectual horizons. "The new Asianists and Africanists know next to nothing about European or American history," Curtin complained. "Americanists know less European history than they did thirty years ago."[1] Historians nowadays would smile at Curtin's words: most Americanists know next to nothing about many of the scores of subfields within *American* history. The trend toward specialization is even more pronounced in the sciences. In the 1930s nearly all of the members of the American Physical Society subscribed to *Physical Review*. Now, the APS has thirty separate divisions and *Physical Review* is published in nearly as many parts; few physicists subscribe to the entire publication.[2]

General education emerged as a curricular antidote to specialization. Most liberal arts colleges, seeking to ensure that students were exposed to a wide range of fields and ideas, required that they choose from a "menu" of courses beyond their major. An à la carte sampling would expose them to multiple intellectual traditions and the skills that would help them become productive workers and engaged citizens.[3] Nowadays, the mission statements of liberal arts colleges commit plenty of fine words to this cause. Princeton's catalogue, for example, maintains that its general education courses "transcend the boundaries of specialization and provide students with a common language and common skills." In reality, however, most general education courses are taught by faculty who are hired by departments. Often the "general" education offerings are indistinguishable from departmental courses. Princeton undergraduates may fulfill their science and technology requirement by taking an introductory physics course whose sole reading is a standard physics text. At the other extreme, Princeton students can fulfill the literature and the arts requirement by choosing from among hundreds of boutique courses, ranging from "Animation from Ovid to Disney" to "Soccer and Latin America." Students who enroll in introductory physics or a quirky literature class doubtless are confused by Princeton's rhetoric about "transcending" disciplinary boundaries and inculcating a "common language."

General education requirements are the result of deals brokered (and defended) by powerful department chairs. Chairs insist that undergraduates be required to take their department's introductory survey: How can students graduate from college without having studied American history, biology, or psychology? Then comes the wheeling and dealing. Louis Menand described the process as akin to *Jarndyce v. Jarndyce*, the impossibly protracted lawsuit in Charles Dickens's *Bleak House*.[4]

Yet because most scholars focus on ever-narrowing fields of specialization, they are increasingly ill-equipped to teach the courses students are required to take. Being assigned to teach the departmental survey is tantamount to a professional death sentence—a time-consuming diversion from scholarly work. That's why the task often devolves to untenured faculty, adjuncts, or graduate students.

In consequence, first- and second-year students are often herded into large introductory surveys staffed by overworked and inexperienced teachers. Such courses are money-makers—they generate far more tuition revenue than they cost in instructional salaries—and they build the enrollments that justify staffing levels for the entire department. This enables tenured professors to hide out in the upper-level seminars—or to avoid undergraduate teaching entirely. This convergence is often an unhappy one for undergraduates, who must struggle to make sense of huge, content-clotted lecture courses taught by the least experienced faculty. Although originally conceived as a way of buttressing the ivory tower, general education now sags against it, threatening to bring it down.

Vartan Gregorian, former president of Brown University, is among the many who have called for a reorganization of the curriculum "to give coherence to our specialized and fragmented base of knowledge."[5] Leon Botstein, president of Bard College, has specifically called for an end to the departmental monopoly on general education. Colleges must find a "curricular structure beyond the major" that "engages all students and spans disciplinary divisions." Such an education, he noted, would focus on issues, questions, and problems rather than disciplinary concerns.[6] A blue-ribbon study by the Association of American Colleges similarly recommended "interdisciplinary science courses that would focus on concepts and enigmas" and emphasize "the human, social, and political implications of scientific research."[7]

Proposals to reform general education often make sense to college presidents, parents, students, and even many professors. But from the perspective of academic departments, bent on advancing knowledge within their disciplines, such proposals make no sense at all. How can scientists who were hired to conduct specialized research be expected to "emphasize the human, social, and political implications" of their work? How can researchers who burrow into ever-narrower fields within their specialization perceive the broad horizons of multiple disciplines? Rather than think the unthinkable, professors circle their wagons around the departmental box and defend it stoutly from menacing presidents and accreditation committees.

Role-immersion pedagogies, however, provide an alternative approach. A single Reacting game not only builds many of

the skills that the mission statements of most colleges purportedly address, as previous chapters have sought to illustrate, but
it can also fulfill the interdisciplinary mandate of general education. *The Trial of Galileo,* for example, provides an introduction to motion physics, optics, and astronomy; and it also explores the impact of religion on scientific thinking as well as the
impact of science on religion. Furthermore, the game shows
how the 1632 debate over Galileo's system of scientific thought
was influenced by the struggle for military dominance between
the Spanish empire and France, by the advance of Protestantism in northern Europe, and by new philosophical and aesthetic
movements. Students *see* how individuals change science—and
in so doing, everything else. They *experience* how seemingly dis-
crete subjects—physics, political science, religion, history—are
indissolubly joined in the real world.

Reacting faculty have devised general education courses in
which groups of Reacting games draw students into multiple
intellectual traditions within a general framework. As the accompanying table suggests, faculty seeking to introduce students
to the complex relationship of scientific ideas and society can run
three games in a semester, perhaps beginning with *The Trial of
Galileo* followed by *Darwin and the Rise of Naturalism* and then
Acid Rain and the European Environment. Other faculty have
created Reacting courses on global problems in the twentieth
century, on democratic theory and practice, on Western religious
traditions, major philosophical and aesthetic systems, and so on.

At present, nearly sixty teams of scholars are designing Reacting games. Within a few years, the curricular possibilities
will be even richer.[8]

strative Reacting general-education courses

neral-education gory	Reacting game 1	Reacting game 2	Reacting game 3
nce and society	*The Trial of Galileo*	*Darwin and the Rise of Naturalism*	*Acid Rain and the European Environment, 1979–1989*
bal issues in he twentieth entury	*The Struggle for Palestine in the 1930s*	*Defining a Nation: The Indian Subcontinent on the Eve of Independence, 1945*	*The Collapse of Apartheid and the Dawn of Democracy in South Africa, 1993*
erican emocracy, Part I	*Patriots, Loyalists, and Revolution in New York City, 1775–1776*	*America's Founding: The Constitutional Convention*	*Frederick Douglass, Slavery, Abolitionism, and the Constitution, 1845*
stern religious raditions	*Josianic Reform: Deuteronomy, Prophecy, and the Israelite Religion*	*Constantine and the Council of Nicaea*	*The Trial of Anne Hutchinson*
manities and iterature	*Marlowe and Shakespeare, 1582*	*Modernism versus Traditionalism: Art in Paris, 1888–1889*	*Modern Music in Crisis: Darmstadt, 1958*

Because much of the "content" is embedded within the structural elements of a Reacting game, many instructors choose games outside their specialization—or even their discipline. No longer obliged to function as authority-bearing dispensers of knowledge, they enjoy being guides and motivators who help students surmount the many obstacles every game imposes. Uncertain gamemasters, when obliged to make a ruling on a contentious or debated point, simply respond that they need time to research the matter. And they do.[9] After spending years within a particular academic burrow, many exult in the opportunity to come up and take a look at what is going on elsewhere. Some even believe that this revitalizes their scholarship.

General education was also conceived, as Columbia's John Erskine explained, as a way of providing "the basis for an intellectual life in common."[10] In his view, the great books of Western civilization constituted the ideal foundation for that shared student experience. If everyone on campus read Plato, issues of rhetoric and justice might supplant the usual discussions of football or the dining hall food. But while St. John's College, with its four-year prescribed curriculum, and Columbia University, among other schools, have proudly retained their great books programs, relatively few institutions have followed suit. Few professors are trained to teach such works and fewer are inclined to do so. Other colleges have proposed common curricula, usually for first-year students, but few of these have gained wider acceptance.[11]

However, some colleges and universities create Reacting courses, with the same set of games, played by the entire first-year or second-year class. Thus when a student mentions that he was James Madison in *his* class's Constitutional Convention game, "William Paterson" may describe how she scuttled the Virginia Plan in *her* class. In this way, education on campus can become general as well as academic. To further bind this social network, these schools hold game-related art exhibits, plays, lectures, athletic competitions, and festivals.

Yet radical curricular innovation of this character is not common. Faculty on curriculum committees often balk at granting general education credit for Reacting courses. The irony is that while Reacting courses address the avowed purposes of general education, often far better than existing courses, the expansiveness of the games means that they don't fit neatly into existing general education categories. Many colleges wouldn't approve *The Trial of Galileo* for introductory science *or* introductory religion precisely because the game encompasses both categories of knowledge. Reacting courses are sometimes denied general education credit because they are too general.

Some special programs, such as first-year seminars, have provided an ideal curricular home for Reacting games. Honors programs and honors colleges, which seek a distinctive curriculum and pedagogy, have also embraced Reacting with few curricular obstacles. But at present, most professors offer Reacting games within their disciplinary courses. In large lectures, they often devote discussion sections, run by teaching assistants, to a complementary Reacting game. Increasingly, however, instructors of introductory courses in history, political science, or religion sacrifice breadth of coverage for depth of understanding and devote an entire semester to three games. Professors of introductory American history run *Forest Diplomacy: War, Peace, and Land on the Colonial Frontier, 1756–1757*; *Patriots, Loyalists, and Revolution in New York City, 1775–1776*; and *Kentucky, 1861: Loyalty, State, and Nation*. Political scientists feature *The Threshold of Democracy: Athens in 403 BCE*; *Henry VIII and the Reformation Parliament*; and *Rousseau, Burke, and Revolution in France, 1791.* The creation of more games will facilitate the development of Reacting-based courses for many disciplines.

The Turn to Pedagogy and Assessment

For decades, reform of higher education was nearly synonymous with changing the curriculum, especially the requirements for general education. Faculty committees debated such matters endlessly, and the hiring of a new president or provost inevitably resulted in promulgation of an adjectivally engorged "Bold New Educational Initiative." But the ensuing reshuffle of the familiar curricular deck seldom led to discernible changes in what or how students learned. During the past decade, however, leaders in higher education have shifted their gaze from curriculum to pedagogy. As with the debates on curriculum, however, discussion of pedagogical change has run smack into the solid wall of disciplinary tradition. Faculty who have learned their craft from esteemed mentors are skeptical—and rightly so—of the latest pedagogical fads. Confronted with much-ballyhooed (and often expensive) pedagogical "improvements," ranging from Power-Point to classroom clickers, many instructors ignore the latest trends and just go about their business. Fads come—and, mercifully, they go.

During the past decade, however, calls for pedagogical reform have been trumped by a new emphasis on assessment. And assessment itself has undergone a conceptual sea change. No longer do assessment teams focus solely on educational inputs—the credentials and training of faculty, the design of syllabi and the content of courses, and student evaluations of it all; nowadays the emphasis is on *outputs*: What have students learned—from individual courses and from college as a whole?

The new assessment assumes that once teams of administrators and faculty have determined what works—and what does not—instructors will embrace the successful pedagogies.[12] This has contributed to many worthy proposals. The American Association of Colleges and Universities, guided by George Kuh, has endorsed a set of "high-impact" educational practices, including first-year seminars, collaborative assignments and projects, writing "across the curriculum," student-faculty research initiatives, community-based and experiential learning, and capstone courses and projects, among others.[13] Furthermore, many faculty, working on their own (though often supported by their institution's newly energized teacher development centers), have developed innumerable active-learning pedagogies—and imaginative enhancements to traditional teaching modes.

Despite these and other demonstrable successes, many instructors are disinclined to change the way they teach.[14] In 2012 Carl Wieman, a Nobel Prize–winning physicist, bemoaned the failure of his three-decade campaign to persuade American colleges to adopt scientifically validated methods of teaching. "I'm not sure what I can do beyond what I've already done," he declared.[15] After studying a century of undergraduate education at Stanford, Larry Cuban was similarly "baffled" by the professors' steadfast adherence to pedagogical conventions. Despite major transformations in nearly all aspects of the university, teaching had exhibited a "perplexing continuity." He concluded that faculty attitudes were so completely embedded in the university's departmental structures and traditions that "no magical programs, awards, or charismatic leaders" could solve "age-old dilemmas."[16] Derek Bok concluded that, with respect to pedagogy, most colleges and universities find it next to impossible to break through "the crust of inertia and complacency."[17]

Proponents of Reacting have encountered the same resistance. In 2006, for example, an assessment team at Washington and Jefferson College did an intensive study of its twenty-eight "Freshman Forum" seminars, one-fourth of which were devoted to Reacting. The researchers issued a report that showed that the Reacting students rated their course as better than did students in the other seminars, and that Reacting students surpassed the other students in end-of-semester, critical-thinking essay writing.[18] But when presented with this report, "almost all" of the non-Reacting instructors said they would teach as they had in the past. Furthermore, about a fourth of these instructors expressed doubts about whether Reacting sections should even be offered in the future.[19]

Most faculty members cling to familiar practices even when offered financial incentives to try something else. (If pecuniary considerations had been their primary motivation, few would have set their sights on a career in academia.) Most professors take their obligations seriously and resolve to do their duty—*as they have learned it*; many scoff at the nostrums proposed by educational consultants, learning researchers, and well-meaning administrators and assessment teams. But this may be changing.

Distance Learning: "The Coming Tsunami"

"There's a tsunami coming," Stanford president John Hennessy warned in 2012. Online education, with the University of Phoe-

nix in the lead, had already dug deep channels in the undergraduate enrollment pool. But now Stanford, Harvard, Michigan, Penn, Princeton, and other universities had formed online
consortia that would inevitably siphon off still more. College
administrators almost instantly discovered a technological solution to their two biggest problems: rising costs and poor retention. Online learning, though initially expensive, would reach
a point at which additional enrollments would cost virtually
nothing, and students who complained about inconvenient
class schedules and insufficient campus parking could happily
log in to "class" in their pajamas whenever they wanted.

Many professors expressed misgivings over online courses,
but the iron law of economics, reinforced by the harshest of assessment metrics (retention), muted their objections. For example, when the Florida legislature imposed a 25 percent funding
cut for the University of Florida, Provost Joe Glover announced
plans to contract with a "private partner" to provide cheaper
online courses. When the professoriate complained, Glover
counterattacked: poor graduation rates nationwide, he observed,
showed that higher education had not proven to be "tremen-
dously effective in the face-to-face mode." A few months later
the University of Florida signed a ten-year $186-million contract
with Pearson, the education conglomerate, to run the University of Florida's online education program.[20]

"What happened to the newspaper and magazine business,"
New York Times columnist David Brooks declared, "is about to
happen to higher education: a rescrambling around the Web."
Professors would go the way of journalists, whose jobs had in-
creasingly been rendered obsolete by the Internet. Although
Brooks regarded the impending demise of traditional college

education with "trepidation," he saw no reason for despair. After all, studies had shown that online education was "roughly as effective as classroom learning." If students could learn as well by logging onto the Internet as by trooping to class, so be it.[21] The coming tsunami, in other words, would crash through the ivory tower at its weakest point: the bricks and mortar classroom. Swiftly, MOOCs (Massive Open Online Courses) began morphing into McCROCs (Massive Closed Credit-bearing Online Courses). By early 2013, venture capitalists were pouring hundreds of millions into online education. The MOOC rush was on.

College administrators assured jittery faculty that there would always be a place for live instructors in "flipped" classrooms. Students would still want to interact with a real person. But many instructors could read the handwriting on the blackboard—which was inexorably being moved online. Complacency, the default response to pedagogical innovation, no longer seemed tenable.

But in late 2013 several major studies found that MOOC students weren't logging on—at least not with sufficient regularity to learn much.[22] There were exceptions. Students with advanced degrees did well in MOOCs, as did those who were highly motivated; but less-motivated students—the same ones who fared poorly in regular college classes—usually failed to log in, watch the videos, and do the online assignments. In a bizarre reversal of arguments, defenders of online learning increasingly championed the *social* aspects of the experience. One study showed that while students in regular classes were sitting passively, alone and inattentive, distance learners were "often more engaged than their campus-based counterparts." (The exceptions were classes with collaborative learning activities.)[23] Another study found that students in face-to-face seminars were half as likely to participate in discussions as were students in online discussions.[24] For proponents of bricks-and-mortar colleges, this was the cruelest irony: distance learning was proving to be more successful at bringing students together than classes in which small groups of students were sitting next to each other.

The savviest thinkers in the MOOC camp were unfazed by the poor success rates of the early MOOCs. They regarded the videos of superstar lecturers as merely transitional, a temporary marriage of the pedagogy of the past with the delivery mode of the future. Online videos of even excellent lecturers would seldom be as effective as flesh-and-blood teachers. When staring at their iPads or smartphones, students were irresistibly lured to their social media or enticed by a new mission in *World of Warcraft*. The real revolution in distance learning would come when MOOCs exploited the advantages of the medium. John Seely Brown, former director of the Palo Alto Research Center (PARC) for Xerox and a proponent of new forms of online learning, envisioned a "new world of education" in which students solved problems through "team quests" and cultivated the imagination in approaches to learning characterized by "experiencing, playing, and occasionally failing."[25] Jane McGonigal, a game designer with a PhD from the University of California, Berkeley, was already designing multiplayer collaborative games for business, the arts, social and political movements, and environmental activists.[26] Commenting on McGonigal's pioneering work, Duke professor and administrator Cathy Davidson observed that video games tapped into players' longing to initiate change and undermine conventions[27]—a craving, as the present book suggests, for subversive play.

Educational gaming, used widely in elementary schools, has advanced upward in the curriculum. Higher education game designers have learned that the sophisticated historical visual reconstructions in *Assassin's Creed*, a popular action-adventure online game, can be enlisted for games containing historical content. Data-rich disciplines, such as political science, sociology, psychology, and art history, can be adapted to online gaming even more readily.[28] Within five years, perhaps fewer, a new generation of higher education games, based on software templates and graphics from popular video games, will likely transform online learning. College students may soon *experience* the dynamics of presidential politics by playing an online game entitled, say, "Electing a President, 2020." Or they may discover the difficulties of planting a colony in seventeenth-century North America by playing an online game entitled "Proprietors' Challenge: Founding a Successful New World Colony." Using the instant feedback systems devised by commercial video game designers, creators of the new online education games will continuously improve the games and make them more compelling. When college students at last prefer their for-credit video games to *Grand Theft Auto* or *World of Warcraft*, the educational millennium will have arrived. Then many professors, especially those charged with teaching content-heavy introductory courses, may see their enrollments evaporate. The online tsunami, when it finally arrives, may hit with more force than anyone has imagined.

Most administrators, though uncertain of the timing and extent of the looming threat, are leading the charge to shore up the undergraduate classroom. Creative faculty, too, supported by newly energized faculty development centers, have devised innumerable active-learning pedagogies and strategies. Building on many of these initiatives, José Antonio Bowen, president of Goucher College, has offered a sweeping reconceptualization of higher education to ensure that it better accords with the culture and expectations of students. Rather than function as dispensers of information, which students can find instantly online, professors must become motivators and coaches. Instead of holding office hours, they should schedule virtual interactions on Facebook, pose frequent questions and observations on Twitter, and encourage students to join online chat groups. Instructors should especially exploit the students' powerful social networks for pedagogical purposes. "In other words," Bowen explained, "we need to make college more like a video game."

Or, he notes, more like a Reacting class.[29]

The Halfway Revolution

To promote real learning, we must shift our focus from the performance of teachers to the creation of structures that will stimulate learning. But persuading instructors to rethink their professional practice is no easy task. That's why administrators usually greet Reacting proponents on their faculty with open arms. Even administrators who are skeptical of role-immersion games often support their Reacting vanguard in order to stimulate wider discussions of teaching on campus.[30]

The proponents of role-immersion games, moreover, inevitably play their trump card over traditionalists. Few regular instructors enter traditional classrooms confident that their lectures and open-ended discussions will produce an intellectually vibrant experience. Even exceptional teachers who deliver razzle-dazzle performances find the effort exhausting and the results uncertain. Andrew Hamilton, a biology professor at the University of Colorado, observed that he and his prize-winning colleague, after learning that two-thirds of the students hadn't clicked on the readings for their large course, redesigned it completely, eliminating the textbook and incorporating interesting new readings. Yet one-third of their students failed to pass the redesigned course. Hamilton concluded that he had to "come to grips" with the reality that the problem wasn't the curriculum or readings; the basic pedagogy of the standard course was "fundamentally broken."[31] Hamilton's words echoed those of Henry Seidel Canby, who as a young English professor at Yale a century earlier nerved himself for class "as for an ordeal" and relapsed after each class into "a limp vacuity."[32] If this anxiety grinds down the superstars, it proves even more burdensome to the numerous teachers who, though knowledgeable and conscientious, lack the master teacher's ready humor or charisma. Too often, our regular classrooms resemble a movie in which excellent actors struggle to breathe life into a so-so script. It's a lot of work and not many find the performance all that satisfying.

This, too, explains why Reacting has spread. *Instructors* find Reacting classes provocative, stimulating, and enjoyable. Their enthusiasm startles (and often unsettles) colleagues, some of whom eventually visit a Reacting class. There they see students taking charge and working through difficult material. The visitors also realize that a class sparkling with such energy might be satisfying to "teach." Eventually these professors attend a Reacting workshop and experience a miniversion of a game. Some become converts on the spot; most remain skeptical until they try a Reacting game in their own classes. Many then become enthusiasts of role-immersion games; some go further and join the Reacting community. Within a few years—or months—most join game-design teams, give Reacting presentations at professional conferences, and participate in the governance of the Reacting Consortium.

Role-immersion pedagogies have spread rapidly in recent years for another reason. They *differ* from conventional pedagogies and also *complement* them. To be sure, some students report that the experience of a Reacting class has caused them to become impatient with lectures; but most students insist that after a role-immersion experience, they better appreciate the reflective elements of regular classes. The Reacting teaching mode, though nearly antithetical to conventional instruction, can never supplant it, if only because no student wants to play more than one Reacting game at a time. Moreover, the imaginative loops of a Reacting game result in uncertain content coverage. Some classes playing *The Trial of Galileo* focus on theology, and others, on motion physics and astronomy; some, on whether the Earth moves, and others, whether the universe is infinite. Regular lectures and discussions cover more material and do it in a more predictable way. Reacting exposes students to smaller but deeper pools of knowledge, extending through multiple disciplines. Regular classes encourage critical detachment; Reacting encourages empathetic identification. And where conventional pedagogies depend on solitary study, Reacting builds community and promotes engagement. Conventional and Reacting pedagogies are very different—and mutually supportive.

Perhaps most important, Reacting obliges students to address messy, unstructured problems: these range from solving interpersonal dynamics within a team to devising arguments based on difficult texts and rapidly changing situations. This requires imaginative thinking of the sort one seldom learns through passive pedagogical modes. Indeed, normal classrooms and even quiet dorm rooms (an oxymoron?) are often inhospitable to creativity. Learning researchers have found that when students are placed in novel and unfamiliar environments, they find it easier to think "outside the box."[33] Not only do Reacting students long remember their debates as Roman senators and Puritan divines, they find that in such strange contexts all sorts of new and interesting ideas come naturally.

In a jibe at Plato, Aristotle insisted in the *Poetics* that imaginative thinking was a "higher thing" than the hard facts of reality and logic. Poetry, encompassing music and other creative arts, was a realm of intuition, emotion, and imagination that explored "that which may happen." By posing the question, "What if?" we pass through a magic portal into another realm: we end up outside the box.[34]

Our mental boxes consist of well-trodden neural pathways, structures of thought that make us who we are.[35] Those pathways that generate the most traffic, freighted with the strongest emotional ties, pertain to our self. When students take on Reacting roles, they move into a new imaginative realm. Soon they are outside the box of their (former) self. Then they find themselves ensconced in a new social network where they are obliged to articulate unfamiliar and even alien ideas. Inevitably, they ask (themselves): What if I were a different person?

This question unleashes tremendous imaginative power. Students whose beliefs have been prescribed by familiar religious or political texts rethink who they are and what they believe. Students who shrink from public speaking feel impelled to stand on chairs, sing songs, and deliver spontaneous orations. Students who fear failure, lest it reveal deep insufficiencies of the self, push their new personas into emotionally perilous waters. Students who cling to a small circle of like-minded friends reach out to others and form close and empathetic bonds with them. Students who take on roles as teammates cultivate leadership skills and agonize over moral dilemmas.

The suggestion that role-immersion games can solve almost all the problems afflicting higher education is so sweeping that sensible readers will likely dismiss it out of hand. But those who venture beyond the box in any field often discover a landscape that extends far beyond anything they had imagined.

Beyond Plato's Cave

The box as a metaphor for blinkered thinking perhaps originated with Plato's cave, whose denizens knew nothing of the illumined world of reason beyond the walls. Plato maintained that those who had escaped the cave and seen the real world were obliged to help those who remained trapped in the cave; but he also knew from painful experience that a solitary instructor could achieve little. To endure, ideas must be housed within institutional structures. If the *Republic* provided a blueprint for the Platonic utopia, Plato's Academy was its institutional embodiment. Its rational purposes were inscribed above its front door: "Let none but geometers enter here." Logic constituted its foundation, and solid blocks of reason, its walls.

The Platonic ideal continues to inform the debate over higher education, usually as an unstated and unexamined premise. When contemporary critics complain that corporate influence and managerial models corrupt the academy, or that professors or legislators impose their own political agendas on it, the critics often assume that higher education somewhere existed in a purer form—and usually they have in mind, if vaguely, some variant of the Platonic ideal.

But the Platonic ideal has long been part of the problem, because it deprives higher education of the motivational and imaginative power of subversive play. Nietzsche made a similar observation in 1872: the emergence of the modern university and its "scholar-scientists" constituted the culmination of the Socratic vision and the ascendancy of Plato's "logical universe."[36] Nietzsche bemoaned the university's repudiation of the "ecstatic dream world" of music and art, of unfettered creativity. He advocated combining Socratic logic with the imagination, ecstasy, and creative destruction symbolized by Dionysus, the god who could change his identity at will.

Yet Nietzsche erred in assuming that the academic world was suffused solely with reason. Higher education has always been animated by subversive play—the competition for prizes and chaired professorships, the thrill of overturning accepted wisdom, the wonder of imagining that the world can be different. When Galileo published his *Dialogue on the Two Chief World Systems* in 1632, for example, he knew he was treading on thin papal ice. He had nearly been silenced by the Inquisition in 1616, and in the intervening years his caustic tongue had earned him many bitter enemies. Yet he structured his masterwork as a dialogue among three characters, including a dull-witted figure named Simplicio—simpleton—who insisted that the Earth did not move. Many thought that Simplicio resembled Pope Urban VIII, including the outraged pope himself. Friends and colleagues had long pleaded with Galileo to refrain from humiliating those who disagreed with him, but Galileo could not resist. The "father of modern science," as Einstein called him, was hopelessly lost in subversive play. Galileo worked so hard partly because he was having so much mischievous fun.

Humans have always succumbed to the allure of subversive play. Adam and Eve had it as good as it gets, living eternally in paradise. Yet when the serpent tempted Eve to compete with God (by eating of the tree of knowledge), to assume a new identity ("for ye shall be as gods"), and to flout His laws, Eve just couldn't say no. Paradise had everything except fun, which is what Eve craved most.

God smacked them down, consigning Adam and Eve to work, suffering, and death—which proves that opposition to subversive play goes way back, too. Plato, Freud, Dewey, Piaget, Erikson—along with generations of college administrators and faculty who battled against fraternities and college athletics—also assumed that subversive play could be suppressed. They were wrong.

The critics have plenty of good reasons for opposing subversive play. Many subversive play worlds, such as opium dens, gambling casinos, and beer pong matches, do much harm. Gamblers and binge drinkers may claim that their subversive play helps them let off a little steam, making it easier to knuckle down later and do some work; but these meager benefits hardly offset their costs to society.[37] Plato's Socrates, too, condemned the pervasive play of the male citizens of Athens. Freed from hard labor through the exploitation of slaves, they did little *but* play. Athenians consequently turned many aspects of life into contests, ranging from beard growing to choral singing. Socrates especially condemned the rhetorical competitions in the Assembly and law courts, where Athenians shouted and clapped "till the rocks and the whole place re-echo, and redouble the noise of their boos and applause."[38] Athenians conjured fantasy worlds that they mistook for reality. By transforming social and political life into competitions, by pretending that their own selves contained glorious multitudes, by undermining the natural social order, Athenians inhabited a colossal subversive play world. Plato's Socrates proposed to replace it with an antithetical utopia founded on work and structured by occupation.

But democratic Athens also shows the creative power of subversive play. The achievements of that single city-state stagger the imagination. The contests among its playwrights and rhetoricians (including Plato's Socrates!) gave rise to many classic works of literature and philosophy. In political theory, law, historical method, science, mathematics, medicine, sculpture, architecture, and numerous other fields, the relentlessly playful Athenians added more to the storehouse of knowledge than any people before or since. They achieved so much not because they worked so doggedly but because they played so brilliantly.

Role-immersion games in higher education today hold the promise of restoring the churning passions and subversive impulses that have always invigorated the life of the mind. Yet many faculty and administrators remain wary. They regard with suspicion those who tinker with the ivory tower, and for good reason: a stream of pedagogical fads, most of them hawked by corporate vendors, has sloshed around its base for much of the past half-century. Nearly always these waters recede, having done little harm. Traditionalists then breathe a sigh of relief; sometimes, wiping their brow, they cite illustrious forebears such as psychologist William James, who disapproved of "namby-pamby attempts of the softer pedagogy to lubricate" the hard work of learning.[39]

And so the ivory tower stands as a proud monument to the intellectual achievements of the past century. Most of us who work within its increasingly partitioned and uniquely adorned rooms love the place. If we find it difficult to think outside the box, it's because our eyes linger within, drawn to a glittering wonderland of scholarly accomplishment. That's why so many of us are willing to mount its ramparts in defense of tradition.

But often we stand alone. For over a century the minds of our students have been imprisoned within subversive play worlds, captives of the sophomoric creations of fraternity brothers and Mark Zuckerberg, of the NCAA and ESPN, of Anheuser-Busch and Coors, of *Grand Theft Auto* and *World of Warcraft*, and of all of the giant corporations that usurp the motivational power of subversive play to generate profits.[40]

Students (and teachers) deserve an academic world that is as exciting as intercollegiate football, as enchanting as *World of Warcraft*, as subversive as illegal boozing, and as absurd as fraternity initiations. As faculty and administrators, we can help students glimpse the intellectual wonderland that attracted us to academia in the first place: the invigorating scholarly debates, the transformational power of new ideas, the exhilarating risk of looking at the world in a different way, and the thrill of challenging accepted beliefs and practices. We must encourage students to experience the revitalizing contests and churning passions that have always breathed life into the republic of knowledge for which the academy must stand.

Socrates at Sunset

The semester was drawing to a close and, as had happened with Nate Gibson's French Revolution class, my class's game on woman suffrage and radical labor would end before it had reached a proper conclusion. We needed additional classes to complete the game. While Nate and his peers had volunteered to come to extra early morning sessions, my students chose an extra class in the evening.

Aviva Buechler, who played Mabel Dodge, a socialite patron of radical causes, offered to host a "salon" at her "mansion" on Fifth Avenue on Saturday evening. Though I would be out of town, I encouraged Aviva to hold the class without me.

When I returned on Sunday I saw no emails about Mabel Dodge's Evening so I assumed that Aviva had canceled it for lack of interest.

But during the regular class on Monday, several students turned in papers based on their presentations at "Mabel Dodge's." Other students challenged remarks that had been made that evening.

After class, as students were leaving the classroom, I grabbed Aviva.

"Well, how did it go?"

She looked at me blankly.

"Your salon."

"Oh," she said, "very well. Emma Goldman gave a terrific speech."

"But what was it like?"

"What do you mean?" she asked.

"What *happened*?"

"It was a regular class," she said matter-of-factly.

"How could that be? You held it late on Saturday night without an instructor!"

"It was a regular *Reacting* class," she clarified.

Emily Alpern Fisch followed Aviva out the door. I asked if she had attended "Mabel Dodge's." "Of course," she said. "Everybody came." She mentioned that Aviva had reserved a classroom and tracked down a custodian to unlock it, and she and Aviva had decorated the room and laid out cookies and soda. When other students first arrived they attacked the cookies and chatted like regular students, but after Aviva gave her welcoming remarks as Mabel Dodge, everyone went into "game mode."

That seemed perfectly natural, Emily explained, because throughout the semester her classmates had repeatedly slipped into their roles during faction meetings and secret get-togethers in the dorms.

> Two nights before my faction in [Ming] China had to come up with our big collective presentation, we went to the Sulz Tower, thirteenth floor, at 1:00 A.M. and ate junk food and searched for the *perfect Analect* to prove the emperor was *wrong*. We kind of felt like we *were* Chinese scholars. I forgot I was trying to "win" a game. That happened with all of the games.

Six years later, I tracked down Aviva and Emily to confirm this account of their class without a professor. Both were now elementary school teachers. I also invited them to crash the Big Pnyx, scheduled the following week, when first-year students from four different Reacting classes would come together for a large collective meeting of the Athenian Assembly. Aviva and Emily accepted instantly.

On the evening of the Big Pnyx, they showed up, along with most students from all four classes. Some wore togas (in lieu of *chitons*); most didn't. The main issue for debate was whether to give tax-paying foreigners (metics) voting rights in the Athenian Assembly. Some students read prepared speeches or spoke from notes; others hammed it up. I was reminded of Socrates's critique of the real Pnyx, particularly his account of a young man who, after chewing lotus leaves, loses his inhibitions, "takes to politics," and goes to the Assembly where he could be seen "jumping to his feet or saying whatever comes into his head."[1] The students' Big Pnyx had some silly moments, but also some provocative ones, such as when a Latina student spoke against giving the *metics* the right to participate in the Assembly: "They came here to make money. How can they care as much about Athens as those of us who were born and raised here?"

Afterwards, as we were walking down the stairs, Aviva and Emily said the evening had brought back fond memories. I pressed them to recall the class Aviva had held in my absence six years earlier: *Why* did they work so hard if no instructor was around to grade them? Aviva said that, having been assigned a leadership role, she wanted to prove to herself and her classmates that she could do it. Emily made a similar point.

> I was in charge of how much I got out of a Reacting class. The instructor wasn't going to hold my hand and tell me how many pages to read for next Wednesday. The instructor was like the GPS: he mapped out options, but we had to decide both the destination and the route. It was magical when we were all screaming around the table about women's suffrage. I wanted to keep bringing more and more props to make it more real and tangible.

Then I realized that we were walking along the same brick path where, some fifteen years earlier, I had lingered to ponder the fate of wind-blown leaves rather than hasten to a class I dreaded.

"Don't you see?" Emily said, misunderstanding my silence. "It was *my* world. I felt like I could do *anything* I wanted."

APPENDIX: LIST OF REACTING GAMES

All Reacting games are approved by the Editorial Board of the Reacting Consortium. Some games are published by W. W. Norton in the "Reacting to the Past Series" while others are under review by the Reacting Consortium Press. Descriptions of these games, and others still in development, can be found at the main Reacting website: www.barnard.edu/reacting.

"REACTING TO THE PAST SERIES"
(PUBLISHED BY W. W. NORTON)

Charles Darwin, the Copley Medal and the Rise of Naturalism, 1861–64, by Marsha Driscoll, Elizabeth Dunn, Dann Siems, and Kamran Swanson

Confucianism and the Succession Crisis of the Wanli Emperor, 1587, by Daniel Gardner and Mark Carnes

Defining a Nation: India on the Eve of Independence, 1945, by Ainslie Embree and Mark Carnes

Greenwich Village, 1913: Suffrage, Labor, and the New Woman, by Mary Jane Treacy

Henry VIII & the Reformation Parliament, by J. Patrick Coby

Patriots, Loyalists & Revolution in New York City, 1775–76, by William Offutt

Rousseau, Burke, and Revolution in France, 1791, by Mark Carnes, Jennifer Popiel and Gary Kates

The Threshold of Democracy: Athens in 403 BCE, by Josiah Ober, Mark Carnes, Naomi Norman, Lisa Cox, Rebecca Kennedy, Kenny Morrell, and Bret Mulligan

Trial of Anne Hutchinson: Liberty, Law, and Intolerance in Puritan New England, by Michael Winship and Mark Carnes

Trial of Galileo: Aristotelianism, the "New Cosmology," and the Catholic Church, 1616–33, by Frederick Purnell, Jr., Michael Pettersen, and Mark Carnes

THE REACTING CONSORTIUM PRESS (2014)

Acid Rain and the European Environment, 1979–89, by David E. Henderson and Susan K. Henderson

America's Founding: The Constitutional Convention, by J. Patrick Coby

Beware the Ides of March: Rome in 44 BCE, by Carl A. Anderson, T. Keith Dix, and Naomi Norman

The Collapse of Apartheid and the Dawn of Democracy in South Africa, 1993, by John C. Eby and Fred Morton

Constantine and the Council of Nicaea: Defining Orthodoxy and Heresy in Christianity, 325 CE, by David E. Henderson and Frank Kirkpatrick

Forest Diplomacy: War, Peace, and Land on the Colonial Frontier, 1756–1757, by Nicolas W. Proctor

Frederick Douglass, Slavery, Abolitionism, and the Constitution, 1845, by Mark Higbee

Japan, the West, and the Road to World War, by John Moser

Kentucky, 1861: A Nation in the Balance, by Nicolas W. Proctor and Margaret Storey

Kansas, 1999: Evolution or Creationism, by David E. Henderson and H. Taz Daughtrey

Korea at the Crossroads of Civilizations: Confucianism, Westernization, and the 1894 Kabo Reforms, by John Duncan and Jennifer Jung-Kim

NOTES

1. For further information, see the main Reacting website: www.barnard.edu/reacting.

2. Nate Gibson is this student's real name. Protocols in some disciplines discourage the use of the real names of students, even when students grant permission, because students may not fully appreciate the consequences of such disclosure. When I informed the students in this book that I would not use their names, many insisted that their ideas were their intellectual property; they had a right to be identified with their views. This book therefore includes the real names of all of the students who requested that their names be included—and who have graduated from college. All other students are identified by a fictitious first name only, indicated with quotation marks on first mention.

3. On perfect attendance in Reacting classes, see William Gorton and Jonathan Havercroft, "Using Historical Simulations to Teach Political Theory," *Journal of Political Science Education* 8, no. 1 (2012): p. 56. Gorton noted that his Reacting classes at Alma College often had perfect attendance. Havercroft found that attendance in his Reacting classes at the University of Oklahoma ranged from 95 percent to 100 percent, whereas

the norm in other classes at midsemester hovered near 50 percent. Other Reacting faculty have reported perfect attendance for Reacting classes: David Henderson, a chemistry professor at Trinity College (Hartford); Gretchen Galbraith, a history professor at Grand Valley State University; Daniela Mansbach, a political science professor at the University of Wisconsin (Superior). On Reacting students volunteering to attend subsequent Reacting classes: this first happened in my second or third year of teaching Reacting to first-year students. A sophomore asked if she could just sit in and observe the current group of first-year students. I said that her presence might make the first-years feel uncomfortable. She said that she could be there as a helper, someone who could serve as a sounding board for arguments or as a coach on public speaking. I agreed, and thus began the use of "student preceptors," which some colleges now build into Reacting courses. The use of preceptors has had several unintended and beneficial consequences: for one, it provides game designers with more feedback on design problems ("this student can't find sufficient texts on which to base her papers"); for another, it generates innumerable suggestions on *how* to teach through Reacting. For example, Lily Lamboy, a Reacting student at Smith College and now a graduate student in political science at Stanford, devised an online tutorial in which students pair up and critique each other's speaking according to particular mechanics of effective oral presentations. This ingenious device helps students teach each other public speaking.

4. This class was videotaped, and an edited version can be seen on YouTube (Google Reacting to the Past, Henry VIII game, Part 1). The sick student appears on camera (she is wearing a gray beret and is identified as the Burgess of Colchester). She can be heard defending Machiavellian tactics—and, throughout the video—coughing.

5. Plato, *The Republic*, trans. Desmond Lee (New York: Penguin, 1953), p. 270; Plato, *The Laws of Plato*, Book 7, trans. Thomas Pangle (New York: Basic Books, 1979), p. 193.

6. Biographer Alan Ryan concluded that Dewey's educational philosophy was "determinedly teleological—at every stage the child was soon as a creature about to embark on the *next* stage of growth," in *John Dewey and the High Tide of American Liberalism* (New York: W. W. Norton, 1995), pp. 147, 349. See also John Dewey, *Democracy and Education* (New York:

Macmillan, 1916), p. 239: "Play then changes to fooling and if habitually indulged in is demoralizing," and "Children . . . are anxious to engage in the pursuits of adults . . . setting the table, washing dishes . . ."

7. Jean Piaget, *Play, Dreams and Imitation in Childhood*, trans. C. Gattegno and F. M. Hodgson (New York: W. W. Norton, 1962), p. 160. See also Brian Sutton-Smith, "Piaget, Play, and Cognition Revisited," in Willis F. Overton, *The Relationship between Social and Cognitive Development* (Hillsdale, NJ: Lawrence Erlbaum, 1983), p. 230. Sutton-Smith wrote that Piaget regarded play as "a predominantly infantile state of development." Mihai Spariosu outlines how Piaget described play in negative terms in *Dionysus Reborn: Play and the Aesthetic Dimension in Modern Philosophical and Scientific Discourse* (Ithaca, NY: Cornell University Press, 1989), p. 195. On Piaget's "attempts to discipline play, yoking it to rational rules and social order," see Spariosu, *Dionysus Reborn*, pp. 190–196.

8. Erik Erikson, *Toys and Reasons: Stages in the Ritualization of Experience* (New York: W. W. Norton, 1977), pp. 89–109; see also Erik Erikson, *Childhood and Society* (New York: W. W. Norton, 1963), p. 258. "The child must forget past hopes and wishes, while his exuberant imagination is tamed and harnessed. . . . For before the child, psychologically already a rudimentary parent, can become a biological parent, he must begin to be a worker."

9. John Dewey, *The Middle Works* (Carbondale: Southern Illinois University Press, 1976–1983), p. 340; Ryan, in *John Dewey*, p. 141, noted that for Dewey, children were "always being propelled toward adult competence."

10. John Dewey, *How We Think* (Boston: D. C. Heath, 1910), p. 162: "In order, then, that playfulness may not terminate in arbitrary fancifulness and in building up an imaginary world alongside the world of actual things, it is necessary that the play attitude should gradually pass into a work attitude." Dewey told parents and teachers that he had washed dishes himself and not found it "unimaginative and prosaic" in John Dewey, *Democracy and Education* (New York: Macmillan, 1916), p. 239.

11. The argument that Plato propounded the theory of bad and good play is developed in Spariosu, *Dionysus Reborn*.

12. James M. Sloat, "Freshman Forum: Thematic v. Reacting—a Multi-Stage Assessment," (unpublished, January 26, 2007): p. 10. The study's assessment is forthright: "As is apparent [from the data on student performance], students in the Reacting sections outperformed their Thematic peers in all groups and on all measures—with the exception of the Best students' treatment of the quotation from the exam." Sloat's researchers surveyed students and faculty, and examined student essays on a common theme at the end of the semester, pp. 11–13. Sloat also found that while the Thematic seminars seemed to work better for the middling students, the "best" and "worst" students flourished in Reacting. Sloat hypothesized: "Our Best students likely thrived in a setting where they were challenged to learn in different ways. Our Worst students likely benefited from the required engagement which is part of Reacting. Our Middling students, though, may have found the different curriculum to be unsettling—and occasionally disorienting. For such students, a Thematic curriculum may have provided the comfort level that allowed them to do their best work" (p. 13).

13. Sloat, "Freshman Forum," p. 4. When asked about the workload, students in the Thematic sections gave an average score of 3.2, whereas those in Reacting reported 4.0 (when 3.0 had been designated as "average," and 1.0 as "less than average"). And when students were asked about the amount of effort expended in the course, the Thematic average was 3.6 and the Reacting average was 2.7, when 3.0 had been designated "average" and 1.0 as "more than average."

14. Plato, *The Laws of Plato,* trans. Thomas Pangle (New York: Basic Books, 1980), p. 193.

15. Plato (Lee), *The Republic,* pp. 214, 265, 266. Classicist Josiah Ober noted that public speaking in Athens was a contest—"a game": "At least one object of the game [of giving speeches in the Assembly] was victory in making one's own distinct critical voice recognized," in *Political Dissent in Democratic Athens* (Princeton, NJ: Princeton University Press, 1998), p. 47.

16. Plato, *The Republic,* (Lee), p. 92.

17. See *HBS Case Development* at www.hbs.edu/faculty/research/Pages/case-development.aspx; last accessed June 19, 2013.

18. Candace C. Archer, Melissa K. Miller, "Prioritizing Active Learning: An Exploration of Gateway Courses in Political Science," *PS: Political Science and Politics*, 44, no. 2 (April 2011), pp. 431–432; Michelle Inderbitzin and Debbie A. Storrs, "Mediating the Conflict Between Transformative Pedagogy and Bureaucratic Practice," *College Teaching* 56, no. 1 (Winter 2008), p. 49. To be sure, some of the political science "simulations" included Reacting games, which usually last a full month.

19. Liz Grauerholz, "Getting Past Ideology for Effective Teaching," *Sociological Viewpoints* (Fall 2007): pp. 18–20; Leanne C. Powner, "Teaching the Scientific Method in the Active Learning Classroom," *PS: Political Science and Politics* 39, no. 3 (July 2006) p. 521.

20. See Corinne Auman, "Using Simulation Games to Increase Student and Instructor Engagement," *College Teaching* 59 (2011): pp. 154–161; E. J. Langer, *The Power of Mindful Learning* (Cambridge, MA: Da Capo Press, 1997); Jonathan Moizer, Jonathan Lean, Mike Towler, and Caroline Abbey, "Simulations and Games: Overcoming the Barriers to Their Use in Higher Education," *Active Learning in Higher Education* 10 (2009): pp. 207–224. Over the past decade scores of professors, after attending a Reacting training session, have told me that they tried "something like this" themselves. I always ask how it went and *without exception* they replied that such classes had been successful. Nearly all added that they didn't take their simulation "as far" as Reacting. Simulations are an effective active-learning pedagogy, but role-immersion games have a deeper psychological resonance and cognitive power.

21. By proposing a parallel to the pseudoscience of divination, I mean to suggest the insufficiency of reason in matters of pedagogy, while acknowledging that such a stance is preposterous in a book on higher education. In staking out this impossible position, however, I am emboldened by Kieran Egan's iconoclasm in *Getting It Wrong From the Beginning: Our Progressivist Inheritance from Herbert Spencer, John Dewey, and Jean Piaget* (New Haven: Yale University Press, 2002). Egan assumed the role of a "licensed fool" to argue that "most empirical research in education isn't empirical in the way commonly assumed," pp. 164–165. He added that educational researchers had neglected issues of imagination and emotion because such topics were difficult to research. Egan insisted that the "main problem" in educational theory is "our poverty in conceptions of

education"—for instance, this book asserts, its neglect of role-immersion games, p. 180.

22. Steve Kolowich, "In Deals With 10 Public Universities, Coursera Bids for Role in Credit Courses," *Chronicle of Higher Education* (May 30, 2013); Tamar Lewin, "Master's Degree Is New Frontier of Study Online," *New York Times* (August 17, 2013).

23. The apostles of doom are legion, though Harvard Business School professor Clayton Christensen may be high priest of the doomsayers: he predicts that half of the nation's universities (including public) will be bankrupt by 2028, in Cromwell Schubarth, "Disruption Guru Christensen: Why Apple, Tesla, VCs, Academia May Die," *Silicon Valley Business Journal* (February 7, 2013), online; last accessed July 25, 2013.

24. José Antonio Bowen, *Teaching Naked: How Moving Technology Out of Your College Classroom Will Improve Student Learning* (San Francisco: John Wiley and Sons, 2012), p. 13.

25. In December 2013 the Reacting Board, a dozen faculty and administrators and student alumni who govern the Reacting Consortium, affirmed that its mission is to promote in-class role-immersion games; it has not endorsed online variants.

1. "ALL CLASSES ARE SORTA BORING"

1. Adams, *The Education of Henry Adams* (New York: The Library of America/Viking, 1983), pp. 770, 777, 783.

2. Adams, *Education*, pp. 995–996, 997, 998.

3. Cited in Robert McCaughey, *Stand Columbia: A History of Columbia University in the City of New York, 1754–2004* (New York: Columbia University Press, 2003), p. 170.

4. Kim Townsend, *Manhood at Harvard: William James and Others* (New York: W. W. Norton, 1996), p. 120.

5. Cited in Donald Fleming, "Eliot's New Broom," in Bernard Bailyn, Donald Fleming, Oscar Handlin, and Stephan Thernstrom, *Glimpses of the Harvard Past* (Cambridge, MA: Harvard University Press, 1986), p. 70.

6. Cited in William Howe Tolman, *History of Higher Education in Rhode Island* (Washington, DC: Government Printing, 1894), p. 166.

7. Cited in McCaughey, *Stand Columbia*, p. 170.

8. Cited in McCaughey, *Stand Columbia*, p. 162.

9. George Santayana, *Character and Opinion in the United States* (New York: W. W. Norton, 1921), p. 53.

10. A. Lawrence Lowell, "Competition in College," *Atlantic Monthly* 31 (1909): p. 831.

11. Cited in Morton Keller and Phyllis Keller, *Making Harvard Modern: The Rise of America's University* (New York: Oxford University Press, 2001), p. 43. David Riesman, more temperate, shared the faculty skepticism toward undergraduates: apart from a "small minority" of potential scholars and future teachers, "the great majority" of his classmates cared little about academics, in David Riesman, "Education at Harvard," *Change* 5, no. 7 (September 1973), p. 26.

12. Judith N. Shklar, "A Life of Learning," *ACLS Occasional Paper*, no. 9 (1989): pp. 1041–1053. http://www.acls.org /Publications/OP/Haskins /1989_JudithNShklar.pdf.

13. Harry R. Lewis, *Excellence Without Soul: How a Great University Forgot Education* (New York: PublicAffairs Books, 2006). Derek Bok argues that notions of a golden age of higher education "have little foundation in fact," in *Our Underachieving Colleges* (Princeton, NJ: Princeton University Press, 2006), p. 29.

14. This paragraph is based solely on materials from Harvard, because it was widely regarded as the university that most embodied excellence in higher education. But the same story of student disengagement could be told for nearly any school with sufficient archival resources. Political scientist Philip E. Jacob, *Changing Values in College: An Exploratory Study of the Impact of College Teaching* (New York: Harper, 1957), found that in the 1940s only a minority of students at any college valued their education "primarily in terms of its intellectual contribution," cited in Tim Clydesdale, *The First Year Out: Understanding American Teens after High School* (Chicago: University of Chicago Press, 2007), p. 173. Or consider the University of Chicago, commonly cited as an institution that possessed resources comparable to Harvard and attracted more serious students. But future journalist Vincent Sheean described his cohort of undergraduates, himself included, as "a couple

thousand young nincompoops whose ambition in life was to get into the right fraternity or club, go to the right parties, and get elected to something or other." "No teacher," he added, "could have compelled full attention" from such students, in Vincent Sheean, *Personal History* (Boston: Houghton Mifflin, 1969), p. 9. Andrew Delbanco's evocation of liberal arts education at its finest includes plenty of examples of faculty who bemoaned the legions of disengaged students, in *College: What It Was, Is, and Should Be* (Princeton, NJ: Princeton University Press, 2011), pp. 17–18, 69–70. "One should always be wary of accounts of college life that posit some golden age" (p. 18).

15. Cited in *Declining by Degrees: Higher Education at Risk* (Learning Matters, 2005). Quotes are from the PBS Home Video.

16. See especially Charles Blaich, "Overview of Findings from the First Year of the Wabash National Study of Liberal Arts Education" (Wabash College, Center for Inquiry in the Liberal Arts, 2007, http://www.liberalarts.wabash.edu/storage/Overview_of_Findings_from_the_First_Year_web_07.17.09.pdf; last accessed April 2014). The Wabash study further found that two-thirds of fourth-year college students reported that their motivation either stayed the same or declined while they were in college: see Dan Berrett, "Can Colleges Manufacture Motivation?" *Chronicle of Higher Education* (April 15, 2012); and Mark Bauerlein, "A Very Long Disengagement," *Chronicle of Higher Education* (January 6, 2006).

17. These studies are summarized in Dan Berrett, "Can Colleges Manufacture Motivation?" *Chronicle of Higher Education.*

18. Richard Arum and Josipa Roksa, *Academically Adrift: Limited Learning on College Campuses* (Chicago: University of Chicago Press, 2011), p. 69. See also Philip Babcock and Mindy Marks, "Leisure College, USA: The Decline in Student Study Time," *Education Outlook,* no. 7 (August 2010): pp. 2–5.

19. Annie Beth Fox, Jonathan Rosen, and Mary Crawford, "Distractions, Distractions: Does Instant Messaging Affect College Students' Performance on a Concurrent Reading Comprehension Task?" *CyberPsychology and Behavior* 12, no. 1 (2009): p. 52. See also Matt Richtel, "Growing Up Digital, Wired for Distraction," *New York Times* (November 22, 2010).

20. Richard Arum and Josipa Roksa, *Academically Adrift,* p. 36. A 2008 survey of employers commissioned by the Association of American Colleges and Universities found that 31 percent of college graduates were not well prepared in critical thinking skills; only 21 percent were rated "very well prepared."

21. Derek Bok, *Underachieving Colleges,* p. 311. "Surveys of student progress in other important dimensions, including writing, numeracy, and foreign language proficiency, indicate that only a minority of undergraduates improve substantially, while some actually regress."

22. Tim Clydesdale, *The First Year Out,* p. 153, 163–164.

23. Rebekah Nathan, *My Freshman Year: What a Professor Learned by Becoming a Student* (Ithaca, NY: Cornell University Press, 2005), pp. 120, 100. "One-half came to class" (p. 120); "most sobering insight" (p. 100).

24. The White House, Office of the Press Secretary, "Remarks by the President in Conference Call with College and University Student-Journalists" (September 27, 2010). http://whitehouse.gov/.

25. See Jeffrey Brainard and Andrea Fuller, "Graduation Rates Fall at One-Third of 4-Year Colleges," *Chronicle of Higher Education* (December 5, 2010).

26. William G. Bowen, Matthew M. Chingos, and Michael S. McPherson, *Crossing the Finish Line: Completing College at America's Public Universities* (Princeton, NJ: Princeton University Press, 2009): pp. 25–26. "Figure 2.2 shows an overall bachelor's degree attainment rate of about 68 percent for the highest socioeconomic group. Although this rate is high relative to the attainment rates of the other groups, it seems low to us in an absolute sense. Common sense suggests that appreciably more than two-thirds of students from the most advantaged families in the country should be expected to earn bachelor's degrees" (p. 25); "We suspect that a combination of weak motivation or interest on the part of students . . . may be more consequential in causing a number of these students not to graduate" (pp. 220–221).

27. Moffatt ultimately blamed the students for their "marginally intellectual mentalities" and a "fairy-tale approach" to culture, in *Coming of Age in New Jersey: College and American Culture* (New Brunswick, NJ: Rutgers University Press, 1989), p. 326, n. 43.

28. Elizabeth A. Armstrong and Laura T. Hamilton, *Paying for the Party: How College Maintains Inequality* (Cambridge, MA: Harvard University Press, 2013), p. 15; George D. Kuh, "What We're Learning about Student Engagement from NSSE: Benchmarks for Effective Educational Practices," *Change* 35, no. 2 (2003): pp. 24–32; Geoffrey L. Collier, "We Pretend to Teach, They Pretend to Learn," *Wall Street Journal* (December 26, 2013); Murray Sperber, *Beer and Circus: How Big-Time College Sports Is Crippling Undergraduate Education* (New York: Henry Holt, 2000).

29. On the mutual incomprehension of students and faculty, see Rebecca D. Cox, *The College Fear Factor: How Students and Professors Misunderstand One Another* (Cambridge, MA: Harvard University Press, 2009), pp. 10–12.

30. Adams, *Education*, p. 996.

31. "Dean Hanford and the Future of the College," *Crimson* (February 10, 1934). On the one student in ten, see also Henry Seidel Canby, *Alma Mater: The Gothic Age of the American College* (New York: Arno, 1975), p. 88. The book was originally published by Farrar and Rinehart in 1936. Anthropologist Michael Moffatt, more optimistic, estimated that "somewhere between 10 and 20 percent" of the undergraduates he studied at Rutgers in the 1980s were "friendly toward the life of the mind," *Coming of Age in New Jersey: College and American Culture* (New Brunswick, NJ: Rutgers University Press, 1989), p. 300.

32. Barack Obama, *Dreams from My Father* (New York: Random House, 1995), p. 96.

33. Michael Ellsberg, "Will Dropouts Save America?" *New York Times* (October 22, 2011). "I'd put my money on the kids who are dropping out of college to start new businesses," he wrote.

34. Bok, *Underachieving Colleges*, p. 318.

35. Bok, *Underachieving Colleges*, pp. 323, 325. "What are the prospects . . . not good" (p. 323); "off the radar screen" (p. 325). See also Larry Cuban, *How Scholars Trumped Teachers: Change Without Reform in University Curriculum, Teaching, and Research, 1890–1990* (New York: Teachers College Press, 1999), p. 4.

36. Purvi Mehta, after completing a Ph.D. in history and anthropology, teaches history at Colorado College. Fiza Quraishi is a staff

attorney at the National Center for Youth Law doing policy reform for foster children and youth in the juvenile justice system. Diana Paquin Morel teaches fourth- and fifth-graders at the John Middleton School in Skokie, Illinois, intent on making the curriculum come alive.

37. The spread of Reacting was likely accelerated in 2004 by its winning the Theodore Hesburgh Award (funded by TIAA-CREF) for pedagogical innovation in higher education.

38. The Reacting Consortium includes an Editorial Board, which provides guidance and oversight to some sixty teams of scholars involved in designing and testing new games; other administrative structures promote development of online resources for Reacting faculty and administrators, including discussions, webinars, and podcasts. The Reacting Consortium also holds a summer institute in New York every year, along with dozens of campus and regional workshops. See www.barnard.edu /reacting. Scores of volunteer faculty and administrators lead all of these initiatives.

2. SUBVERSIVE PLAY: THE BANE OF HIGHER EDUCATION

1. Henry Seidel Canby, *College Sons and College Fathers* (New York: Harper, 1915), pp. 1–2, 5–9, 85–89, 105–109.

2. Canby, *College Sons,* pp. 105–109.

3. This account is described in his memoir, *Alma Mater: The Gothic Age of the American College* (New York: Arno, 1975).

4. Canby, *Alma Mater,* p. 25.

5. Canby, *Alma Mater,* pp. 28, 25.

6. Canby, *Alma Mater,* pp. 40, 29, 49, 73.

7. Historian Helen Horowitz has suggested that the competitiveness of fraternities and athletics "turned the boy into a man prepared for success in the competitive world of American business," in *Campus Life: Undergraduate Culture from the End of the Eighteenth Century to the Present* (Chicago: University of Chicago Press, 1987), p. 41.

8. Johan Huizinga, *Homo Ludens: A Study of the Play-Element in Culture* (Boston: Beacon Press, 1950), pp. 5, 71.

9. Huizinga, *Homo Ludens,* pp. 2, 71. Also, deep play engendered feelings of "rapture and enthusiasm" and of "exaltation and tension" (p. 132). Huizinga finally proposed that the "primary thing" was the "desire to excel others," in *Homo Ludens,* p. 50.

10. Canby, *Alma Mater,* p. 19.

11. Canby, *Alma Mater,* pp. 19, 29.

12. Plato, *The Republic,* trans. Desmond Lee (New York: Penguin, 1953), p. 126.

13. Victor Turner, *The Forest of Symbols: Aspects of Ndembu Ritual* (Ithaca, NY: Cornell University Press, 1967), pp. 265–266, 271–272. See also Robert Anchor, "History and Play: Johan Huizinga and His Critics," *History and Theory* 17, no. 1 (February 1978): p. 93.

14. Victor Turner, *Dramas, Fields and Metaphors: Symbolic Action in Human Society* (Ithaca, NY: Cornell University Press, 1974), p. 243; also Turner, "Poverty: Religious Symbols of Communitas," in Joan Vincent, ed., *The Anthropology of Politics: A Reader in Ethnography, Theory, and Technique* (Malden, MA: Blackwell Publishers, 2002), p. 99.

15. Mikhail Bakhtin, *Rabelais and His World,* trans. Helene Iswolsky (Bloomington, IN: Indiana University Press, 1984), p. 251.

16. Bakhtin held that in such contexts the "peculiar logic" of "inside out" prevailed, in *Rabelais,* p. 11. Victor Turner observed a similar inversion of mental processes among the Ndembu, whose circumcision rituals featured songs in which high-flying birds improbably laid eggs in the nests of ground-loving storks; and a type of lizard, famously known for its skittishness, attacked deadly snakes. To the Ndembu, whose lives were regulated by nature, such juxtapositions were nonsense, "a complete reversal of the natural order," in *The Forest of Symbols,* p. 192.

17. Turner identified these special rituals as "liminal," from the Greek for "threshold," because they occurred as individuals (or society itself) moved from one state (or status) to another. (Puberty rites were an obvious example.) Turner further described such rites as "social dramas" in which one's former identity was challenged or the normal workings of society were "breached," in Turner, *From Ritual to Theatre,* p. 10. See also Turner, "Social Dramas and Stories about Them," in W. J. T. Mitchell, ed., *On Narrative* (Chicago: University of Chicago Press, 1981), p. 162.

Turner, citing Jung, argues that symbols are the "best possible expression" of an "*unknown* fact" (emphasis in original), in *The Forest of Symbols*, p. 26.

18. White, "College Fraternities," *The Forum* (May 1887), p. 249.

19. Huizinga, *Homo Ludens*, p. 8.

20. Canby, *Alma Mater*, pp. 25, 26.

21. Canby, *Alma Mater*, pp. 19, 25, 29, 35, 43, 72, 73.

22. Canby, *Alma Mater*, p. 35.

23. Bakhtin, *Rabelais*, p. 6. For a briefer chronicle of student resistance to the academic side of higher education, see Andrew Delbanco, *College: What It Was, Is, and Should Be* (Princeton, NJ: Princeton University Press, 2011), pp. 17–21.

24. Henry Sheldon, *Student Life and Customs* (New York: D. Appleton, 1901), p. 126; also Nicholas L. Syrett, *The Company He Keeps: A History of White College Fraternities* (Chapel Hill: University of North Carolina Press, 2009), pp. 38–41.

25. Steven Sowards, "Library Systems Under a Dual Collection, Hanover College, 1827–1909," *Libraries and Culture* 4, no. 3 (Summer 1989): pp. 319–320.

26. Faculty often bitterly opposed the society's debates, orations, and other "exhibitions," one student recalled, "on the ground of their engrossing too much attention from the students." See Lyman Hotchkiss Bagg, *Four Years at Yale* (New Haven: C. C. Chatfield, 1871), p. 203; also Syrett, *The Company He Keeps*, p. 39. On the failure to combine rival literary societies, see Sheldon, *Student Life*, p. 128.

27. On the fraternities' role in crushing the debating societies, see Frederick Rudolph, *The American College and University: A History* (New York: Alfred A. Knopf, 1962), pp. 144–145; also Sheldon, *Student Life*, pp. 133–135.

28. The competitive ethos within the fraternities was bound up with issues of masculinity, notes Nicholas Syrett, in *The Company He Keeps*, pp. 38–39, 150. But proving one's masculinity is itself a social competition.

29. Cited in Sheldon, *Student Life*, p. 185; also E. E. Aiken, *The Secret Society System* (New Haven: O. H. Briggs, 1882), p. 185. Into the twenty-first century, the competitions within fraternities and sororities remain as brutal as ever. Social scientists Armstrong and Hamilton found it "heart-

wrenching" to observe the pain inflicted upon women who had "failed" in these social competitions at a large midwestern university; see Elizabeth A. Armstrong and Laura T. Hamilton, *Paying for the Party: How Colleges Maintain Inequality* (Cambridge, MA: Harvard University Press, 2013), p. 95; see also 74–81.

30. On the prevalence of death in such rituals, see Sheldon, *Student Life,* p. 173.

31. Cited in Horowitz, *Campus Life,* p. 53. This attitude persisted. For example, in the late twentieth century, a fraternity initiate described the speech he had listened to after a brutal hazing, when members had dumped excrement and urine on him, inducing him to vomit, and then obliging him and the other pledges to clean it up. The fraternity official explained that "the shackles of sense have been burst once again." He alluded to the "chaos" of the hazing, and praised the initiates for having endured "a full day of insanity." "Your mind," he added, "was miraculously transformed into a yo-yo," cited in Peggy Reeves Sandy, *Fraternity Gang Rape: Sex, Brotherhood, and Privilege on Campus* (New York: New York University Press, 2007), pp. 157–158.

32. Horowtiz, *Campus Life,* pp. 36, 39.

33. James McCosh, "Discipline in American College," *North American Review* 16: p. 440.

34. Syrett, *The Company He Keeps,* pp. 34–37. Syrett notes that the "point" of the fraternities was that they were "illicit, illegal, and clandestine," p. 37. See also Edward Hitchcock, "Reminiscences of Amherst College," pp. 321–325, cited in Sheldon, *Student Life,* p. 180. Rudolph wrote that in fraternities, "students erected within the gates a monster," in *American Colleges and Universities,* p. 155.

35. On fraternities and the demise of the debating societies, see Syrett, *The Company He Keeps,* pp. 38–39; also Bagg, *Four Years at Yale,* p. 219.

36. *Annual Report of President and Treasurer of Harvard College, 1892–93,* p. 14, cited in Sheldon, *Student Life,* p. 239, also p. 242 fn.

37. Cited in Kim Townsend, *Manhood at Harvard* (New York: W. W. Norton, 1996), p. 111, from a section of a 1904 report entitled "The Evils of Football."

38. See an 1897–1898 report to the United States Commissioner of Education, as cited in Sheldon, *Student Life,* p. 243 fn.

39. Cited in John R. Thelin, *A History of American Higher Education* (Baltimore: Johns Hopkins Press, 2004) p. 178. As late as 1897, after Harvard administrators proposed to wrest intercollegiate athletics from students, a faculty committee declared that students "ought to be given so far as possible, a free hand in the management of *their* sports (emphasis added)," cited in Townsend, *Manhood at Harvard,* p. 119.

40. Robert McCaughey, *Stand Columbia: A History of Columbia University in the City of New York, 1754–2004* (New York: Columbia University Press, 2003), pp. 279–280.

41. Woodrow Wilson, "What Is a College For?" *Scribner's Magazine* 46, no. 5 (November 1909): p. 576.

42. Wilson's impotence confirmed Canby's judgment that while faculty might deplore the world the students made, it was "folly and destruction to attack it," in *College Sons and Fathers,* pp. 10–14, 24.

43. See Horowitz, *Campus Life,* p. 142; Syrett, *The Company He Keeps,* pp. 144–149; and Armstrong and Hamilton, *Paying for the Party,* pp. 59, 217.

44. Horowitz, *Campus Life,* p. 39.

45. See Ann Schnoebelen, "After a Ban of 80 Years, Sisterhood Takes Hold at Swarthmore," *Chronicle of Higher Education* (June 3, 2013).

46. Henry Wechsler and Bernice Wuethrich, *Dying to Drink: Confronting Binge Drinking on College Campuses* (New York: Rodale Books, 2002), p. 118; also see Bruce Horovitz, Theresa Howard, and Laura Petrecca, "Alcohol Makers on Tricky Path in Marketing to College Crowd," *USA Today* (November 16, 2005).

47. Murray Sperber, *Beer and Circus: How Big-Time College Sports Is Crippling Undergraduate Education* (New York: Macmillan, 2000), p. 157. Advertisers were likely aware of the theoretical power of alcohol as a "liminal" cultural construct through articles in consumer research publications. See, for example, Robert V. Kozinets et al., "Ludic Agency and Retail Spectacle," *Journal of Consumer Research* 31 (December 2004), p. 658.

48. Cited in Sperber, *Beer and Circus,* p. 188.

49. Hoyt Alverson, "Students' Social Life at Dartmouth College: Reflections in Their Looking Glass," (February 15, 2005): pp. 12–13; last accessed October 18, 2011: http://www.dartmouth.edu/~dcare/pdfs/dartmouth-drinking.pdf. Beer pong became so popular that it was banned by scores of colleges and universities. Yet the appeal of the drinking game

itself was such that many students continued to play—with water. In 2007 officials at Dartmouth, concerned over reports of water intoxication, banned water pong as well, in Meaghan Haire, "The War Against Beer Pong," *Time* (July 31, 2008); and Ben Nunner, "Water Pong Banned, Risks of Overhydrating Cited," *Dartmouth* (February 5, 2007).

50. Barrett Seaman, *Binge: Campus Life in an Age of Disconnection and Excess* (Hoboken, NJ: John Wiley and Sons, 2005), p. 116.

51. Alverson, a senior anthropologist at Dartmouth who had been assigned to head up a task force, concluded that binge drinking was not a problem of student behavior but of student culture, in "Students' Social Life," p. 11. That college drinking is best understood as a "cultural" phenomenon is also the thesis of George W. Dowdall, *College Drinking: Reframing a Social Problem* (Westport, CT: Praeger, 2009), p. 5. "Culture powerfully shapes the way those seeking to study or to change college drinking operate." Dowdall added that at one-third of American universities, where more than half of the students reportedly engage in binge drinking, drinking had become the "expected behavior" of most students, p. 152.

52. Claire Potter, "Forget the SATS. How Many Days Did Your Students Drink Last Week?" *Chronicle of Higher Education* (September 24, 2011).

53. Drinking has always played a prominent part in the lives of college students: The original literary and debating societies met in taverns. But college drinking has changed substantially in the past half-century. A statistical study of college drinking in 1949 concluded that the proportion of students who drank frequently and heavily was "very small." One male student in five, and one female student in fifty, reported that he or she had been drunk more than five times in college, in Robert Strauss and Selden D. Bacon, *Drinking in College* (New Haven: Yale University Press, 1953), pp. 116, 133. The percentage of students drinking was "very small" (p. 116); 8 percent of males, 1 percent of females, drunk more than five times (p. 133). Comparable data for subsequent decades is unavailable. But by 1993, when the Harvard School of Public Health conducted the first of four large statistical studies of college drinking, one male student in four, and one female in six, reported that he or she had been drunk three or more times during the previous thirty *days,* in Dowdall, *College Drinking,*

pp. 27, 28. Data was extrapolated from tables 2.1 and 2.2, pp. 27 and 28, respectively. The studies further showed that nearly half of the students in the 1993 sample were "binge drinkers" ("five or more alcoholic drinks at a sitting in past two weeks") and one in five was a "frequent binge drinker"—having gone on a binge *three* times or more within the previous two weeks; Dowdall, *College Drinking*, pp. 29–31, summarizes the studies. The data is from the Harvard School of Public Health College and Alcohol Studies; it uses the definition of "binge drinker" as a male who has had five drinks "at a sitting" or "within two hours" or a female who has had four drinks in the same conditions. See Dowdall, *College Drinking*, p. 83, on the stability since 1980 of two-fifths of college students as binge drinkers, with one-fifth as "frequent binge drinkers," moving slowly up to nearly one-fourth.

54. Craig Brandon, *The Five-Year Party: How Colleges Have Given Up On Educating Your Child and What You Can Do About It* (Dallas, TX: Benbella Books, 2010), p. 87.

55. See especially Henry Wechsler and Bernice Wuethrich, *Dying to Drink*, pp, 4–6; also, R. W. Hingson, W. Zha, E. R. Weitzman, "Magnitude of and Trends in Alcohol-Related Mortality and Morbidity Among U.S. College Students Ages 18–24, 1998–2005," *Journal of Studies on Alcohol and Drugs Supplement* 16 (2009): pp. 20–20. For updated information, see www.niaaa.hin.gov.

56. Jennifer Conlin, "University of Shmacked," *New York Times* (September 23, 2012).

57. Horovitz, Howard, and Petrecca, "Alcohol Makers on Tricky Path." By 2011, surveys showed that 99 percent of teenage boys and 94 percent of teenage girls played video games regularly, in Jane McGonigal, *Reality Is Broken: Why Games Make Us Better and How They Can Change the World* (New York: Penguin Press, 2011).

58. A 2012 Pew Research survey of twenty-seven colleges and universities found that 65 percent of college students played video and online games every day and that 77 percent were video "gamers," in Lee Rainie, "Homo Connectus," *Pew Research Center Internet and American Life Project* (2007): http://www.pewinternet.org/2007/11/05/homo-connectus-the-impact-of-technology-on-peoples-everyday-lives/; last accessed April 2014. See also Marisa Hivner, "Video Game Culture: College Students' Obsession with Gaming," *Reporting and the Internet* (August 4, 2012).

59. See David Golumbia, "Games Without Play," *New Literary History* 40 (2009), pp. 188–189. See also T. L. Taylor, *Play Between Worlds* (Cambridge, MA: MIT Press, 2006), p. 76.

60. Elena Bertozzi, "Marking the Territory: Grand Theft Auto IV as a Playground for Masculinity," in David Embrick, ed., *Social Exclusion, Power and Video Game Play: New Research in Digital Media and Technology* (Blue Ridge Summit, PA: Lexington Books, 2012), p. 3. Conversely, even brilliantly conceived online games that eschew competition and subversive elements often fail; for example, see Celia Pearce, *Communities of Play: Emergent Cultures in Multiplayer Games and Virtual Worlds* (Cambridge, MA: MIT Press, 2009), p. 15.

61. Jeannine Stein, "For College Students, Video Games May Not Be an Innocuous Pursuit," *Los Angeles Times* (January 27, 2009).

62. Ernest Cavalli, "FCC Commissioner Blames WoW for College Dropouts," *Wired.com* (December 18, 2008): http://www.wired.com/2008/12/fcc-commish-bla/; last accessed April 2014.

63. Ben Mezrich, *Accidental Billionaires: The Founding of Facebook* (New York: Doubleday, 2009), pp. 44–45.

64. Howard Gardner and Katie Davis, *The App Generation: How Today's Youth Navigate Identity, Intimacy, and Imagination in a Digital World* (New Haven: Yale University Press, 2013), p. 63. Gardner and Davis report: "We gathered considerable evidence that [young people] take care to present a socially desirable, *polished self* online."

65. These quotes are from author interviews with Columbia and Barnard undergraduates who preferred to remain anonymous. On the intense competition that characterizes social media, Neeraj Vedwan writes: "An aspect of sociality that is often neglected by the social media cheerleaders is the tendency of participants to engage in competitive status enhancement by strategically positioning themselves as superior to others," in "Does Facebook Make Us Happy?" *Anthropology Now* 5, no. 2 (September 2013): p. 89; a Stanford study found that a large majority of undergraduates felt more inadequate and unhappy after using social media, in Alexander H. Jordan, Benoit Monin, Carol Dweck, Benjamin Lovett, Oliver John, and James Gross, "Misery Has More Company Than People Think: Underestimating the Prevalence of Others' Negative Emotions," *Personality and Social Psychology Bulletin* 37, no. 1 (2011): pp. 120–135.

66. See also Sherry Turkle, *Alone Together: Why We Expect More From Technology and Less From Each Other* (New York: Basic Books, 2011), pp. 153, 212.

67. Rick Nauert, "New College Addiction? Social Media, Facebook or Friends," psychcentral.com (April 23, 2010): psychcentral.com/news/2010/04/23/new-college-addiction-social-media-facebook-or-friends/13108.html; last accessed August 24, 2011.

68. "U. of Nebraska Bans Assassins Game," *USA Today* (March 7, 2008). I appreciate the comments of Jonathan Truitt, who provided first-person testimony on the origins of "Assassins," email of October 6, 2013.

69. Julianna Baggott, "Tag for the Gamer Generation," *Boston Globe* (March 16, 2010).

70. Armstrong and Hamilton, *Paying for the Party*, p. 251.

71. Canby, *Alma Mater*, pp. 46, 48.

72. In 2011 David Rosengrant, a physicist at Kennesaw State University, persuaded a sampling of his students to wear eye-tracking glasses during his lecture classes; he found that they were looking at him only 30 percent of the time; most of the time they were on Facebook or texting. "I thought the students would really spend a large majority of the time focused on me," he reported. See Angela Chen, "Eye-Tracking Study Finds Students' Attentiveness Depends on Location, Location, Location," *Chronicle of Higher Education* (August 1, 2012); another study found that 91 percent of the students in another lecture class used their phones to text message during classes, in Deborah R. Tindell and Robert W. Bohlander, "The Use and Abuse of Cell Phones and Text Messaging in the Classroom," *College Teaching* 60, no. 1 (2012).

73. Of the fifty-three students they studied who lived on a single dormitory floor, Hamilton and Armstrong concluded that "a tiny fraction"—perhaps only seven—exited the university "with the kind of credentials or human capital that many expect all college graduates to acquire" (p. 251). Armstrong and Hamilton call for elimination of the Greek system; but they note that "no large public university has taken this step," in *Paying for the Party* (p. 235). They also sensibly call for "scaling back college athletics" (p. 236), but concede that this is unlikely (pp. 236–237).

3. CREATING AN ACADEMIC SUBVERSIVE PLAY WORLD

1. The account of that class was based on several sources, including interviews with Nate Gibson, Linda Schroedermeier, and other students in 2013 and 2014; these were supplemented by six newspapers, containing some two dozen student essays—that have survived, nine years after the class. The newspapers also included photographs of the students: Linda's face, for example, was Photoshopped onto Lafayette's body. Because the essays referred to actions the previous week, and because the students had some strong recollections, it was fairly simple to reconstruct the debates and the course of the game.

2. On reviewing these words, Nate sent an explanatory follow-up: Prior to Reacting, he wrote, he "truly believed" that he was a hard worker and good student: "My reasoning was that good grades were a sign of hard work. I simply didn't have a context to understand what hard work was." His Reacting course had provided a "wake-up call" because the stakes had to do with something other than grades. "Reacting," he added, "helped to broaden my view on what it meant to work hard and to really learn." The other students cited in this chapter said almost exactly the same thing.

3. Cited in Andrew Delbanco, *College: What It Was, Is, and Should Be* (Princeton, NJ: Princeton University Press), p. 33. Shapiro is now president of the Teagle Foundation.

4. CRITICAL THINKING AND OUR SELVES

1. A video of this class, including Fareeda and Joshua (and many of the quotes cited here), appears online, in "The Struggle for Palestine in the 1930s," at www.barnard.edu/reacting.

2. In response to such encounters, Reacting game designers have created "neutral" roles that allow students to observe or respond to a Reacting class without being obliged to voice opinions that contravene their core beliefs. I created such a role for Angela: she was to keep a diary, commenting on what transpired in the class's Boston, 1636–1637, modeled after Samuel Pepys's chronicle of London. This gave her something to do; I doubt it was an especially good educational experience.

3. Kathleen Taylor, *Brainwashing: The Science of Thought Control* (New York: Oxford University Press, 2004), pp. 124–125, p. 129. See also Dominic Streatfeild, *Brainwash: The Secret History of Mind Control* (New York: St. Martin's Press, 2006), p. 348; and David L. Morgan and Michael L. Schwalbe, "Mind and Self in Society: Linking Social Structure and Social Cognition," *Social Psychology Quarterly* 53, no. 2 (June 1990): p. 150. The "overwhelming empirical evidence for the stability of self-concepts" is summarized in J. M. Cheek and R. Hogan, "Self-concepts, Self-presentations, and Moral Judgments," in J. Suls and A. G. Greenwald, eds., *Psychological Perspectives on the Self,* Vol. 2 (Hillsdale, NJ: Lawrence Erlbaum, 1983), p. 256.

4. Some neurobiologists contend that a fixed self is likely part of our genetic heritage. This argument is summarized by Carl Zimmer, "The Neurobiology of the Self," *Scientific American* (November 2005): p. 100.

5. The neurological hierarchy of the "self" is outlined in Todd E. Feinberg, *From Axons to Identity: Neurological Explorations of the Nature of the Self* (New York: W. W. Norton, 2009).

6. Antonio Damasio, *Self Comes to Mind: Constructing the Conscious Brain* (New York: Vintage, 2010), pp. 62–64; see also Todd E. Feinberg, *From Axons to Identity,* pp. 151–152.

7. Damasio, *Self Comes to Mind,* p. 25.

8. George Northoff, Alexander Heinzel, Moritz de Breck, Felix Bermpohl, Henrik Dobrowolny, and Jaak Panksepp, "Self-Referential Processing in Our Brain—A Meta-analysis of Imaging Studies of the Self," *NeuroImage* 31, no. 2 (February 2, 2006): pp. 440–457; Georg Northoff and Felix Bermpohl, "Cortical Midline Structures and the Self," *Trends in Cognitive Sciences* 8, no. 3 (March 2004): p. 103; and Jennifer J. Summerfield, Demis Hasasbis, and Eleanor A. Maguire, "Cortical Midline Involvement in Autobiographical Memory," *NeuroImage* 44, no. 3 (February 1, 2009): pp. 1188–1200.

9. Psychologists have found, for example, that test subjects recall and process words and associations related to their "self aspects" more rapidly than other familiar words; see Kurt Hugenberg and Galen Bodenhausen, "Category Membership Moderates the Inhibition of Social Identities," *Journal of Experimental Social Psychology* 40 (2004): pp. 233–238; Allen

R. McConnell, Tonya M. Shoda, and Hayley M. Skulborstad, "The Self as a Collection of Multiple Self-Aspects: Structure, Development, Operation, and Implications," *Social Cognition* 30, no. 4 (2012), pp. 384–385.

10. William James, *Principles of Psychology*, Vol. 1 (New York: Henry Holt, 1890), p. 294.

11. George Herbert Mead, *Mind, Self, and Society* (Chicago: University of Chicago Press, 1962), p. 182. Originally published in 1934.

12. James, *Principles of Psychology*, p. 310.

13. Kathleen Taylor, *Brainwashing*, pp. 124–125; see also Morgan and Schwalbe, "Mind and Self in Society," p. 150; and James E. Zull, "The Art of Changing the Brain," *Educational Leadership* 62, no. 1 (2004): pp. 68–72.

14. Linda J. Sax, Alexander W. Astin, William S. Korn, and Shannon K. Gilmartin, *The American College Teacher: National Norms for the 1989–1999 HERI Faculty Survey* (1999), p. 36; cited in Derek Bok, *Our Underachieving Colleges* (Princeton, NJ: Princeton University Press, 2006), p. 68. A study from 1998–1999, found that 99.5 percent of faculty in four-year colleges regarded "ability to think clearly" to be "essential" or "very important," Bok, *Underachieving Colleges*, p. 68, fn 20.

15. Cited in Richard Arum and Josipa Roksa, *Academically Adrift: Limited Learning on College Campuses* (Chicago: University of Chicago Press, 2011), p. 35.

16. Statistics from *College Learning for the New Global Century: A Report from the National Leadership* (Washington, DC: American Association of Colleges and Universities, 2007), p. 8.

17. Bok, *Our Underachieving Colleges*, p. 116; see also Ernest T. Pascarella and Patrick T. Terenzini, *How College Affects Students*, Vol. 2 (San Francisco: Jossey-Bass, 2005), p. 205. Bok observed that "the gains reported by Pascarella and Terenzini merely show that average seniors raise their ability from the fiftieth to the sixty-ninth percentile of *their entering freshman cohort*" (emphasis in original)," p. 116. Timothy Clydesdale argues that even these unimpressive results were inflated because the studies were funded "to a substantial degree" by the colleges and universities themselves, in Clydesdale, *The First Year Out: Understanding American Teens after High School* (Chicago: University of Chicago Press, 2007), p. 171.

18. Arum and Roksa, *Academically Adrift*, p. 121. See also Charles Blaich, "Overview of Findings from the First Year of the Wabash National Study of Liberal Arts Education" (Wabash College, Center for Inquiry in the Liberal Arts, 2007): www.liberalarts.wabash.edu/research/. A 2008 survey of employers commissioned by the Association of American Colleges and Universities found that 31 percent of college graduates were not well prepared in critical thinking skills; only 21 percent were rated "very well prepared": www.aacu.org/leap.

19. Lee S. Shulman, *Teaching as Community Property* (San Francisco: Jossey-Bass, 2004), p. 36. See also Susan A. Ambrose, Michael W. Bridges, Michele DiPietro, Marsha C. Lovett, and Marie K. Norman, eds., *How Learning Works: Seven Research-Based Principles for Smart Teaching* (San Francisco: John Wiley and Sons, 2010), pp. 11–27; Ken Bain, *What the Best College Teachers Do* (Cambridge, MA: Harvard University Press, 2004), pp. 27–32.

20. Cited in Daniel Garber, "Descartes, or the Cultivation of the Intellect," in Amelie Rorty, ed., *Philosophers of Education* (London: Routledge, 1998), p. 125.

21. Jean-Jacques Rousseau, *Emile,* trans. Allan Bloom (New York: Basic Books, 1978), p. 207.

22. Bok, *Our Underachieving Colleges*, pp. 126, 117.

23. Allan Bloom, *The Closing of the American Mind* (New York: Simon and Schuster, 1987), p. 272; Martha Nusssbaum, *Cultivating Humanity: A Classical Defense of Reform in Liberal Education* (Cambridge, MA: Harvard University Press, 1997), p. 19.

24. Andrew Delbanco, *College: What It Was, Is, and Should Be* (Princeton, NJ: Princeton University Press, 2012), p. 53.

25. Friedrich Nietzsche, *Twilight of the Idols,* trans. Walter Kaufmann, in *The Viking Portable Nietzsche* (New York: Viking, 1968), p. 476. Alexander Nehamas wrote that Nietzsche's conclusion that the Socratic dialectic "is not very persuasive . . . seems to me to be exactly right," in Alexander Nehamas, *Virtues of Authenticity: Essays on Plato and Socrates* (Princeton, NJ: Princeton University Press, 1999), p. 71.

26. Gregory Vlastos, ed., *The Philosophy of Socrates: A Collection of Critical Essays* (Garden City: Doubleday, 1971), p. 2; John Beverslius, *Cross-Examining Socrates: A Defense of the Interlocutors in Plato's Early Dialogues*

(Cambridge: Cambridge University Press, 2000), p. 5, fn 5. Beverslius notes that twenty years later Vlastos slightly modified this language, replacing "never" with "seldom, if ever," p. 5, fn 5. See also Thomas Schmid, "Socratic Dialectic in the *Charmides*," in Gary Alan Scott, ed., *Does Socrates Have a Method? Rethinking the Elenchus in Plato's Dialogues and Beyond* (University Park, PA: Penn State University Press, 2002), pp. 235ff.

27. Gary Alan Scott, *Plato's Socrates as Educator* (Albany, NY: SUNY Press, 2000), p. 162.

28. Beverslius, *Cross-Examining Socrates*, p. 34.

29. Some classicists suggest that Plato asserted Socrates's limitations as a teacher in order to rebut the principal charge leveled during Socrates's trial. If Socrates never persuaded anyone of anything, then he could not have been guilty of "corrupting" the youth of Athens.

30. Cited in Beverslius, *Cross-Examining Socrates*, p. 38.

31. On the Socratic *elenchus* as a form of ad hominem attack, see Charles H. Kahn, *Plato and the Socratic Dialogue: The Philosophical Use of a Literary Form* (Cambridge: Cambridge University Press, 1996), pp. 125–147. "As we have seen, the Socratic *elenchus* was originally more a testing of persons than of propositions," p. 133; also Richard Robinson, *Plato's Earlier Dialectic* (Ithaca, NY: Cornell University Press, 1941), pp. 15–17.

32. Classicists have consigned forests to pulp in response to this question. Alexander Nehamas put it this way: "How do two people who are ignorant of the answer to a given question discover that answer and how do they realize that they have discovered it? If the *elenchus* [the interrogatory method of Socrates] presents a serious methodological question, this is it," cited in Alexander Nehamas, "Meno's Paradox and Socrates as a Teacher," in Jane M. Day, ed., *Plato's Meno in Focus* (New York: Routledge, 1994), p. 233.

33. Cited in Richard Robinson, *"Elenchus,"* in Vlastos, *The Philosophy of Socrates*, p. 81.

34. See, for example, Hayden W. Ausland, "Forensic Characteristics of Socratic Argumentation," in Gary Alan Scott, *Does Socrates Have a Method?* (University Park, PA: Penn State University Press, 2001), p. 37. Ausland observed that the Greek verb for *elenchus* means "primarily 'to impugn the honor of' a person" and he claimed that the use of the term in Socratic literature was "clearly at least shaped by this background" (p. 37).

See also François Renaud, "Humbling as Upbringing: The Ethical Dimension of the Elenchus in the *Lysis*," in Scott, *Does Socrates Have a Method?* pp. 194–195, including fn 42.

35. Robert Wellman argues that "shame" is "a bit too weak" a translation: "It is perhaps better rendered disgraceful, base, or ugly," in Robert R. Wellman, "Socrates and Alcibiades: The Alcibiades Major," *History of Education Quarterly* 6, no. 4 (Winter 1966): p. 10. See Gary Alan Scott, *Plato's Socrates as Educator* (Albany: SUNY Press, 2000), p. 7; and Schmid, "Socratic Dialectic in the *Charmides*," in Scott, *Does Socrates Have a Method?* p. 247.

36. Socrates perhaps conceived of his *elenchus* as an alternative to the Eleusinian rites, which broke an adolescent male's ties to childhood and initiated his rebirth into the brotherhood of men. Socratic interrogations functioned in a similar way. The "true *elenchus*," one scholar observed, was "no mere philosophical conversation" but a "'going down' of the whole self" that prepared the interlocutor for a rebirth of a new self, in Schmid, "Socratic Dialectic in the *Charmides*," in Scott, *Does Socrates Have a Method?* p. 247. Scott writes that a precondition for the *elenchus* is a letting go "of their former selves, relinquishing the identity they presently have," in *Socrates as Educator*, p. 167.

37. Alexander Nehamas, *The Art of Living: Socratic Reflections from Plato to Foucault* (Berkeley: University of California Press, 1998), p. 65; P. T. Geach called Socratic dialectic morally harmful in "Plato's *Euthyphro:* An Analysis and Commentary," *The Monist* 50 (1966): p. 372. Cited in Beverslius, *Cross-Examining*, p. 15.

38. Cited in Robinson, "*Elenchus*," in Vlastos, *The Philosophy of Socrates*, p. 91.

39. Paul D. Carrington, "Hail! Langdell!" *Law and Social Inquiry* 20 (1995): pp. 748, 740. Eliot's reference to Langdell's method as "intensely active" was cited in Peggy Cooper Davis and Elizabeth Ehrenfest Steinglass, "A Dialogue About Socratic Teaching," *NYU Review of Law and Social Change* 23 (1997): p. 249.

40. One law student, looking back on the "brutally aggressive" Socratic approach of William Keener, dean of the Columbia law school, recalled that students' first reaction was "a bitter hatred of this man who had

so humiliated them," which later shifted to deep respect; in Carrington, "Hail! Langdell!" p. 743.

41. Charles Warren, ed., *Centennial History of the Harvard Law School 1817–1917* (Boston, MA: The Harvard Law School Association, 1918), pp. 34–35; Franklin G. Fessenden, "Rebirth of the Harvard Law School," *Harvard Law Review* 33 (1920): pp. 493, 497–501, 711.

42. Stephen Bainbridge, "Why I Don't Use the Socratic Method": http://www.professorbainbridge.com/professorbainbridgecom/2013/08/bainbridge-on-why-not-to-use-the-socratic-method-and-teaching-corporate-law.html; last accessed April 4, 2014.

43. Brian Leiter, "The Socratic Method: The Scandal of American Legal Education": leiterlawschool.typepad.com/leiter/2005/09/the_socratic_me.html.

44. Scott Turow, *One L: The Turbulent True Story of a First Year at Harvard Law School* (New York: Grand Central Publishing, 1988), p. 215; Lani Guinier, Michelle Fine, Jane Balin, Ann Bartow, and Deborah Lee Stachel, "Becoming Gentlemen: Women's Experiences at One Ivy League Law School," *University of Pennsylvania Law Review* 143, no. 1 (November 1994): p. 4.

45. Cited in Burnele Powell, "A Defense of the Socratic Method: An Interview with Martin B. Louis (1934–1994)," *North Carolina Law Review* 73 (1995): pp. 967, 957. That same year Duke law professor Paul Carrington similarly lamented the disappearance of hard-nosed Socratic instructors in Carrington, "Hail! Langdell!" p. 748.

46. J. T. Dillon, *The Practice of Questioning* (New York: Routledge, 1990).

47. Plato, *The Republic,* trans. Desmond Lee (New York: Penguin, 1953), p. 265. On the emotional foundations of the Socratic method, see Robert R. Wellman, "Socrates and Alcibiades: The Alcibiades Major," *History of Education Quarterly* 6, no. 4 (Winter 1966): pp. 9–10.

48. Nietzsche, *Twilight of the Idols,* p. 476.

49. Beverslius, *Cross-Examining Socrates,* p. 9. Beverslius observes that while the "apparently devastating" arguments of Socrates are momentarily "paralyzing," they have "no lasting effect" largely because his interlocutors "often manifest deep resistance" toward the process, p. 9.

50. Kenneth Branagh interview with Cary Mazer: www.english. upenn.edu/~cmazer/branagh.html.

51. Some neuroscientists have found that the regions of the brain most closely associated with self-focused thoughts are especially active during sleep. It's hard to focus on our self when we're caught up in the swirl of daily events and experiences. Sleep is perhaps a time for us to reassess our self. From time immemorial, ascetics (and yoga instructors) have insisted that we must close out the world to find our inner self. See, for example, Antonio Damasio, *Self Comes to Mind*, pp. 230–241.

52. Some argue that people nowadays suffer from information overload, a product of our data saturation through high-tech devices. But human brains have always been swamped with information. Pioneers and explorers seldom complained of being distracted while trailblazing impenetrable forests or sailing treacherous seas, even though their minds were awash with sensory inputs—images, sounds, smells—any one of which might signal impending doom. The brain is adept at filtering out what doesn't matter. But the proliferation of information-hungry subversive play selves, each tagging information and demanding that it be analyzed, may overload our processing capacity. We're distracted not by information per se, but by the high-priority demands of media-made subversive play selves.

53. I had met Isabella during a test play among Reacting faculty of the Josiah game. She was a preceptor to the prophets and Judahite factions, helping them track down biblical references and citations. After the game, I asked if anyone had a problem playing a game that examined the foundations of their faith. When none of the professors voiced objections, Stewart interjected, "Ask Isabella." She proceeded to tell the story that appears here.

54. Charles Taylor, *Sources of the Self: The Making of the Modern Identity* (Cambridge, MA: Harvard University Press, 1989), p. 116.

55. Rousseau, *Emile* (Bloom), p. 243; Sigmund Freud, *Civilization and Its Discontents*, trans. James Strachey (New York: W. W. Norton, 1961), p. 28.

56. Anthony G. Greenwald, "Is Anyone in Charge? Personalysis versus the Principle of Personal Unity," in Suls and Greenwald, eds., *Psychological Perspectives on the Self*, pp. 167, 157. "It is surprising that the personal

unity principle remains so deeply entrenched, albeit implicitly, in both lay and psychological thought" (p. 167). Greenwald adds that "psychological researchers, like most lay persons, have a theory of the self as a unified entity that extends to the boundaries of the person" (p. 157) and cites S. Epstein, "The Self-Concept Revisited: Or a Theory of a Theory," *American Psychologist* 28 (1973): pp. 404–416.

57. Erik Erikson, *Childhood and Society* (New York: W. W. Norton, 1950). On the "danger" of "role confusion," see pp. 262 and 273; on "the search for and the insistence on identity," see p. 263. See also Erik Erikson, *Identity: Youth and Crisis* (New York: W. W. Norton, 1968).

58. In 1963, for example, several psychologists explained that the lack of "proper adult models" could result in schizophrenic psychosis in children. Such a "family milieu" failed to provide "appropriate sex-linked roles," in T. Lidz, S. Fleck, Yrjo Alanen, and Alice Cornelison, "Schizophrenic Patients and Their Siblings," *Psychiatry* 26 (1963): p. 3. See also Allen P. Webb, "Sex-Role Preferences and Adjustment in Early Adolescents, *Child Development* 34, no. 3 (September 1963): p. 615. "We are seeing in the high anxiety group signs of role identity problems which may be symptomatic of maladjustment." When "role confusion" was based on doubt as to one's sexual identity, Erikson added, "outright psychotic episodes are not uncommon," in Erikson, *Childhood and Society*, p. 262.

59. Erik Erikson, *Toys and Reasons: Stages in the Ritualization of Experience* (New York: W. W. Norton, 1976), pp. 21, 26, 95, 102–103, 109, 163–164. See also Eric Berne, a psychologist who attempted to salvage Freud's thesis by contending that the adult penchant for competitive social posturing—for game playing—was a type of mass derangement. He called on adults to get back onto their proper developmental track. The "most perfect form of human living," he contended, was a "games-free intimacy." If people would just give up their subversive play, they could get down to the real work of being human; in Eric Berne, *Games People Play: The Basic Handbook of Transactional Analysis* (New York: Ballantine Books, 1996), pp. 18, 62.

60. See, for example, Leonie Huddy, "From Social to Political Identity: A Critical Examination of Social Identity Theory," *Political Psychology* 22, no. 1 (2001): pp. 129–130, Steven Hitlen, "Values as the Core of Personal Identity: Drawing Links between Two Theories of Self," *Social Psychology Quarterly* 66, no. 2 (June 2003), p. 118.

61. McConnell, "The Self as a Collection of Multiple Self-Aspects," p. 381; Stanley Klein and Cynthia Gangi, "The Multiplicity of Self: Neuropsychological Evidence and Its Implications for the Self as a Construct in Psychological Research," *Annals of the New York Academy of Sciences* 1191 (2010), pp. 1–2, 5, 10.

62. Some of this research is summarized in Stephen R. Marks, Shelley M. MacDermid, "Multiple Roles and the Self: A Theory of Role Balance," *Journal of Marriage and the Family* 58, no. 2 (May 1996): p. 418; see also Peggy A. Thoits, "Identity-Relevant Events and Psychological Symptoms: A Cautionary Tale," *Journal of Health and Social Behavior* 36 (March 1995): pp. 72, 105.

63. Isabella volunteered an additional point: "I have no idea whether Professor Stewart agrees with the conclusions I came to!"

64. Mead had anticipated the possibility that multiple selves would help individuals experience "enlarged and more adequate personalities" in George Herbert Mead, *Selected Writings* (Indianapolis, IN: Bobbs-Merrill, 1964), p. 148.

65. Tracy Lightcamp, a political scientist at LaGrange College, was struck by the disparity in student evaluations of his large lectures and Reacting classes. In response to the question, "Were you encouraged to think critically and analytically?" 65 percent of his Reacting students cited "very often," while only 37 percent of his other students did so. Another question asked: "Were you actively involved in the learning process?" Seventy-seven percent of the Reacting students said "very often" compared to only 16 percent of the others, in Tracy Lightcamp, "Creating Political Order: Maintaining Student Engagement through *Reacting to the Past*," *PS: Political Science and Politics* (January 2009): p. 178.

66. This literature is summarized in Allen R. McConnell, "The Multiple Self-Aspects Framework: Self-Concept Representation and Its Implications," *Personality and Social Psychology Review* 15, no. 1, 2011.

5. OVERCOMING THE SILENCE OF THE STUDENTS

1. This conversation was taken from a videotape of the class.
2. See "Debate at Dawn."

3. Greg Lukianoff, "Feigning Free Speech on Campus," *New York Times* (October 24, 2012).

4. Paul Massari, "Hammonds Challenges Students," *Harvard Gazette* (September 2, 2011). Former Harvard dean Harry Lewis commented, "Harvard should not condone the sacrifice of rights to speech and thought simply because they can be inconvenient in a residential college," in "The Freshman Pledge," in his blog, *Bits and Pieces* (August 30, 2011).

5. Lukianoff, "Feigning Free Speech on Campus." In 2013, moreover, the UCLA survey of nearly 200,000 first-year students nationwide found that 67.8 percent agreed that colleges should prohibit racist or sexist speech on campus; see John H. Pryor et al., *The American Freshman: National Norms, Fall 2012* (Los Angeles: Higher Education Research Institute at Los Angeles, 2013), p. 37.

6. A research study similarly found that large campuses had more diverse student populations, but that this institutional diversity "led to less diversity among friends," in Lacey Johnson, "More Diversity on Campus Leads to Less Diversity Among Friends," *Chronicle of Higher Education* (September 22, 2011).

7. Cited in Lisa Foderaro, "Roommates Who Click," *The New York Times,* August 20, 2010.

8. Edmund Burke, *Reflections on the Revolution in France* (London: Seeley, Jackson, 1872), p. 159. John Stuart Mill, *On Liberty* (London: Walter Scott Publishing, 1859, Project Gutenberg Ebook [#3490]), p. 67. This position has been updated by Gerald Graff, *Beyond the Culture Wars: How Teaching the Conflicts Can Revitalize American Education* (New York: W. W. Norton, 1992); see also Susan A. Ambrose, Michael W. Bridges, Michele DiPietro, Marsha C. Lovett, and Marie K. Norman, *How Learning Works: Seven Research-Based Principles for Smart Teaching* (San Francisco: John Wiley and Sons, 2010), pp. 186–187. Some scholars have found that argumentation is more effective than the classical view of abstract reasoning, chiefly because it minimizes the tendency toward confirmation bias: "Reasoning does not lead to more accurate beliefs about an object, to better estimates of the correctness of one's answer, or to superior moral judgments. Instead, by looking only for supporting arguments, reasoning strengthens people's opinions, distorts their estimates, and allows them

to get away with violations of their own moral intuitions. In these cases, epistemic or moral goals are not well served by reasoning. By contrast, argumentative goals are: People are better able to support their positions or to justify their moral arguments," in Hugo Mercier and Dan Sperber, "Why Do Humans Reason? Arguments for An Argumentative Theory," *Behavioral and Brain Sciences* 34 (2011): p. 68.

9. John Dewey, *Human Nature and Conduct* (New York: Henry Holt, 1922), p. 300. See also Gerald Graff, *Clueless in Academe: How Schooling Obscures the Life of the Mind* (New Haven: Yale University Press, 2003), pp. 83–95; this subject is also discussed in Chapter 8 of this book.

10. Cathy Small used the pseudonym of Rebekah Nathan, *My Freshman Year: What a Professor Learned by Becoming a Student* (Ithaca, NY: Cornell University Press, 2005), pp. 95, 99. Other professors who have lived with undergraduates, or conducted dorm-based studies, have made the same observation. See Elizabeth A. Armstrong and Laura T. Hamilton, *Paying for the Party: How Colleges Maintain Inequality* (Cambridge, MA: Harvard University Press, 2013); and Michael Moffatt, *Coming of Age in New Jersey: College and American Culture* (New Brunswick, NJ: Rutgers University Press, 1989), p. 300.

11. Greg Lukianoff, "Feigning Free Speech on Campus."

12. Carol Trosset, "Obstacles to Open Discussion and Critical Thinking: The Grinnell College Study," *Change* 30, no. 5 (September/October, 1998): pp. 44–49. "Promising our students" (p. 49). For the study, 93 percent of the students were juniors and seniors, three-fourths of whom majored in the subject of the class. The mean class size for the study was twenty-nine.

13. Nathan, *My Freshman Year*, pp. 97, 98. Another study found that as many as two-thirds of students never or rarely participate in class; see Avner Caspi, and Kelly Saporta, "Participation in Class and in Online Discussions: Gender Differences," *Computers and Education* 50 (2008): pp. 718–724.

14. Claudia E. Nunn, "Discussion in the College Classroom: Triangulating Observational and Survey Results," *Journal of Higher Education* 67, no. 3 (May/June 1996): pp. 250, 259, 261.

15. Suzanne Feigelson, "The Silent Classroom," *Amherst* (Fall 2001): pp. 12, 14.

16. Adams, *The Education of Henry Adams* (New York: The Library of America/Viking, 1983), p. 995.

17. Cited in Polly A. Fassinger, "Understanding Classroom Interaction: Students' and Professors' Contributions to Students' Silence." *Journal of Higher Education* 66, no. 1 (1995): p. 94.

18. Telephone interview with Suzanne Garfinkle in the fall of 2010.

19. See Rebecca D. Cox, *College Fear Factor: How Students and Professors Misunderstand One Another* (Cambridge, MA: Harvard University Press, 2009), pp. 93, 111–112.

20. Cited in Ken Bain, *What the Best College Teachers Do* (Cambridge, MA: Harvard University Press, 2004), p. 109.

21. Mary M. Reda, "What's the Problem with Quiet Students? Anyone? Anyone?" *Chronicle of Higher Education* (September 5, 2010).

22. This video, "The French Revolution on the Hudson," can be seen online: reacting.barnard.edu/headlines/video-french-revolution-hudson.

23. This analysis of the data was provided in an email from Stroessner, August 31, 2011. See Steven Stroessner, "All the World's a Stage? Consequences of a Role-Playing Pedagogy on Psychological Factors and Writing and Rhetorical Skill in College Undergraduates," *Journal of Educational Psychology* 101, no. 3 (2009): pp. 610, 612–614. The colleges were Barnard College (New York City), Trinity College (Hartford, CT), and Smith College (Northampton, MA).

24. Derek Bok, *Our Underachieving Colleges* (Princeton, NJ: Princeton University Press, 2006), p. 106.

25. Ann Davison and Sue Lantz Goldhaber, "Integration, Socialization, Collaboration: Inviting Native and Non-Native English Speakers into the Academy Through 'Reacting to the Past,'" in Judith Summerfield and Crystal Benedicks, eds., *Reclaiming the Public University* (New York: Peter Lang, 2007), pp. 157, 150.

26. Email communication from Barbara Gombach to author, September 15, 2011.

27. Popiel recalled a student from China who had considered dropping the course when she learned how much speaking was required. The student's father agreed: "You're too meek and your English isn't good enough." But his doubts and her own persuaded her to remain in the course. During a pivotal debate—the one Popiel's recent class had bungled—this student

dismantled Galileo's scientific arguments so expertly the others in her faction cheered. "I felt that she and I had done battle together," Popiel recalled. By the end, the Chinese student saw "great new things in herself."

28. Davison and Goldhaber cited the experiences of a young Greek woman at Queens College, who told them: "I had sometimes a difficulty distinguishing reality with Re-acting reality. I was very passionate about it and I felt sometimes that I was actually the person I played. So, I learned a lot about myself, how I reacted to pressure, how I had to control my emotions and how real experiences in my life played a role in the experience of the games," in Davison and Goldhaber, "Integration, Socialization, Collaboration," p. 160.

29. Sherry Turkle similarly describes teenagers who reported that they hated the phone. "No one answers the phone in our house anymore," one mother reported. "It used to be that the kids would race to pick up the phone. Now they are up in their rooms, knowing no one is going to call them, and texting and going on Facebook or whatever instead," as cited in *Alone Together: Why We Expect More From Technology and Less from Each Other* (New York: Basic Books, 2011), p. 15.

30. Jonathan Wickens, a student at Indiana University, explained that on Facebook "there are only smiles," (online interview on September 10, 2011). Reacting debates, by contrast, showed the complex responses of peers: smiles, frowns, confusion, and the myriad facial expressions that have facilitated communication since the dawn of man.

31. See Turkle, *Alone Together,* especially her section, "The New State of the Self: Tethered and Marked Absent," pp. 155–157.

32. "Work Week," *Wall Street Journal* (December 29, 1998), p. A-1.; F. T. I. Consulting, "Key Findings from a Survey of Hiring Decision-Makers (Accrediting Council for Independent Colleges and Schools, [unpublished], released December 5, 2011); also Thomas L. Friedman, "Generation Q," *New York Times* (October 10, 2007); Bok, *Our Underachieving Colleges,* p. 106; see also Chapter 9 of this book.

6. LEARNING BY FAILING

1. The data is summarized in Jean M. Twenge, W. Keith Campbell, and Elise C. Freeman, "Generational Differences in Young Adults' Life

Goals, Concern for Others, and Civic Orientation, 1966–2009," *Journal of Personality and Social Psychology* 102, no. 5 (May 2012), pp. 1045–1062. In response to the statement, "being very well-off financially," 45 percent of those responding from 1966 to 1978 (Boomers) agreed, whereas 74 percent of the Millennials (2000–2009) did so (p. 1049); to the statement, "developing a meaningful philosophy of life," 73 percent of those responding from 1966 to 1978 agreed, whereas only 45 percent of the Millennials did so (p. 1049).

2. On the rise of self-esteem since the 1980s, see Jean M. Twenge, "The Age of Anxiety? The Birth Cohort Change in Anxiety and Neuroticism, 1952–1993," *Journal of Personality and Social Psychology* 79: pp. 1007–1021; also, Jennifer Crocker and Lora E. Park, "The Costly Pursuit of Self-Esteem," *Psychological Bulletin* 130, no. 3: p. 7. See also Lori Gottlieb, "How to Land Your Kid in Therapy," *Atlantic* (July/August 2011): p. 73.

3. The data on long-term trends in narcissism is summarized in Jean M. Twenge and W. Keith Campbell, *The Narcissism Epidemic* (New York: Free Press, 2009), pp. 2, 30–33, 206. "It's the same as an SAT score going up 75 points (out of 1600)" (p. 31). More detailed results are reported in Jean M. Twenge, Sara Konrath, Joshua D. Foster, W. Keith Campbell, and Brad J. Bushman, "Egos Inflating Over Time: A Cross-Temporal Meta-Analysis of the Narcissistic Personality Inventory," *Journal of Personality* 76, no. 4 (August 2008): p. 875. "Almost two-thirds of recent college students are above the mean 1979–1985 narcissism score." Twenge's data is based on the responses from 1979 through 2006 of 37,000 students from thirty-one colleges. Although another survey challenged these results, it was based on data from a handful of campuses, and thus compared 2000s data from UC Davis with 1990s data from Berkeley, as noted in Twenge and Campbell, *Narcissism Epidemic,* p. 32. See also K. D. Stewart and P. C. Bernhardt, "Comparing Millennials to Pre-1987 Students and With One Another," *North American Journal* 12 (2010): pp. 579–602. In 2006, too, one in ten Americans in their twenties had experienced symptoms of narcissistic personality disorder, a serious illness. Twenge and Campbell, *Narcissism Epidemic,* p. 2.

4. Sherry Turkle, *Alone Together: Why We Expect More from Technology and Less from Each Other* (New York: Basic Books, 2011), p. 268.

5. Howard Gardner and Katie Davis have proposed that digital media "support and reinforce youth's general shift toward risk aversion," in *App Generation: How Today's Youth Navigate Identity, Intimacy, and Imagination in a Digital World* (New Haven: Yale University Press, 2013), p. 268.

6. See Paul Tough, "What If the Secret to Success Is Failure?" *New York Times* (September 18, 2011). Barbara Ehrenreich makes a similar argument in *Bright-Sided: How Positive Thinking Is Undermining America* (New York: Picador, 2009).

7. Twenge and Campbell, *Narcissism Epidemic*, p. 232.

8. D. T. Max, "Happiness 101," *New York Times* (January 7, 2007).

9. The HERI data is summarized in Sara Lipka, "Economy Changed Freshmen's Plans But Didn't Shake Their Confidence," *Chronicle of Higher Education* (January 27, 2011). See also Jean M. Twenge, "The Age of Anxiety?" pp. 1007–1021; Jean M. Twenge, and W. K. Campbell, "Age and Birth Cohort Differences in Self-Esteem: A Cross-Temporal Meta-Analysis," *Personality and Social Psychology Review* 5 (2001): pp. 321–344.

10. Jennifer Crocker: L. L. Smith and C. H. Elliott, *Hollow Kids: Recapturing the Soul of a Generation Lost to the Self-Esteem Myth* (New York: Random House, 2001).

11. Cited in Sharon Jayson, "Yep, Life'll Burst That Self-Esteem Bubble," *USA Today*, (December 7, 2010); see also Roy F. Baumeister, Jennifer D. Campbell, Joachim I. Krueger, and Kathleen D. Vohs, "Does High Self-Esteem Cause Better Performance, Interpersonal Success, Happiness, or Healthier Lifestyles?" *Psychological Science in the Public Interest* 4, no. 1 (May 2003): pp. 1–44. The authors answer the question in the title of the essay in the negative: many studies show "that the benefits of high self-esteem are far fewer and weaker than proponents of self-esteem had hoped" (p. 38).

12. Benjamin T. Hand, "On Failure at Harvard," *Harvard Crimson* (January 30, 2012).

13. Cited in Sharon Jason, "Yep, Life'll Burst That Self-Esteem Bubble"; see also Jean M. Twenge, *Generation Me: Why Today's Young Americans Are More Confident, Assertive, Entitled—and More Miserable—Than Ever Before* (New York: Free Press, 2006).

14. Cited in Sharon Jayson, "Yep, Life'll Burst That Self-Esteem Bubble"; see also Crocker and Park, "The Costly Pursuit of Self-Esteem": p. 7.

The authors note that failure at achieving the desired goals commonly results in "intensely negative emotions, increased anxiety, feelings of being at risk of social rejection" (p. 9).

15. Linda Bips, "Students Are Different Now," *New York Times* (October 11, 2010).

16. In history, Gandhi was assassinated a year later, although he did expose himself to great personal danger during the 1946 riots in Calcutta.

17. Steven J. Stroessner, Laurie Susser Beckerman, and Alexis Whittaker, "All the World's a Stage? Consequences of a Role-Playing Pedagogy on Psychological Factors and Writing and Rhetorical Skill in College Graduates," *Journal of Educational Psychology* 101, no. 3: p. 617. On the relation between low self-esteem and depression, see E. L. Deci and R. M. Ryan, "The General Causality Orientations Scale: Self-Determination in Personality," *Journal of Research in Personality* 19 (1985): pp. 109–134; see also S. Gable and J. B. Nezlek, "Level and Instability of Day-to-Day Psychological Well-Being and Risk for Depression," *Journal of Personality & Social Psychology* 74 (1998): pp. 129–138.

18. Stroessner, "All the World's a Stage?" p. 617. The data, Stroessner wrote, had produced an "intriguing" effect that ran "counter to what has often been found in studies on perceived control and well-being." Stroessner concluded that Reacting might "provide a context in which the normal relation between self-esteem and maintaining feelings of control are negated or even reversed."

19. Stroessner, "All the World's a Stage?" p. 617.

20. See Carol S. Dweck, *Self-Theories: Their Role in Motivation, Personality, and Development* (Philadelphia: Psychology Press, 2000), pp. 1–10.

21. Although I use the terms "Solid Selves" and "Malleable Selves," Dweck uses the terms "entity theorists" and "incremental theorists." "Entity theorists" believe that the self is a fixed entity, whereas "incremental theorists" believe the self to be capable of changing and growing incrementally; Dweck, *Self-Theories*, pp. 2–4.

22. They tended to disagree with statements such as this: "The knowledge I gain in school is more important than the grades I receive," in Dweck, *Self-Theories*, p. 35.

23. David Glenn, "Carol Dweck's Attitude," *Chronicle Review* (May 9, 2010).

24. Cited in Glenn, "Carol Dweck's Attitude." Further confirmation of the ways in which one's self intrudes on cognitive function has come from recent studies of stereotyping, such as those of Claude Steele, now dean of the School of Education at Stanford (and my former provost at Columbia). One recent study found that when women used a fictitious name in math tests, they did better than when they used their own name, in Shen Zhang, Toni Schmader, and William M. Hall, "L'Eggo My Ego: Reducing the Gender Gap in Math by Unlinking the Self from Performance," *Self and Identity* 12, no. 4 (2013). (I was alerted to this reference by Amelia Vanderlaan, a former Reacting student who figures prominently in a later section of this chapter [Chapter 6].)

25. Cited in Sharon Jayson, "Yep, Life'll Burst That Self-Esteem Bubble."

26. Dweck, *Self-Theories*, p. 128.

27. Eventually Cohen wrote a game, "The Math Wars," a debate over the role of the Tripos exam, rooted in Euclidean geometry, at Cambridge University during the 1870s.

28. Cohen related the story of Lauren Arthur, a Reacting student who had told him of her excitement on being named governor general of India in 1945. "Oh my gosh," she said on reading her role. "Look at all of my power. I'm in total control: army, navy, civil service, everything." During the game she made full use of her authority, but Cohen kept folding historical complications into the game, making her job more difficult. After one tumultuous session, she asked to speak with him. "I thought I had everything under control, but now I know it is all unraveling," she said matter-of-factly. "I'm going to fail." Cohen was struck by the "precious" look on her face: "a combination of discouragement, bewilderment—and amusement." He understood her perfectly: he had been there, done that. Three years later, just before Lauren was about to graduate, she stopped by Cohen's office. "By failing as governor general," she said, "I learned a lot about what you can control and what you can't." Failure, she said, had been a "growing experience" that helped her cope with the challenges of college. In 2014, when I contacted Arthur to confirm the accuracy of Cohen's account, she mentioned that she was running for a seat in the Missouri legislature: "I know that failure is certainly a possibility.

However, I believe this is an incredible opportunity, regardless of outcome. And for me, that was one of the most important lessons I learned in Reacting."

29. Amanda Houle, "Reacting to 'Reacting,'" *Change* (July 27, 2006).

30. See Chapter 4.

31. Houle, "Reacting": p. 52.

32. The questions were drawn from Albert Mehrabian's Balanced Emotional Empathy Scale (BEES), a standard tool for ascertaining the empathy of nurses, police officers, social workers, and potential foster parents.

33. Stroessner, "All the World's a Stage?" pp. 612, 614. "Students who participated in Reacting to the Past showed a significant endorsement of incremental beliefs ["Malleable Selves"], whereas students in the control seminars did not" (p. 614). "It is not particularly surprising," Stroessner concluded, "that students in Reacting to the Past did not develop a stronger internal locus of control, given the frequent occurrence of random and chance events in the game scenarios" (p. 612).

34. See, for example, Charles S. Carver, *On the Self-Regulation of Behavior* (Cambridge: Cambridge University Press, 1998); Susan A. Ambrose et al., *How Learning Works* (San Francisco: Jossey-Bass, 2010), pp. 76–77; Ken Bain, *What the Best College Teachers Do* (Cambridge, MA: Harvard University Press, 2004), pp. 35, 41. "Rather than pitting people against each other, [the best teachers] encouraged cooperation and collaboration" (p. 35); "the teachers we observed usually abstain from appeals to competition" (p. 41).

35. For this description of flow see Mihaly Csikszentmihalyi, *Flow: The Psychology of Optimal Experience* (New York: Harper and Row, 1990), p. 64.

36. Educators, too, can lead students into a state of flow by creating "positive" learning experiences, often through imaginative adaptations of play activities. In this respect, Csikszentmihalyi and his adherents have offered refinements to the basic educational theories of Piaget, Dewey, and, of course, Plato. See especially I. Dee Fink, *Creating Significant Learning Experiences: An Integrated Approach to Designing College Courses* (San Francisco: Jossey-Bass, 2003).

37. Mihaly Csikszentmihalyi and Isabella Csikszentmihalyi, eds., *Optimal Experience: Psychological Studies of Flow in Consciousness* (Cambridge: Cambridge University Press, 1988), pp. 34, 59.

38. Susan Jackson and Mihaly Csikszentmihalyi, *Flow in Sports: The Keys to Optimal Experiences and Performances* (Champaign, IL: Human Kinetics, 1999), p. 9.

39. Mihaly Csikszentmihalyi, *Creativity: Flow and the Psychology of Discovery and Invention* (New York: Harper, 1996).

40. Csikszentmihalyi, *Optimal Experience: Psychological Studies of Flow in Consciousness*, p. 34.

41. See Brett N. Steenbarger, *Enhancing Trader Performance: Proven Strategies from the Cutting Edge of Trading Psychology* (New York: Wiley Trading Series, 2006).

42. Jim Bouton, *Ball Four* (New York: Wiley, 1990), p. 51.

43. See T. L. Taylor, *Play Between Worlds: Exploring Online Game Culture* (Cambridge, MA: MIT Press, 2006), pp. 74–75.

44. The author is indebted to Donna Heiland's essay, "Approaching the Ineffable: Flow, Sublimity, and Student Learning," in Donna Heiland and Laura J. Rosenthal, *Literary Study, Measurement, and the Sublime: Disciplinary Assessment* (New York: Teagle Foundation, 2011), and to a subsequent discussion with Heiland. Sublime art usually conveyed an element of danger: plunging chasms, dizzying heights, foreboding, dark forests. The resulting *frisson* may be caused by the adrenaline jolt that triggers peak experiences.

45. José Antonio Bowen, *Teaching Naked: How Moving Technology Out of Your College Classroom Will Improve Student Learning* (San Francisco: John Wiley and Sons, 2012), p. 92.

46. See Rebecca D. Cox, *College Fear Factor: How Students and Professors Misunderstand One Another* (Cambridge, MA: Harvard University Press, 2009), pp. 24–25, 40.

47. When the dean of students at Harvard College learned that the Ivy League was cutting down on the number of students who could be admitted as football players, he was dismayed: "They are the only people here who know how to lose," as cited in Harry Lewis, *Excellence Without a Soul: How a Great University Forgot Education* (New York: Public Affairs, 2006), p. 213.

48. To illustrate the point, she described how the manager of her unit pulled her aside and asked if she would consider applying for a job as head of a research team. Rivka had only worked for a short time as an analyst; she knew the promotion was a stretch. "I waffled for a few days. I hated the idea of gunning for something and failing. But at the end of the day, I knew that I could work hard enough to deserve it, and that was what was important. If I didn't get it, I could wrap my head around the failure. So I gunned for it and, to my utter surprise, I got it."

7. BUILDING COMMUNITY AND GLOBAL CITIZENSHIP

1. After telling this story at a workshop several years ago, one professor said afterwards that she didn't believe it. I was too surprised to say much in response. Who could invent such a screwy story? I hope that when these words appear in print, the students in this discussion will confirm it.

2. Tom Wolfe, *I Am Charlotte Simmons* (New York: Farrar Straus Giroux, 2004), p. 354.

3. Elizabeth A. Armstrong and Laura T. Hamilton, *Paying for the Party: How College Maintains Inequality* (Cambridge, MA: Harvard University Press, 2013), p. xi: "swept up onto the party pathway" and "I just can't imagine"; also, "I tried so hard to fit in" (p. 161).

4. *American College Health Association—National College Health Assessment: Reference Group Report, Fall 2007* (Baltimore, MD: American College Health Association, 2008): www.acha-ncha.org/reports_ACHA-NCHAoriginal.html.

5. Tamar Lewin, "Record Level of Stress Found in College Freshmen," *New York Times* (January 26, 2011). The title of an article about another study of 25,000 students conveyed its conclusions: Lauren Sieben, "Nearly a Third of College Students Have Had Mental-Health Counseling, Study Finds," *Chronicle of Higher Education* (March 14, 2011).

6. About half of the nation's colleges and universities run a 24-hour-a-day suicide or crisis hotline. See *A Report of the Anxiety Disorders Association of America* (Silver Spring, MD: Anxiety Disorders Association of America, 2006) p. 5. http://www.adaa.org/sites/default/files/FINALCollegeReport.pdf; last accessed April 2014.

7. Daniel F. Chambliss and Christopher G. Takacs also emphasize the centrality of social ties, in *How College Works* (Cambridge, MA: Harvard University Press, 2014), p. 17.

8. Mary Grigsby, *College Life Through the Eyes of Students* (Albany: SUNY Press, 2009), pp. 54–55, 68, 88.

9. Lori Gottlieb, "How to Land Your Kid in Therapy," *Atlantic* (July/August, 2011): p. 70; see also Abigail Sullivan Moore, "Off Off Off Campus," *New York Times* (February 3, 2013).

10. Justin Pope, "'Helicopter Parents' Hover Over College Students' Lives, *News and Observer* (November 5, 2007); also Ralph Gardner, Jr., "In College, You Can Go Home Again and Again," *New York Times* (December 14, 2006).

11. Brian Baker, "Wake Up Call: Unpack the Suitcase Campus," *Carolinian* (March 18, 2002). College officials and resident advisers rarely organize events on campus on weekends, as an RA at Kent State University observed, "because we know there's a low turnout," in Kristine Gill, "Kent State: A Suitcase Campus," *Kentnewsnet* (December 5, 2007); http://www.kentwired.com/latest_updates/article_103c79ca-6d61-5218 -91a3-e8296495a91b.html; last accessed April 6, 2014. See also Elizabeth Kunde, "College Addresses Suitcase Campus," *Ripon College Days* (December 6, 2006).

12. Victoria Vlisides, "Whitewater on Its Way to Losing Suitcase Stigma," *Royal Purple* (February 27, 2008): "In the Fall, 33.9 percent of students stayed in the residence halls and 35.6 percent stayed in the spring semester." Although this data was for the Whitewater campus of the University of Wisconsin, officials reported similar results at most other Wisconsin campuses.

13. See Neeraj Vedway, "Does Facebook Make Us Happy?" *Anthropology Now* 5, no. 2 (September 2013): p. 89.

14. Turkle, *Alone Together: Why We Expect More from Technology and Less from Each Other* (New York: Basic Books, 2011), p. 294. "We are so enmeshed."

15. Richard Powers, *Galatea 2.2* (New York: Farrar Strauss and Giroux, 1995), p. 9. See also Stephen Marche, "Is Facebook Making Us Lonely," *Atlantic Monthly* 309, no. 4 (May 2012).

16. In 2013 Amin Saberi, a Stanford professor and the founder and CEO of Coursera, announced that MOOCs had learned that peer interaction would be a key new component of the online learning experience. "With this transition from brick-and-mortar classes to online learning, you shouldn't lose the social, collaborative aspects of learning. It should be able to enable it," as cited in Jake New, "New MOOC Provider Says It Fosters Peer Interaction," *Chronicle of Higher Education* (April 16, 2013).

17. Marybeth Hoffman, Jayne Richmond, Jennifer Morrow, and Kandice Salomone, "Investigating 'Sense of Belonging' in First-Year College Students," *Journal of College Student Retention*, 4, no. 3: pp. 227, 229. "One-quarter of all new college students do not return" (p. 227). Their chief explanation is that students lack a "sense of belonging": that is, they are lonely (p. 229).

18. Alexander Astin, *What Matters in College? Four Critical Years Revisited* (San Francisco: Jossey-Bass), p. 398.

19. Vincent Tinto, *Leaving College: Rethinking the Causes and Cures of Student Attrition* (Chicago: The University of Chicago Press, 1993), pp. 106–108. Subsequent researchers found that the only strong correlation was between retention and social integration; see John M. Braxton, A. V. Sullivan, and R. M. Johnson, Jr., "Appraising Tinto's Theory of College Student Departure," in J. C. Smart, ed., *Higher Education: A Handbook of Theory and Research*, Vol. 12 (New York: Agathon Press, 1997), pp. 107–164.

20. Richard Light, *Making the Most of College* (Cambridge, MA: Harvard University Press, 2001), pp. 35, 98.

21. Ernest T. Pascarella and Patrick T. Terenzini, *How College Affects Students: A Third Decade of Research* (San Francisco: Jossey-Bass, 2005), p. 426. "Our review . . . leads us to conclusions generally consistent [with other studies] suggesting that students' institutional commitments exert an important and positive effect in shaping their persistence decisions. . . . The phenomenon appears to be general across a variety of settings" (p. 426). See also Mary J. Fischer, "Settling into Campus Life: Differences by Race/Ethnicity in College Involvement and Outcomes," *Journal of Higher Education* 78, no. 2 (March/April 2007): pp. 145–148. Fischer's

study of data from NSSE for several years after 1999 found that, regardless
of their race or ethnicity, students who had more friends on campus were
happier with college and were more likely to graduate than students who
had fewer. She also found students' ties to their professors had *no impact*
on satisfaction and persistence rates, with one exception: black students
were slightly more likely to persist if they had had positive interactions
with professors (pp. 151–152). See also J. P. Bean, "Dropouts and Turnover:
The Synthesis and Test of a Causal Model of Student Attrition," *Research
in Higher Education* 12 (1980): pp. 155–187.

22. Alexander W. Astin, "Student Involvement: A Developmental
Theory for Higher Education," *Journal of College Student Personnel* 25
(1984); see also George D. Kuh and Patrick G. Love, "New Theoretical
Directions: A Cultural Perspective on Student Departure," in John
M. Braxton, *Reworking the Student Departure Puzzle* (Nashville: Vander-
bilt University Press, 2000), p. 207; and Gary R. Pike, George D. Kuh,
and A. C. McCormick, "An Investigation of the Contingent Relationships between Learning Community Participation and Student Engagement," *Research in Higher Education* 52, no. 3: pp. 300–322.

23. Alexander W. Astin, "What Matters in College?" *Liberal Education* 79, no. 4 (Fall 1993): pp. 1–4.

24. Sam Dillon, "Share of College Spending for Recreation is Rising," *New York Times* (July 8, 2010).

25. On the proliferation of programs for undergraduate students, and
the ubiquitous lament that too few students attend, see Armstrong and
Hamilton, *Paying for the Party,* p. 99; Robert A. Bonfiglio, "Doing Less:
Do Students Really Need So Many Programs?" originally in *About Cam-
pus* 7, no. 1 (2002), cited in Elizabeth Whitt, ed., *ASHE Reader on College
Student Affairs Administration* (New York: Pearson, 2004), pp. 429–430.
One of the most thoughtful assessments was written by George D. Kuh,
Elizabeth J. Whitt, and Jill D. Shedd, "A Reexamination of Core As-
sumptions in Student Affairs," *Student Affairs Work, 2001: A Paradigmatic
Odyssey* (Washington, DC: American College Personnel Association,
1987), reprinted in *ASHE Reader,* pp. 184–185.

26. Harry R. Lewis, *Excellence Without a Soul: How a Great University Forgot Education* (New York: PublicAffairs Books, 2006), pp. 154,
155, 167.

27. University of Northern Colorado website: www.unco.edu/provost /enroll-retain/Quality%20of%20Campus%20Life%20&%20Facilities .pdf; last accessed July 9, 2012.

28. Herbert S. Newman Partners website, http://www.newmanarchi tects.com/; last accessed in February 2012.

29. A major survey of several-score studies shows that first-year semi-nars and learning communities slightly increase the likelihood of first-year students re-enrolling as sophomores. Ernest Pascarella and Patrick Teren-zini saw the effect in the range of 7 percent; another study of random assignment came up with 13 percent. That learning communities, broadly defined, likely contribute to students' success in college is the thesis of Chun-Mei Zhao and George D. Kuh, "Adding Value: Learning Com-munities and Student Engagement," *Research in Higher Education* 45, no. 2 (March 2004); see also Hoffman, Richmond, Morrow, and Salomone, "Investigating 'Sense of Belonging'": pp. 229–230, 233–34; see also M. W. Sidle and J. McReynolds, "The Freshman Year Experience: Student Re-tention and Student Success," *Journal of College and Character* 36 (1999), pp. 60–74.

30. Ohio State University and Kentucky learning community web-sites, [http://housing.osu.edu/learning-communities/ and http://www .uky.edu/Housing/undergraduate/llp/communities.html; last accessed January 2011. See also Armstrong and Hamilton, *Paying for the Party,* pp. 64–65.

31. Cited in Lewis, *Excellence Without a Soul,* pp. 78–79.

32. Gary R. Pike, "The Influence of Fraternity or Sorority Member-ship on Students' College Experiences and Cognitive Development," *Research in Higher Education* 41 (2000): pp. 117–139; also Richard Arum and Josipa Roksa, *Academically Adrift: Limited Learning on College Campuses* (Chicago: University of Chicago Press, 2011), pp. 101–103. See also Chapter 2 of this book.

33. See Sam Dillon, "Share of College Spending for Recreation Is Rising."

34. Email correspondence in February 2012 with Purvi Mehta, Fiza Quraishi, and Diana Paquin Morel.

35. I said nothing because my own attempts to make the dinner spe-cial were so pitiful, and yet nearly every one of my students attended; to

cite my unearned "success" would have offended those who worked hard on the dinners. I suspect the other Reacting faculty felt the same way. Funding for the dinners was later restored.

36. Jeff Webb and Ann Engar, "Exploring Classroom Community: A Social Network Study of Reacting to the Past," pp. 14–15 (forthcoming). Jeff Webb is the associate director of the LEAP program at the University of Utah. "Thus, students in the Reacting factions showed a propensity to form ties, but not homophilous ties" (p. 16).

37. "Edward A. Shils," in John A. Garraty and Mark C. Carnes, eds., *American National Biography* (New York: Oxford University Press and the American Council of Learned Societies, 1999).

38. A study of thirty-five introductory history classes at Eastern Michigan University for 2008 and 2009 indicated that students who had taken Reacting versions had a retention rate that was about 10 percent higher than those who had taken courses without the Reacting pedagogy; see Joe Scazzaro, "Faculty Development Center Report," June 22, 2010 (unpublished).

39. Jeffrey R. Young, "Bill Gates Predicts Technology Will Make 'Place-Based' Colleges Less Important in Five Years," *Chronicle of Higher Education* (August 9, 2010). "College, except for the parties, needs to be less place-based," said Bill Gates.

40. Derek Bok observed that determining which nations will prove consequential in students' lives remains "clouded by uncertainty and confusion," in Derek Bok, *Our Underachieving Colleges* (Princeton, NJ: Princeton University Press, 2006), p. 76.

41. Martha C. Nussbaum, *Cultivating Humanity: A Classical Defense of Reform in Liberal Education* (Cambridge, MA: Harvard University Press, 1997), p. 69.

42. Nussbaum, *Cultivating Humanity,* p. 67.

43. Sarabeth took three separate Reacting courses and then worked as a preceptor for several faculty workshops.

44. One of the challenges in game design is to ensure that some players are not assigned to factions, and thus have freedom to be persuaded by the debates; but these roles often lack the rich social dynamics of the factional players. Sometimes these players feel left out. Game designers have devised various ways to script such roles so that players have tasks that

oblige them to interact with the other players and yet allow them a measure of freedom in choosing historically appropriate positions on particular debates.

45. See, for example, Matthew J. Mayhew, Gregory C. Wolniak, and Ernest T. Pascarella, "How Educational Practices Affect the Development of Life-Long Learning Orientations in Traditionally-Aged Undergraduate Students," *Research in Higher Education* 49, no. 4 (June 2008): pp. 353–354; Chambliss and Takacs, *How College Works*, p. 5; Dawson Hancock, "Cooperative Learning and Peer Orientation Effects on Motivation and Achievement," *Journal of Educational Research* 97, no. 3 (January/February, 2004): pp. 159–166; and Erica McWilliam and Shane Dawson, "Teaching for Creativity: Towards Sustainable and Replicable Pedagogical Practice," *Higher Education* 56, no. 6 (December 2008): pp. 633–643.

8. INCULCATING MORALITY AND EMPATHY (!)

1. This account is taken from a videotape of the class in 2010, provided by filmmaker Vinnie Massimino.

2. Jack Meacham and Jerry G. Gaff, "Learning Goals in Mission Statements: Implications for Educational Leadership," *Liberal Education* (Winter 2006): p. 53.

3. Denison University's mission statement:

www.denison.edu/academics/catalog/missionstatement.html;

Dartmouth's mission statement: www.dartmouth.edu/home/about /mission.html;

University of South Dakota's mission statement:

www.usd.edu/arts-and-sciences/mission-statement.cfm; adopted by the faculty of the College of Arts and Sciences, January 14, 2003.

4. Cited in Harry R. Lewis, *Excellence Without a Soul: How a Great University Forgot Education* (New York: PublicAffairs Books, 2006), p. 97.

5. Lewis, *Excellence Without a Soul,* pp. 97, xiii.

6. David Brooks, "'Moral Suicide,' a la Wolfe," *New York Times* (November 16, 2004).

7. Stanley Fish, "Will the Humanities Save Us?" *New York Times* (January 6, 2008).

8. Stanley Fish, "The Uses of the Humanities," *New York Times* (January 8, 2008).

9. Fish, "Uses of the Humanities."

10. Derek Bok, *Our Underachieving Colleges* (Princeton, NJ: Princeton University Press, 2006), p. 154.

11. Donald L. McCabe and Linda K. Trevino, "Honor Codes and Other Contextual Influences," *Journal of Higher Education* 64 (1993): p. 522; Margaret P. Jendrek, "Faculty Reactions to Academic Dishonesty," *Journal of College Student Development* 30 (1989): p. 401; Donald L. McCabe, Linda K. Trevino, and Kenneth D. Butterfield, "Cheating in Academic Institutions: A Decade of Research," *Ethics and Behavior* 11 (2001): pp. 219, 223. See also Jean M. Twenge and W. Keith Campbell, *The Narcissism Epidemic* (New York: The Free Press, 2009), p. 206.

12. Sociologist Tim Clydesdale, after interviewing over one hundred students, was struck by how easily they admitted to their cheating, in *The First Year Out: Understanding American Teens after High School* (Chicago: University of Chicago Press, 2007), p. 165. Two decades earlier, sociologist Tim Moffatt held similar conversations, but many peers "disapproved" of cheating, in *Coming of Age in New Jersey* (New Brunswick, NJ: Rutgers University Press, 2008), pp. 296–297.

13. Adam Smith, *The Wealth of Nations* (London: Methuen & Co., 1904), p. 4. Originally published in 1776.

14. Remarks by Chairman Adam Greenspan, "Adam Smith," February 6, 2005, Federal Reserve Board website: www.federalreserve.gov /boarddocs/speeches/2005/20050206/default.html.

15. See Jerry Evensky, "Adam Smith's *Theory of Moral Sentiments:* On Morals and Why They Matter to a Liberal Society of Free People and Free Markets," *Journal of Economic Perspectives* 19, no. 3 (Summer 2005): pp. 117, 126–127.

16. Adam Smith, *The Theory of Moral Sentiments* (London: Henry G. Bohn, 1853), p. 4. Originally published in 1790.

17. Cited in Evensky, "Adam Smith's *Theory,*" p. 121.

18. The results of several large surveys are summarized in Jean M. Twenge, W. Keith Campbell, and Elise C. Freeman, "Generational Differences in Young Adults' Life Goals, Concern for Others, and Civic Orientation, 1966–2009," *Journal of Personality and Social Psychology* 102, no. 5

(May 2012), pp. 1045–1062. The data shows, for example, that in 1966, over 80 percent of the respondents agreed on the importance of a "meaningful philosophy of life." But that percentage declined steadily until it slipped below 50 percent in the early 1980s; conversely, those agreed on the importance of "becoming very well-off financially" were about 35 percent in 1972 and rose above 50 percent by the end of the decade, approaching 80 percent by 2009.

19. On the rise in narcissism, see Chapter 6 in this book, "Learning by Failing."

20. Sara Konrath, "The Empathy Gap," *Psychology Today*, blog, June 28, 2010, http://www.psychologytoday.com/blog/the-empathy-gap; also Edward H. O'Brien, Courtney Hsing, and Sara Konrath, "Changes in Dispositional Empathy Over Time in American College Students: a Meta-Analysis": sitemaker.umich.edu/skonrath/files/empathy_decline.pdf; last accessed Mar. 28, 2011. This survey was based on data in seventy-two studies involving 13,737 students. The empathy scale was the Davis Interpersonal Reactivity Index.

21. Howard Gardner and Katie Davis, *The App Generation: How Today's Youth Navigate Identity, Intimacy, and Imagination in a Digital World* (New Haven: Yale University Press, 2013), pp. 111–112. "The decline" quote begins on p. 112.

22. Eric L. Dey and Sylvia Hurtado, "College Students in Changing Contexts," in Philip G. Altbach, Robert O. Berdahl, and Patricia J. Gumport, *American Higher Education in the Twenty-First Century: Social, Political and Economic Challenges* (Baltimore: Johns Hopkins University Press, 2005), pp. 322–327.

23. Jean-Jacques Rousseau, *Emile*, trans. Barbara Foxley (London: Dent, 1993), p. 79.

24. Martha C. Nussbaum, *Cultivating Humanity: A Classical Defense of Reform in Liberal Education* (Cambridge, MA: Harvard University Press, 1997), pp. 10–11, 85, 90.

25. Martha Nussbaum adds: "The imaginative component of democratic education requires careful selectivity" in *Not For Profit: Why Democracy Needs the Humanities* (Princeton, NJ: Princeton University Press, 2010), p. 109. Michael S. Roth, president of Wesleyan University, observed that Nussbaum's careful selection of texts results in a process with a

"specific political content," in "Good and Risky: The Promise of a Liberal Education," *Chronicle Review* (July 11, 2010).

26. Lewis, *Excellence without a Soul,* p. 98.

27. See, for example, Roy A. Sorensen, "Self-Strengthening Empathy," *Philosophy and Phenomenological Research* 58, no. 1, (March 1998), pp. 87–90.

28. Plato, *The Republic,* trans. Desmond Lee (New York: Penguin, 1953), pp. 349, 350.

29. Cited in Bok, *Our Underachieving Colleges,* p. 166. Richard Kahlenberg, a senior fellow at the Century Foundation, thought that colleges might best counteract declining empathy scores by "teaching empathy through role-playing"—such as having students spend a day in a wheelchair or go a night without eating; in "Should We Teach Empathy in College?" *Chronicle of Higher Education* (April 9, 2011).

30. Steven Stroessner, "All the World's a Stage? Consequences of a Role-Playing Pedagogy on Psychological Factors and Writing and Rhetorical Skill in College Undergraduates," *Journal of Educational Psychology* 101, no. 3 (2009): p. 611.

31. The central task for students playing Reacting games is writing papers advancing the views of the figures they represent. Historical figures whose own thoughts lacked intellectual depth or complex textual foundations do not provide students with much scope for scholarly research or imaginative inquiry. Role-immersion games lacking such sources would be a contradiction in terms: How can a student immerse herself in a historical figure who lacked intellectual depth?

32. See the website for the BEES scale: www.kaaj.com/psych/scales/emp.html.

9. TEACHING LEADERSHIP THROUGH TEAMWORK

1. Jack Meacham and Jerry G. Gaff, "Learning Goals in Mission Statements: Implications for Educational Leadership," *Liberal Education* (Winter 2006).

2. Princeton mission statement (2010): www.princeton.edu/campuslife/mission/.

3. Cited in Richard Greenwald, "Today's Students Need Leadership Training Like Never Before," *Chronicle of Higher Education* (December 5, 2010).

4. James MacGregor Burns, *Leadership* (New York: Harper and Row, 1978), p. 2.

5. Derek Bok, *Our Underachieving Colleges* (Princeton, NJ: Princeton University Press, 2006), p. 81.

6. Cited in Lori Gottlieb, "How to Land Your Kid in Therapy," *Atlantic* (July/August, 2011): p. 72.

7. David Hackett Fischer, *Washington's Crossing* (New York: Oxford University Press, 2004), pp. 316, 266; "community of open discourse" (p. 316); on Washington's "maturing style of quiet, consultative leadership" (p. 266).

8. Ronald A. Heifetz, Riley M. Sinder, Alice Jones, Lynn M. Hodge, and Keith A. Rowley, "Teaching and Assessing Leadership Courses at the John F. Kennedy School of Government," *Journal of Policy Analysis and Management* 8, no. 3 (Summer 1989): pp. 536–562.

9. Joseph Rost, "Leaders and Followers Are the People in This Relationship," in J. T. Wren, ed., *The Leader's Companion* (New York: Free Press, 1995), p. 192, cited in Richard L. Morrill, *Strategic Leadership: Integrating Strategy and Leadership in Colleges and Universities* (Lanham, MD: American Council on Education/Rowman and Littlefield, 2007), p. 9.

10. James MacGregor Burns, *Transforming Leadership: A New Pursuit of Happiness* (New York: Atlantic Monthly Press, 2003), pp. 25–26. The author is grateful for the insights of Richard L. Morrill, former president of the Teagle Foundation, on these and other issues pertaining to the academic study of leadership.

11. Students can and do learn such skills through experiential activities, such as by organizing lead-abatement task forces in inner cities or raising funds for cancer programs.

12. Thomas L. Friedman, "How to Get a Job at Google," *The New York Times* (February 23, 2014). "Too many colleges," the executive continued, "don't deliver on what they promise. You generate a ton of debt, you don't learn the most useful things for your life. It's [just] an extended adolescence."

13. Leon Botstein, "The Curriculum and College Life: Confronting Unfulfilled Promises," in Richard H. Hersh and John Merrow, eds., *Declining by Degrees: Higher Education at Risk* (New York: Palgrave Macmillan, 2005), p. 211.

14. Joe Hogan, "'Reacting to the Past' and the Future of GVSU," *Grand Valley Lanthorn* (February 10, 2014).

10. TEACHING THE PAST BY GETTING IT WRONG?

1. R. G. Collingwood, *The Idea of History: Revised Edition* (London: Oxford University Press, 2005), p. 297.

2. David Hackett Fischer, *Historians' Fallacies: Toward a Logic of Historical Thought* (New York: Harper and Row, 1970), pp. 196–197. Arnold Toynbee sniffed that Collingwood's dictum would require a biographer of Tamerlane to go on a rampage in the streets; see his *A Study of History,* Vol. 9 (Oxford: Oxford University Press, 1954), pp. 733–734. For a thoughtful analysis of Collingwood's position, see William H. Dray, *History as Re-Enactment: R. G. Collingwood's Idea of History* (Oxford: Oxford University Press, 1995).

3. Michael Oakeshott, *Rationalism in Politics* (New York: Basic Books, 1962), p. 9.

4. Oakeshott, *Experience and Its Modes* (Cambridge: The University Press, 1933), p. 99.

5. Oakshott, *Experience and Its Modes,* p. 100.

6. Oakeshott's skepticism about the historical past dovetailed with Collingwood's views; for his part, Collingwood praised Oakeshott's work as "the high-water mark of English thought upon history." Collingwood, *Idea,* p. 159.

7. Gertrude Himmelfarb, *The New History and the Old* (Cambridge, MA: Harvard University Press, 1987), pp. 181–182.

8. Hayden White, *Metahistory: The Historical Imagination of Nineteenth-Century Europe* (Baltimore: Johns Hopkins University Press, 1973), p. x.

9. See, for example, Peter Novick, *The Noble Dream: The 'Objectivity Question' and the American Historical Profession* (New York: Cambridge University Press, 1988).

10. Evans is cited in Julia Nitz, "History, a Literary Artifact? The Traveling Concept of Narrative in/on Historiographic Discourse," *Interdisciplinary Literary Studies* 15, no. 1 (2013): p. 76; see also pp. 74–77.

11. Cited in Berkhofer, *Beyond the Great Story: History as Text and Discourse* (Cambridge, MA: Harvard University Press, 1995), p. 75.

12. Cited in Michael Lackey, ed., *Truthful Fictions: Conversations with American Biographical Novelists* (New York: Bloomsbury Press, 2014), p. 207.

13. Cited in David D. Hall, ed., *The Antinomian Controversy, 1636–1638* (Durham: Duke University Press, 1990), pp. 21, 22.

14. For an example of nearly unintelligible theological jargon, consider John Cotton's reply to questions put to him by church elders: "It is not an unsafe, but a lawfull way to conclude a mans safe Estate by way of Practicall Reasoning, so the Reason be not carnall but spirituall. One proposition being expressed in the Word, or safely deducted thence; the other being the experimental observation of a good Conscience, enlightened by the Spirit of God, and looking up to Christ to cleare the Conclusion from both," from Hall, ed., *Antinomian Controversy*, p. 58.

15. Cited in Hall, ed., *Antinomian Controversy*, p. 11.

16. Michael Winship, *Making Heretics: Militant Protestantism and Free Grace in Massachusetts, 1636–1641* (Princeton, NJ: Princeton University Press, 2002), p. 10.

17. Cited in Larry Cuban, *How Scholars Trumped Teachers: Change Without Reform in University Curriculum, Teaching, and Research, 1890–1990* (New York: Teachers College Press, 1999), p. 112. Cuban added, "It is uncommon for historians to recognize publicly these differences between teaching introductory history courses and the essential academic duty of writing for other scholars."

18. See, for example, Vincent Leitch's summary of Jacques Lacan's post-structuralist pedagogy in "Deconstruction and Pedagogy," in Cary Nelson, ed., *Theory in the Classroom* (Urbana: University of Illinois Press, 1986), p. 51.

19. Stanley Fish, *There's No Such Thing as Free Speech* (Oxford: Oxford University Press, 1994), p. 238.

20. Cited in Berkhofer, *Beyond the Great Story*, p. 75.

21. In 2014, when I interviewed Nate Gibson and Linda Schroeder-meier, students in the early-morning class cited at the beginning of this book, what they recalled best about the class they had taken nine years ago were the ideas of Rousseau, whose *Social Contract* was the chief text for the game. Which faction prevailed in the particular debates had slipped from their memories.

22. What surprised Crider the most about his quiz was that some students completed it, unthinkingly, as if they were still in their roles. That is, they answered that the universe has a center because they were still thinking as if they were conservatives. "They really got into their characters!" Crider wrote. After discovering that many of his students remained persuaded by the Aristotelian view that the universe was bounded, Crider created a video showing the expansion of the universe, pointing out the specific failings of the Aristotelian paradigm. Nowadays, Reacting faculty playing the Galileo game include this video as part of the postmortem discussion.

23. Game designers have found ways to keep the basic historical events "on track" until the final class sessions. Thus games have contingency, but usually it does not alter the historical record in a dramatic way until the end phase of a game.

24. See, especially, Hayden White, *The Fiction of Narrative: Essays on History, Literature, and Theory, 1957–2007* (Baltimore: Johns Hopkins University Press. 2010).

25. Throughout this book, I have not included the actual names of students who are still enrolled in college. I have made an exception here at the request of the student.

26. Leon Litwack, "The Birth of Nation," in Mark C. Carnes, ed., *Past Imperfect: History According to the Movies* (New York: Henry Holt, 1995), p. 136.

27. Although the production costs were staggering, the movie became a box-office bonanza. When de Mille's career faltered in the 1930s, he again turned to history with *The Sign of the Cross* (1932), about Christians in ancient Rome, and *Cleopatra* (1934), both huge successes.

28. Paul Veyne, *Did the Greeks Believe in Their Myths* (Chicago: University of Chicago Press, 1988), p. 60.

29. Homer, *The Iliad,* trans. Michael Reck, p. 602. Iliad 22, 329–364 lines. Cited in Homer, *The Iliad,* trans. Michael Reck (New York: HarperCollins, 1994), p. 19.

30. Jeffrey Hart, *Smiling Through the Cultural Catastrophe: Toward the Revival of Higher Education* (New Haven: Yale University Press, 2001), p. 15. "Homer is always there."

31. Plato, *The Republic,* trans. Desmond Lee (New York: Penguin, 1953), pp. 87, 92.

32. Homer's "falsehoods," of course, were devoid of deceit. Greek audiences did not regard their orators or actors as gods or ancient kings. And Socrates himself endorsed myths—falsehoods!—when they served the purposes of his ideal state.

33. Plato, *The Republic* (Lee), p. 89.

34. Plato, *The Republic* (Lee), pp. 92, 351.

35. Plato, *The Republic* (Lee), pp. 349, 335, 97–98, 351, 352, 342, 348; "power to corrupt" (p. 349); "among all the excellent features of our ideal state, there's none I rank higher than its treatment of poetry" (p. 335); "cumulative psychological damage" (pp. 97–98); "definitely harms," "insensibly led" to become a buffoon at home (p. 351); "childish and vulgar passion (p. 352); "natural magic" (p. 342); "lower elements of the mind" (p. 348).

36. Plato, *The Republic* (Lee), p. 87.

37. Compare Plato's flat non-*mimetic* narration with Homer's own *mimetic* representation of Chryses's words:

"Atreus' sons and you other Achaeans,

May the gods on Olympus grant that you

sack Priam's city and return safe home,

but take the ransom, release my dear child,

respect Apollo's unspeakable power." (Homer, *The Iliad,* Book 1, Reck, p. 19.)

38. Nietzsche, ed., *The Birth of Tragedy,* trans. Francis Golfing, p. 88. On Plato's sly appropriation of *mimesis,* see Lesie Kurke, "Plato, Aesop and the Beginnings of Mimetic Prose," *Representations,* no. 94 (Spring 2006): p. 11; see also pp. 12–13. "By so strongly identifying *mimesis* with

poetry, Plato conjures the illusion that his own prose is nonmimetic" (p. 11). Ekaterina Haskins, a professor of rhetoric at the Rensselaer Polytechnic Institute, observes that in *Phaedrus* and *Menexenus,* Plato's Socrates himself speaks "in voices other than his own," in "'Mimesis' between Poetics and Rhetoric: Performance Culture and Civic Education in Plato, Isocrates, and Aristotle," *Rhetoric Society Quarterly* 30, no. 3 (Summer 2000): p. 11. On the "effectiveness of Plato's fiction of Socrates"—especially on inspiring philosophers "to *follow* Socrates," see Kurke, "The Beginnings of Mimetic Prose": pp. 37–38.

39. Amanda Houle, "Reacting to Reacting," *Change* 38, no. 4 (July/August 2006): p. 52.

11. THE STRANGE WORLD OUTSIDE THE BOX

1. Philip D. Curtin, "Depth Span and Relevance," *American Historical Review* 89 (1984): pp. 2–3.

2. See John J. Hopfield, "Reflections on the APS and the Evolution of Physics," *APS News* 16, no. 8 (August/September, 2007): p. 8.

3. Perhaps the best summary of this phenomenon appears in Louis Menand, *The Marketplace of Ideas: Reform and Resistance in the American University* (New York: W. W. Norton, 2010), especially the chapter "The Problem of General Education," pp. 34–57.

4. Louis Menand, *Marketplace of Ideas,* p. 24.

5. Vartan Gregorian, "Six Challenges to the American University," in Richard H. Hersh and John Merrow, eds., *Declining by Degrees: Higher Education at Risk* (New York: Palgrave Macmillan, 2005), p. 79.

6. Leon Botstein, "The Curriculum and College Life: Confronting Unfulfilled Promises," *Declining by Degrees,* p. 222.

7. *Integrity in the College Curriculum: A Report to the Academic Community* (Washington, DC: Association of American Colleges, 1985), p. 20.

8. The Reacting Editorial Board, established by the Board of the Reacting Consortium, supervises the development of all proposed Reacting games, from inception to publication. Once the Reacting Editorial Board has approved a game for publication, W. W. Norton has the first option to publish it; approved games that Norton declines to publish are published and marketed by the Reacting Consortium Press. A list of all of the games

at various stages of development can be found by Googling BLORG—the Big List of Reacting Games.

9. Often faculty pose questions and share research in online discussion groups for Reacting faculty. These discussion sites include those relating to particular games at the main Reacting website (www.barnard.edu /reacting) and on the Facebook Reacting Faculty Lounge; both of these sites are restricted to faculty and administrators. For information, consult the main Reacting website: www.barnard.edu/reacting.

10. Cited in Robert A. McCaughey, *Stand Columbia: A History of Columbia University in the City of New York, 1754–2004* (New York: Columbia University Press, 2003), p. 297. Erskine was one of the founders of the great books movement.

11. See Derek Bok, *Our Underachieving Colleges* (Princeton, NJ: Princeton University Press, 2006), pp. 262–265.

12. Serious assessment is time-consuming and expensive. But enterprising administrators can streamline the process. The cheapest and easiest test is to determine what percentage of students attends class. It's hard to argue that students are learning in class if they're not there. This sort of bare-bones assessment rankles teachers: it's not *their* fault students skip classes. This judgment, though often true, is irrelevant. Students who don't come to class—for whatever reason—do not derive much benefit from it; and the no-shows are most at risk of dropping out. Administrators can also ask graduating seniors to list all the courses for which they have earned credit. If students can't remember taking a course, chances are that they didn't retain much content. And because "community building" is so central to students' persistence to a degree, administrators can also ask students at the end of the first year to indicate the first names of all of the friends they have made on campus and then tabulate the results. If students haven't made many friends, they are less likely to return the next year.

13. George D. Kuh, *Educational Practices: What They Are, Who Has Access to Them, and Why The Matter* (Washington, DC: Association of American Colleges and Universities, 2008).

14. See, for example, Bok, *Our Underachieving Colleges,* p. 325.

15. Paul Basken, "Crusader for Better Science Teaching Finds College Slow to Change," *Chronicle of Higher Education* (June 17, 2013).

16. Larry Cuban, *How Scholars Trumped Teachers: Change Without Reform in University Curriculum, Teaching, and Research* (New York: Teachers College Press, 1999), pp. 4, 200; "perplexing continuity," "age old dilemmas" (p. 200).

17. Bok, *Our Underachieving Colleges*, p. 330.

18. James M. Sloat, "Freshman Forum: Thematic v. Reacting—A Multi-Stage Assessment," (unpublished, January 26, 2007): p. 10.

19. Sloat, "Freshman Forum": p. 8. Details on the study are cited in the "Debate at Dawn" section of this book.

20. Cited in Trip Gabriel, "Learning in Dorm, Because Class Is on the Web," *New York Times* (November 4, 2010). See especially Jeff Schweers, "Firm Will Get About $186 Million to Manage UF Online," *The Gainesville Sun* (March 27, 2014). While public trustees of large university systems increasingly insist on the lower cost and pedagogical effectiveness of online education, some faculty are seeking to reinvigorate the classroom by using Reacting in large, general education survey courses. For example, within the California State University system, where elected representatives have pressed for greater online degree and course access, history professor Bridget Ford and a team of faculty at CSU East Bay, abetted by state funding, will incorporate sequences of Reacting games in the U.S. history survey courses, which more than a fifth of all enrolled CSU undergraduates currently fail.

21. David Brooks, "The Campus Tsunami," *New York Times* (May 3, 2012).

22. See Thomas M. Rollins, "MOOCS: Been There, Done That," *Chronicle Review* (January 20, 2014).

23. Pu Shih Daniel Chen, Robert Gonyea, and George Kuh, "Learning at Distance: Engaged or Not?" *Innovateonline* 4, no. 3 (February/March 2008); http://cpr.iub.edu/uploads/Learning%20at%20a%20Distance.pdf; last accessed April 10, 2014.

24. Kerstin Hamann, Philip H. Pollock, and Bruce M. Wilson, "Assessing Student Perceptions of the Benefits of Discussions in Small-Group, Large-Class, and Online Learning Contexts," *College Teaching* 60 (2012): p. 69. "Students stated that they were significantly more likely to participate in the online discussions: Two-thirds (67.7%) reported high participation, compared with one-third (32.9%) of small-group discussants and about one-quarter (23.9%) in the full-class environment."

25. Cited in Goldie Blumenstyk, "Manifesto for a New Culture of Learning," *Chronicle Review* (May 15, 2011); on building a new culture of play, see Douglas Thomas's Ted talk, "A New Culture of Learning": www.ted.com/tedx/events/4548; last accessed March 11, 2013.

26. Jane McGonigal, *Reality Is Broken: Why Games Make Us Better and How They Can Change the World* (New York: Penguin Books, 2011). Earlier proponents of video game learning include James Paul Gee, *Good Video Games and Good Learning: Collected Essays on Video Games, Learning, and Literacy* (New York: Peter Lang, 2007), and Steven Johnson, *Everything Bad Is Good for You: How Popular Culture Is Making Us Smarter* (New York: Penguin Books, 2005).

27. Cathy N. Davidson, *Now You See It: How the Brain Science of Attention Will Transform the Way We Live, Work, and Learn* (New York: Viking Press, 2011), pp. 141–145.

28. See, for example, David Embrick, ed., *Social Exclusion, Power and Video Game Play: New Research in Digital Media and Technology* (Blue Ridge Summit, PA: Lexington Books, 2012); Noah Wardrip-Fruin, *Expressive Processing: Digital Fictions, Computer Games, and Software Studies* (Cumberland, RI: MIT Press, 2009); and Nicola Whitton, "Games for Learning: Creating a Level Playing Field or Stacking the Deck?" *International Review of Qualitative Research* 6, no. 3 (Fall 2013).

29. José Antonio Bowen, *Teaching Naked: How Moving Technology Out of Your College Classroom Will Improve Student Learning* (San Francisco: Jossey-Bass, 2012), pp. 71, 75–102, 192–193. See especially his chapter, "Designing College More Like a Video Game," pp. 75–102; on Reacting, see pp. 192–193.

30. Derek Bok recommends such an "active process of enlightened trial and error," in which administrators and faculty mount multiple active-learning experiments and determine which works best; in *Our Underachieving Colleges*, p. 322 fn.

31. Andrew Hamilton, "The Teachable Moment: Rethinking the Large Lecture," *Change* (May/June 2013).

32. Henry Seidel Canby, *Alma Mater: The Gothic Age of the American College* (New York: Farrar and Rinehart, 1936), p. 108.

33. See, for example, Judy Willis, "Building a Bridge from Neuroscience to the Classroom," *Phi Delta Kappan* 89, no. 6 (February 2008): p. 427;

see also Benedict Carey, "How Nonsense Sharpens the Intellect," *New York Times* (October 5, 2009).

34. Friedrich Nietzsche, *Birth of Tragedy and the Genealogy of Morals*, trans. Francis Golffing (New York: Doubleday Anchor Books, 1956), p. 90; also Aristotle, *Poetics*, IX.1,3, in Hazard Adams, ed., *Critical Theory since Plato* (New York: Harcourt Brace Jovanovich, 1971), p. 53.

35. Sociologist Tim Clydesdale used the similar term "identity lockbox" to describe the mindset of the first-year college students he interviewed, in *The First Year Out: Understanding American Teens After High School* (Chicago: University of Chicago Press, 2007).

36. Nietzsche, *The Birth of Tragedy*, pp. 89, 109. "logical universe," "ecstatic dream world" (p. 89). "All our pedagogic devices are oriented to this ideal," whose "archetype and progenitor" was Plato's Socrates (p. 109).

37. Scholars of play have more recently focused on its anarchic, destructive, and irrational bases. See, for example, Mihai Spariosu, *Dionysus Reborn: Play and the Aesthetic Dimension in Modern Philosophical and Scientific Discourse* (Ithaca, NY: Cornell University Press, 1989) and his *God of Many Names: Play, Poetry, and Power in Hellenic Thought from Homer to Aristotle* (Durham: Duke University Press, 1991), p. xii: "Play may well be one of those phenomena that ultimately elude power and point to an anarchical, nonviolent kind of mentality." See also Brian Sutton-Smith, *The Ambiguity of Play* (Cambridge, MA: Harvard University Press, 1997), p. 229: "So in conclusion, I have presented here the view that variability is the key to play, and that structurally play is characterized by quirkiness, redundancy, and flexibility."

38. Plato, *The Republic*, trans. Desmond Lee (New York: Penguin, 1953), p. 214. Stanford classicist Josiah Ober noted that public speaking in Athens was a contest—"a game." He added that "one object of the game [of giving speeches in the Assembly] was victory in making one's own distinct critical voice recognized," in *Political Dissent in Democratic Athens* (Princeton, NJ: Princeton University Press, 1998), p. 47.

39. William James, *Talks to Teachers on Psychology* (New York: Henry Holt, 1916), p. 152.

40. On the pecuniary focus of online gaming, see especially anthropologist Tom Boellstorff, *Coming of Age in Second Life: An Anthropologist Explores the Virtually Human* (Princeton, NJ: Princeton University Press,

2008), pp. 206–219. "Second Life was predicated upon and exemplified what I term 'creationist capitalism'" (p. 206).

SOCRATES AT SUNSET

1. Plato, *The Republic*, trans. Desmond Lee (New York: Penguin, 1953), pp. 297–298.

ACKNOWLEDGMENTS

Nearly a decade ago I set out to write a book about teaching, a subject I knew something about. Then I realized I needed to write about learning, a subject that has proven far more elusive. When research in the library failed to answer my questions, I turned to former students—at my institution and dozens of others. Their responses challenged my assumptions about learning—along with much of the scholarly literature on the subject. This book is largely a distillation of the views of hundreds of students. Without them, especially the ninety I interviewed formally, I could not have written this book.

I have learned much, too, from the dozens of faculty cited in this work, and from countless others I cannot name here. I've also received an education in pedagogy, and in many wonderful historical subjects, from the designers of Reacting games, the most creative people I've met in the academic world. Rather than list them here, I have included them—and their ingenious games—in the Appendix.

Reacting to the Past—and thus this book—would not exist if it had not been for the early support and sustained guidance of Judith Shapiro. In 1996, as president of Barnard, she committed herself to Reacting when it was the vaguest of concepts; over the next decade she nurtured the initiative as it spread beyond Barnard and she has continued to champion it as president of the Teagle Foundation. Elizabeth Boylan, then Barnard provost, provided sure-handed administrative support and direction. Debora Spar, who succeeded Shapiro as Barnard president, and Linda Bell, who succeeded Boylan as provost, have continued to promote the program's growth and expansion, most importantly by hosting the Reacting Consortium of colleges and universities. I thank, too, Anna Quindlen, who during her time as board chair, allowed the Barnard trustees to be transformed, at least for one day, into the Hanlin Academy of the Ming dynasty.

The dissemination of Reacting is largely the result of the tireless efforts of Dana Johnson, now the administrative director of the Reacting Consortium, though she began working on Reacting over a decade ago as a Barnard sophomore. Her administrative genius and financial wizardry have not only enabled the program to spread to over 300 colleges and universities but also allowed me to focus on writing this book. Also at Barnard, Susan Campbell has provided solid support for many years, and Madalena Provo, who arrived as I was finishing the book, helped ensure that I did so.

The first Reacting to the Past faculty-training workshop was held in 2001, which prompted a group of venturesome faculty and administrators to try the pedagogy. Pat Coby (Smith College), John Burney (now at Doane College), Marty Braun (Queens College), and Frank Kirkpatrick (Trinity College)—soon followed by Larry Carver (University of Texas at Austin)—were the first of a steadily expanding cohort that transformed my glimmer of an idea into a full-fledged (though still evolving) pedagogical system.

This remarkable group was joined by a dozen or so scholars who have invested much of their lives in the Reacting project by serving on the Board of the Reacting Consortium, which governs the intellectual and editorial aspects of the Reacting initiative. In addition to those mentioned above, I shall always be deeply indebted to Anthony Crider (Elon University), Elizabeth S. Dunn (Indiana University, South Bend), John Eby (Loras College), Nancy Felson (University of Georgia), Mark D. Higbee (Eastern Michigan University), Linda Mayhew (University of Texas at Austin), Gretchen McKay (McDaniel College), Ian McNeely (University of Oregon), Richard Gid Powers (College of Staten Island and the CUNY Graduate Center), Nicolas Proctor (Simpson College), Michael Pettersen (Washington and Jefferson College), Kamran Swanson

(Harold Washington College), and Jace Weaver (University of Georgia). That teacher-scholars of such extraordinary gifts have devoted so much of their lives to Reacting has inspired me to do likewise. The student/ alumni members of the Board have also figured prominently in the Reacting Consortium—and in this book: Amelia VanderLaan (Smith College), who appears in three separate chapters; Lily Lamboy (Smith College and Stanford University); and Dani Holtz (Barnard College and the University of Pennsylvania).

Early on, Reacting benefited from two important grants from the Fund for the Improvement for Secondary Education (FIPSE) of the U. S. Department of Education. David Johnson and Joan Straumanis were pivotal advocates for pedagogical innovation in a bureaucratic culture that was skeptical of "playing games" in college. In recent years, the Teagle Foundation has assisted the Reacting Consortium in attaining self-sufficiency. I especially note Teagle board member Jayne Keith, who went so far as to join my undergraduate class and even play a role in the India game; I have also profited from the ideas and guidance of a succession of innovative and perceptive Teagle presidents: Robert Connor, Richard Morrill, and Shapiro, mentioned earlier. All have read substantial sections and even multiple drafts of this book. Their generosity is surpassed only by their critical acumen.

Other savvy readers included Derek Bok, Ian McNeely, David Thelen, and Frederick Winter. Natasha Gill, author of *Educational Philosophy in the French Enlightenment* (2010), has bested me in countless spirited debates on pedagogical matters—and that, too, has been a learning experience.

Many of the ideas in this book were first developed when I was McAndless Distinguished Professor at Eastern Michigan University in 2010–2011. I thank Mark Higbee for spearheading that invitation, for sharing his excellent ideas and wonderful students, and for introducing me to so many creative and insightful faculty.

As I strayed beyond the normal pastures grazed by professional historians, I have been sustained by longtime friends in the Barnard and Columbia history departments, especially Kenneth T. Jackson, Robert McCaughey, Rosalind Rosenberg, Herb Sloan, Joel Kaye, Lisa Tiersten, and Nancy Woloch. Although John A. Garraty, my mentor and co-author, never understood my peculiar interest in pedagogy, he taught me to cherish short, clean sentences. I hope his legacy shows, though I doubt he would have forgiven the jargon-laden phrase, "subversive play world."

Elizabeth Knoll, a veteran editor at Harvard University Press, has been one of this book's wisest and most perceptive critics. She also proved to be an administrator of astounding talents, bringing the manuscript to publication in record time. I thank three anonymous reviewers for their suggestions, and especially for their criticisms. I also thank Leah Shriro and Kimberly Giambattisto for their fine editorial work.

I'm grateful to Leander Schaerlaeckens, who nudged me to expand my research on play into the realm of sport. Were it not for him, Jim Bouton's *Ball Four* might never have found its way into an academic monograph on higher education.

Being a father has itself been a lesson in learning. My daughter, Stephanie, a pioneering social worker who has explored the use of play in clinical settings, has provided insights on many of the issues in this book. When she was a three-year-old, too, she alerted me to the pedagogical shortcomings of the lecture. We live near the Hudson River and one foggy night, unnerved by the mournful dirge of foghorns, she couldn't sleep. With her on my lap, I launched into a reassuring discourse on how "foghorns are our friends." I explained, perhaps at length, that they guided ships and protected them from harm. "Now do you understand foghorns?" I finally asked. "Yeah," she said in a thoughtful tone. "Sorta like tomatoes."

When I wandered into the oft-impenetrable thickets of this project, Mary Elin Korchinsky held my hand—listening, consoling, teaching. She has led me through a forest of confusion into a gently rolling park, furrowed with streams. We have shared the Reacting project and the writing of this book, along with most everything else. From her, and with her, I have learned about all that matters in life. To her, I dedicate this book.

INDEX